1944

50 YEARS
of
ASSIMILATION

50 Years
of
ASSIMILATION

*From the Midwest
to the Wild West
and All the
Blackness & Whiteness
In Between*

Wanda Lee-Stevens

BOOK YOUR LIFE
1511M Sycamore Avenue, #121
Hercules, CA 94547
(888) 444-7552

Second Edition: March 2018

First Edition: April 2015
Second Printing: October 2015
Third Printing: March 2016
Fourth Printing: May 2017

Content Consulting Editor: Rebecca Salome, Tucson, AZ
Cover Concept: Wanda Lee-Stevens
Cover Photograph: Candy Bright, Hercules, CA
Original Cover Design: Darlene Kong, Oakland, CA
Illustrations: Darnell Jones, Nashville, TN

Sunny Day Publishing, LLC
Cuyahoga Falls, OH 44223

Printed in the United States of America

ISBN: 978-1-948613-02-6

Library of Congress Control Number: 2018938140

This second edition is dedicated to:

All those folks out there (past and present) who are truth-telling, standing up, standing out, and unabashedly unashamed to fight for equality by any means necessary, doing what is right and necessary to make this world a place for EVERYONE! You are my heroes!

A Note from the Author

A very beautiful and wise woman, Josie B. Cummings, from Los Angeles, expressed an adage to me, in a very loving and wishful way, *"Books can travel places you can't."*

In the spirit of that adage that I received wholeheartedly, I hope this book will not only travel places I can't, but that it also takes me to great places I've never been.

May it also be an instrument for open, honest, and healing racial conversations!

Table of Contents

INTRODUCTION

Episode 1 – Psychological

"Shabbat Shalom." Peace on the Sabbath. In 2013, I attended the Bat Mitzvah of my then thirteen-year-old daughter's classmate. This was the first time we visited a synagogue. We arrived in the parking lot just as the host family did. I was relieved to have met them first, and that the parents appeared to be the same age or slightly older than me (age 50). The family quickly walked through the foyer to prepare for their guests, leaving us behind with the older greeters holding boxes of lapis-colored, felt Yarmulkes. One of them began to explain what we should do, after asking if we had ever visited a synagogue before. As we entered the sanctuary, I was glad we arrived right on time. A minor feat for me. I am not sure why I am so typically late. I do believe I have an inherited predisposition and I am sure in my family's case, it has something to do with taking risks. We are gamblers. But I was determined that we would not be the late black people to this event. CP (Colored People) time is reserved for CP events.

We were given the Jewish Bible (the Torah), and the Hebrew Prayer book. The service program seemed logical enough, listing the order of rituals, the names of acknowledged congregants, future events, and prayer requests for the ill and unattended. It was simple in design and different than what I was used to, functional, yet unassuming.

The ambiance of the sanctuary was also unassertive. I think I imagined a more mystic quality. I guess I expected a very sacred and ancient biblical walk-on-water kinda feeling — even though Jesus would not be part of the service. Aside from the mysterious shrine (which I later learned was housing the Ark, and protecting the Torah scrolls on tall, ornate brass rods), everything else felt austere and unemotional.

The seating faced east in three sections, leaving two aisles. Instead of pews, there were broad-back maple chairs, softened by blue-woven upholstered cushions with book cubbies underneath, arranged to form a semi-circle. We sat midway in the left section. I, one away from the aisle seat, was close enough to escape, but not obviously so. My daughter sat in the row in front of me with three schoolmates she recognized. The room began to fill in gradually. We did not know the service was going to be three hours long. Of course I noticed, as I always do, after my cultural auto-scan and calculation, that we were the only black folks out of eighty or so congregants. For the next half-hour, others trickled in. A woman came to my aisle. I uncrossed my legs and made room for her to pass without looking up. She sat in the seat next to the one occupied by my purse on the right. I looked over to do the Christian thing (I'm sure Jewish people do this too) and say hello, and saw that she too was black. She did not return my Judeo-Christian gesture, so I said nothing. I got annoyed. Not because she didn't acknowledge me, which would have been reason enough — especially because we were in a house of prayer. But she chose to locate herself next to me! I didn't know her from Adam, yet she chose to avoid all of the other empty seats (roughly 100) and plop right down in my "only black" sanctified and sacrificial space.

So what is wrong with that, you ask? What was wrong is that her presence put me back in my head. At the very moment I was coming out of my programmed cultural world, she instantly took away from me the *status* (and I use this word facetiously), of being the only black woman there. She turned my soon-to-be, out-of-my-head experience of being present, of me trying to just "be" human, sharing an intimate experience of newness and religious ceremony, into me being incessantly in-my-head and *now* sitting in "the black section." I am sure God was using this as a teaching moment, but I was not being a good student. I wanted to douse her with dark-spot corrector and make her disappear. My presumed mysterious and distinguished solitary attendance, I felt, had been washed away, and "I" had become "they," or "them." So I obsessed most of the rest of the service, two more, long arduous hours, about what the others were thinking of our invasion of "their" space. Were we welcomed? Did they think we were together? Related! Did they want to engage? Or did they think less of us? Did they wonder if we came out of curiosity or as spies? Were we a threat? Did they wish we were gone? I tried hard to focus on the ceremony, the Rabbi, the readings, my daughter's friend, the Torah procession, the "sweet life-candy throw" (cute and I must use that somewhere), the singing, the prayers. But my peripheral view kept pulling me back inside that dangerous headspace of mine. That space that is color-full, not color blind. That space that relentlessly undermines my ability to just be human. The space that has pretty much kept my freedom at bay. It is silent, yet deafening, and it invades continuously. It is always chattering about what is not proper and right and good and mainstream and yes, more white, more USDA-stamped "Approved." It steals my grace, it steals my peace, and it is difficult as hell to shut down.

When the last prayer was said the service ended. I went immediately outside to get some fresh air, to clear my head. On my way back in, I ran into Noah, a co-worker who had helped me out at work on more than one occasion. He had just arrived. He seemed genuinely happy to see me. His presence momentarily silenced my insanity. He told me that he was late, and mainly there to pick up his girlfriend who helped to facilitate the event. I explained my attendance, but he had already guessed, knowing I have a teenage daughter. We chatted about work and the synagogue. He joked that he was on JP time. I had never heard that before. He also admitted he rarely comes for the full length of the service.

Shortly afterward he excused himself to find his girlfriend.

I went back in for the Kiddush (I liked the sound of that word), and while I was waiting in line at the buffet table, I no longer saw the other woman. I was relieved to regain my assumed status, and simultaneously wondered how long I would be under this black plague. Where is my freedom here on earth! Why is this simple freedom so elusive!

I did not see my daughter, so I got in line to fill my plate. I later saw her at a table nearby with her friend and classmates looking right at home. I wondered how much I had already poisoned her with this infectious, dis-eased state of constipated hyper-racial mindfulness, and then took pleasure in the visual harmonious symphony of sisterhood at their table. I sat with the host family's cousins from New York. They'd signaled an invitation, and I spent the next hour embellishing them with my brilliance while annoying the heck out of a younger, twenty-something male cousin. He was put out by my directness toward him. I do not recall what my inquisition was about, but I told him because of my brashness, I was sure he'd never forget me. This remedied my earlier emotional upset. Thank you, Jewish cousin! I needed you.

And this event (rather my behavior) was proof I had not yet evolved. My freedom was, and sometimes still is, smothered under persistent generational, internal, oppressive, repressive dialogues.

Episode 2 - Cultural

I crashed a party given by my friend who is an education administrator. She and her family were hosting relatives, and I happened to call fishing for someplace to go. They asked us over to play some games. My family was more than happy to oblige.

There was a discussion that caused me some grief. My friend had taken undergrad courses with emphasis in African history. She has always been an in-your-face-don't-mess-with-me-African-American. I-know-my-history! She declared that a game called "10,000," was not a "legitimate" game. Wow, I was shocked that these words came out of her mouth! She meant legitimate in the sense of known by mainstream (white stream), commercialized, packaged, distributed and sold to the masses. I was a bit hurt. "Really, did you just say legitimate?" I knew what she meant and was not so shocked that she meant it, but shocked that *she* meant it.

You see, I thought with all her research, education, training, and cultural fortitude that she had actually achieved a re-programming of the socialized cultural sub-thinking we learn at a very early age. That sense of outside validation from things we create to only be legit if someone else, *someone white*, says so. Why does a game need legitimizing? It's play, and play is play! She caught my drift, owned up to her slip, and agreed that if we are having fun, it is legit. But she had me at illegitimate, and I was secretly saddened she had not fully evolved yet either. She was after all a

Gen-Xer, and I thought they were more militant-mindful than us Boomers. And if she had not escaped the sub-thinking cultural programming with her undergrad ethnic studies degree and her graduate degree from UC Berkeley, then the rest of us did not have a prayer.

Episode 3 – Societal

I would be remiss not to mention the very unnecessarily tragic and recent deaths of Trayvon Martin, 2013, Michael Brown, 2014, Eric Garner, 2014, Tamir Rice 2014, Sandra Bland 2015, and more recently, Philando Castile, 2017, (and too many more to painfully name). These young men (and woman) were killed for menial acts of disobedience (or none) and did not deserve to die! Period. Each of their aggressors used their assumed and/or lawful authority to take these lives because of their racists' miens. Our men, particularly our young men, are feared, vilified, and marginalized on a daily basis, and it happens more times than we hear about nationally. But this has got to stop! Black skin is not a weapon!

The "not guilty"verdict for Trayvon Martin's murder, and the "not to indict" verdicts from the grand juries of Michael Brown's and Eric Garner's murderers felt like the clock was dialed back fifty years. Fifty years ago when the JC (Jim Crow) laws ruled the land in the name of the original JC (Jesus Christ). That historical use of Christianity to justify slavery and its subsequent iterations. Those Jim Crow laws that made black injustice legally and socially acceptable: before the protests, before the sit-ins, before the boycotts, before the marches, before the "I Have a Dream" speech, before the Civil Rights Act of 1964, before the Voting Rights Act of 1965. And now, 50 years later, here we are again, marching and protesting — still — to gain true justice, equality, and equal treatment under the law in our "post-racial" society!

I have a native son and he is a wonderful young African-American alpha male. When in this country, his country, my country (and quite possibly the world), will black boys and black men **GAIN THEIR GOD-GIVEN, BASIC MALE HUMAN RIGHT TO BE IMPULSIVELY EXPRESSIVE AND INAPPROPRIATELY INNOCENT, WITHOUT THE FEAR OF BEING KILLED!!! WHEN WILL THEY BE FREE?**

So Dr. King, I have to ask. Desegregation essentially meant assimilation, but is this what you really wanted? I am not sure it is, so I'm sharing with you how the dream played out in my life, because I want to know what real freedom looks like.

THE CAPTURE, 1960s
(The Negro Years)
Humanity Lost, Blackness Found

This is the capture because you are born into a conversation/culture already in existence, and thus a captive of it. I had heard the term Negro as a child, it being stamped on my birth certificate as a declaration and definition of my humanity. So naturally I thought everyone was a Negro, until I didn't.

"Negro get over here."

"Negro get outta my face!"

"Negro...pleez!"

"Look at the new Negro family."

My First White Friend in Black Bottom

Dear Dr. King,

Seven months before your most famous speech, and the same year as the birth of your baby girl Bernice, I was born in Detroit, MI, on January 17th. Negro is what was inked on my birth certificate in 1963. I was the eighth child, and the youngest of three daughters, in a family of nine. My father was from Alabama and worked at a printing factory and a convenience store. He was out of the house 16-20 hours every day. My mother was from Oklahoma and practically lived in the kitchen. She prepared three meals (when we could afford it) for eleven hungry people every single day of her life. Except on the rare occasions when she was able to get away, and go to her friend's house to play Canasta, or attend an Avon or Tupperware party. Or when her father came to visit from Oklahoma. My granddaddy loved to cook.

We shared a two-family flat with my mother's mother, Sadie; Sadie's sister, my Great Aunt Stella; my Aunt Gertrude; and my First Cousin Rochelle. They lived on the upper level. There were always snide remarks about all the "nasty" love-making going on by my parents, "making all 'dem babies and 'dey can't put 'dem nowhere!" But I am happy they kept going because I am here. Besides, they could not resist each other. My handsome daddy with his strength, charm, compassion and height. My momma with her soft-spoken seduction, her supple, flawless cocoa-brown skin, and her voluptuous lips and curvaceous body. She even had what we called "big legs!" My daddy could not help himself. Every woman knows obligation might get you two, three, maybe even four babies. But it takes some real passion, and a fearless love of life itself, to keep making babies after that. I think all the talk was just jealousy and disbelief that two black people could love each other so passionately. I also think I was lucky and got the best of all that goodness rolled into me.

We had what was called a shotgun flat. You opened the front door, and you were right in the living room and could see clearly through the house to the back door. We had two bedrooms. My five older brothers slept in the second bedroom on two beds, outgrowing them more every day. My younger brother and I slept in the bed with my momma, and my two sisters slept in a rollaway bed in the corner of the room. My daddy, whenever he did sleep, it was on the living room couch. However, I have no recollection of actually seeing him sleeping, except in his coffin.

The memories of the first six years of my life are not chronological; they are morphed events that mostly involved my family, our church, and our school. The games we played, the trouble we got into, the fights we had, the cuts and bruises, the toys we got and did not get, and the food we ate. I did not have any recognition of my "blackness." I got some inkling in 1967, when there were fires burning all over our neighborhood, in the shops and nearby factories, and black people rioting and running to get away from the police and the armed soldiers. Under Martial Law, then-Governor George Romney ordered The National Guard to hit the streets. If not all the streets, definitely the streets where we lived; in what was called Black Bottom. They were dressed in army greens like the plastic green soldiers my brothers had. But these soldiers were real, all white as far as we could tell, and they were there to bring order and control. That was tantamount to killing us. Why else would they bring guns? They also had menacing faces, grenades, military trucks, tanks (yes, tanks for real warfare), and the right to beat, arrest, jail, or even kill us. And we had our anger, our baseball bats, our Schwinns, our Buster Browns, and the insulation of knowing that if anyone tried to hurt any of us, they would have to deal with all eleven of us, with my daddy at the head.

One night, we suddenly saw lots and lots of smoke and fire, and people were running all around. My momma was very nervous because my daddy was not home yet and my oldest brothers were not there either. She told us to stay away from the windows, but I wanted to see where all the noise and smoke was coming from and why everyone was running. Just as I moved the curtain to peep outside, when I thought momma was not looking, my big sister Pat yanked my hand and pulled me off the couch. She gave me that "just like momma told you" look, so I knew better than to try again, because an extra pair of mean eyes was watching. I just went over and sat in the corner until my daddy came bursting through the door. He started to call for my momma, but she was already in his arms before he could finish. She said something, and he scanned all over the house. Then he stuffed something in his pocket and went back outside.

A good long time passed, but in my mind it was only a minute. The next thing I knew, two of my brothers came in with a rack of noise and tossed it on the floor in a burst of excitement. I just saw the flicker of the metal and the plastic bags, which made loud crinkling sounds like firecrackers. I screamed and would not stop screaming. My brothers rushed to grab the sprawled bags, and the more they scurried to pile them, the more noise it made, and the louder I cried. They were salivating at the chance to eat an entire rack of looted peanuts. One of them got in my face and yelled at me to shut up. That only made it worse. My screams turned into full-blown hysteria until my daddy returned and ordered them to take the rack outside. This was one of the last times my daddy actually rescued me. I was instantly relieved knowing now that the soldiers would not come in and burn us out or kill us. My brothers, of course, hated me.

Nothing happened to anyone in my family during these riots. But I am sure that the trauma caused by my perception of possible death from the white-armed soldiers, and my family's reactions to them, "sub-planted" into my psyche my first internal message of powerlessness.

I actually knew a white person at this same time. She was my classmate at Bellevue Elementary on the east side of Detroit. I did not see her as the same as the soldiers for obvious reasons. She was little, and had no gun or uniform to threaten me. I didn't really think of her as white either. As a kindergartener, I did not understand that in the socio-cultural sense. She was really, really pale with golden stringy hair that was soft and moved around. I do not remember her name, but we sat together a lot, held hands and swayed together as we sang songs and played games in our circle. She liked to play with me, so you could say she was my first white friend. But we never visited each other outside of school.

My family attended The Church of the Messiah around the corner from our house, and there were a few white members. I recall them helping to hand out Christmas toys to us kids in the basement's fellowship hall. They also gave us gift boxes full of tube socks, underwear, and holiday-themed tin boxes filled with peanut butter brittle and ribbon candy. There was this lady with stinky breath and rattling teeth who used to fuss with my hair, always trying to mash it down and fix it. She was friendly toward my momma, but I cannot say it was mutual. My momma was never rude though.

My daddy was a gambling man, and religiously played "the numbers." He was a binge-drinker too, but reserved that for when the pressures of providing for all of us, keeping his jobs, and dealing with the chaotic civil rights stuff got too heavy for him. He was functional, but he took a hiatus from reality in weekend bouts with the bottle once every three months or so. Kinda like a quarterly tax payment on life's stresses.

The numbers was a black-operated and crowd-sourced lottery of the day. We did not need the state to manage and legalize it. The winner was always someone black in the neighborhood, which was the intention, I believe. Well, as it turns out, my father's pet number was 611. My siblings never knew why he picked that specific number, as no one has that birthday or anniversary in our family. My guess is it had to do with JFK's 1963, civil rights speech on June 11th. In that speech JFK called for the Civil Rights Bill. I think it may have been my daddy's way to pay homage for a struggle he did not participate in on the front lines. His service in the Korean War and the move up north to Detroit interrupted that. Well, in 1969, about a year after you left us Dr. King, my daddy hit the numbers with 611. He won thousands! No one knows exactly how much, but it was enough to give my grandmother some money, his sisters some money, and the bank some money as a deposit for our new house on the northwest side of town. After the '67 and '68 riots, the east side became more dangerous, and we needed a bigger and safer home. We found our new "mansion" on Pinehurst Street between Fenkell and Six Mile Roads. That would be the last grand act my father performed for us. He died before we closed escrow and never even got to live there.

THE SEASONING, 1970s

(The Black Years)
Understanding Blackness

Tell them they are less, sprinkle in some drugs, glamourize the dysfunction, and close the door on open access. Then mix it all together and call it equality.

Say it Loud, "I'm Black and I'm Proud!"

If you're Black, get back
If you're Brown, stick around
If you're Yellow, you're mellow
and if you're White, you're RIGHT...

Black is beautiful, Brown is hip,
Yellow is mellow, and White Ain't Shit!

Why you so light-skinned,
Oh get yo' black ass away from me!

You Black Mutha'...

There Goes the...White Neighbors!

Dear Dr. King,

Our new place was perfect to break up the closeness of ten people living in the same house. It was also a two-family flat, but much bigger. We had an entry with a hall closet, a living room, a kitchen, a dining room, two bedrooms, and one full bathroom on the first floor. Another kitchen, living room, family room, one bedroom, one full bathroom, and a backyard balcony on the second floor. The basement had an engine room, complete with water heater, furnace and incinerator, as well as a laundry room with a laundry chute that started on the second floor. Plus, a bathroom with a shower. The basement shower was more of a mystery. I remember only a brief period when it worked, and it seemed the toilet was always in a state of disrepair. As I think about it now, with six brothers, everything in our house should have been fully functional, in tip-top shape, and it should have been a place of pride. But there was always something broken, or leaking, or just plain raggedy. My brothers did not learn carpentry, plumbing, or have any handyman skills, it seemed, until after they moved out. Their collective skills at home were muscle, sports, womanizing, and kicking ass. There was a second gas oven and stove, in the basement, but I don't remember my mother ever using it. The kitchen on the top floor was never used either. It had an old electric stove, but no refrigerator. Funny, as much as we needed an extra refrigerator, we never installed another. However, we did have the traditional Midwestern freezer in the basement, mostly stocked with meat for reserves or the too-cold-to-go-outside days. The coolest feature by far to us kids, outside of the basement and the extra rooms and two more bathrooms, was the milk cubby, called the milk chute. It was a square opening about the size of a large breadbox cut through to the exterior wall of the house near the side door. It was inlayed with two metal doors, one to open from the outside and one from the inside. The milkman would come once a week to deliver quarts of milk in glass bottles. You would put the empties in the cubby with some money, and he would replace them with fresh milk based on your weekly order. I loved this chute! We used it to talk through when we did not want to open the door. We used it to hide the keys and other items we wanted to throw in to avoid going in the house. We used it in the winter as a snowball storage room for our snowball fights. And we used it to unlock the door once our arms grew long enough to reach it. We never had to worry about robbers using it, though; they did not want to deal with all six of my brothers. My second eldest brother, Willie C, had the reputation of the "bad-est" one of all. No one messed with him. He was hit by a city bus on the east side when he was just a teen. The legendary story goes that my momma was in the middle of E. Jefferson Avenue holding him, waiting for the ambulance, after she stuffed his brains back in his skull. The stitches left a diagonal Frankenstein scar across his forehead. Ever since then people were afraid of him because of the appearance of it, and he would beat the shit out of anyone who tried to hurt him or anyone in our family. I guess it was also because he was 6'1"and strong as an ox.

I know my momma really missed daddy. It was different on Pinehurst. She did not drive, and relying on my two eldest brothers hustling around to take her where she needed to go in my daddy's car was exhausting. She did not have her mother and sister at arm's-reach anymore either, so I know it was a tough and bittersweet transition for her. I remember when the song, "You Got the Best of My Love," by the Emotions came out. She would pop that 45 on the record player and lay down the replay wand over and over, singing and swaying to every beat.

Doesn't take much to make me happy,
And make me smile with glee.
Never ever did I feel discouraged,
Cause our love's no mystery.
Demonstrating, love and affection,
That you give so openly, yeah.
I like the way you make me feel about you baby,
Want the whole wide world to see!
Whoa-whoa, you got the best of my love,
Whoa-whoa, you got the best of my love...

She really missed him. I would see her in quiet moments on bended knee in prayer alongside her bed, head bowed in some kind of despair. Lord knows it was for her sanity and the safety of all of us running all over the entire city doing God knows what. There was no way she could keep up. She probably felt like The Old Lady Who Lived in a Shoe. She used to say a lot, "There's always something to take the joy out of life." I did what I could to add at least a little joy to hers by trying to make good grades and stay out of trouble. But I had my share of family and school fights. I was no angel, but I would cry at the thought of doing something that would put shame on my momma's face. I just could not bear that look she would give me. Fortunately, that look was not directed at me more than three or four times in the fifteen years that I had her. But we had enough black family drama for three households, and three mommas!

Dr. King, most of the white families had moved away by the time we and other black families got settled in. Families moved in with three or four kids, cars, color TVs, and most of the mothers and fathers had factory or good government jobs. Some had their own small businesses. Some of them were even seeking political offices. These were proud hard-working families, all gunning for the American dream. Many households had both parents working. My mom and our next-door neighbor, Ms. Julia, were the only widows on our block.

There were four families that were bigger, but not quite as big as ours: the Thorns, the Mattisons, the Jacksons, and the Walters, each with six kids. The Mattisons had four boys and two girls. The Jacksons, Walters, and the Thorns were split down the middle. My family was friends with all of them. However, Jesse and Carol were my buds from the Jacksons, Sylvia from the Walters, and Ellen was my bud from the Mattisons. I was the eldest but only by a few months. My younger brother Douglass often played with my friends and other boys in the neighborhood. But my brother that was right over me, Ron, hated it when I tried to hang around him. Mostly because he would get in trouble if I got hurt. So he would run to be with his friends as far as he could to get away from me. Even though some of those friends were the older brothers of Jesse, Carol, Sylvia and Ellen.

Our block had fifteen houses, and no two were exactly alike. These were white middle-class homes. These homes were not quickly put together to accommodate a large population swell of factory workers. These homes were planned and built one at a time, with a church and school as the underpinning. There were floor plans with design incorporated. You had to walk around to get from room to room, versus walking straight through. There were framed wooden doors, with glass doorknobs, crown molding, and built-ins. And fireplaces, brandishing carved oak mantels. We had leaded pane windows. There were light fixtures, sconces, and textured ceilings. They had style and substance. All were two-story; many were brick. Some had aluminum siding. Many had a two-car garage behind that matched. But all of them had porches, front and back, and side and back doors. And again, we even had a small balcony in back of the upstairs bedroom.

I especially loved my other good friend Kim's house. Her mom, Laura, had exquisite taste from what I could tell. Not only was her house the prettiest in the neighborhood, but also it had to be the cleanest. She did not play when it came to cleanliness, and she had her kids trained properly. Kimberly had to get on her knees to scrub the toilets. Her mom had the routine down, and all five of those kids would not dare piss her off by not doing it when she said, and the *way* she said it. Laura should have started a maid service or decorator service no doubt 'cause nobody could do it the way she did. She could have trained an army of workers and seriously got paid.

Their kitchen was the best kitchen in the neighborhood too. It was wide with the stove and refrigerator on one side, and the sink and all the cabinets on the other. It had a cool breakfast nook with a built-in bench and pedestal table. The sink was farmhouse-styled, white, and deeper than ours and most of the families. It faced the driveway where her sons played a lot. It was cool too because her house was the only one that I remember where the kitchen could be accessed from both the side door and the backdoor. Their downstairs bathroom was nestled between the kitchen and the den. Most of the other homes had it between two bedrooms. I loved sitting in the nook at that '50s-styled soda fountain table, pretending I was part of their family having dinner. Plus, she could cook her butt off. I can still taste her collard greens today. Everybody did not always get along, but it was superbly functional, and I loved that family. I learned so much from Laura.

There was a Catholic church, St. Francis de Sales. It occupied most of the block; a fortress with manicured patches of lawns, hedges, concrete walkways, and wisps of lots that beckoned play and adventure. The crimson brick buildings were strong and stern with grand doors, a tall steeple, and bell tower. There was an office and rectory rounding the corner of my street. The first building after it was the three-story private elementary school. Behind it, were a gymnasium and a huge parking lot with basketball hoops and a baseball diamond in the north corner. All of it was enclosed with a chain-link fence. Then there was the chapel and convent across the street from our house. The chapel had a seven-foot alabaster, beveled cross, flanked by stained-glass windows. That cross commanded holiness. If you stared at it long enough in a heavy rain and thunderstorm, you could see Jesus hanging there weeping. It felt like he was right there watching us.

We quickly learned to use St. Francis as our play area. Outside of "hooping it up" on the basketball court, we used the front lawn of the school as our baseball field. Each summer, our consistent play wore down the grass until we had a diamond. We used the fences and the trees as a relay and obstacle course field when we got tired of baseball. Then there was the balcony of the chapel, the three-foot-deep corrugated steel, window wells, the shrubs, and the grounds around the chapel as our hide-n-seek depot. The boys had figured out how to climb to the roof of the rectory. They would run from one end to the other throwing pebbles and water balloons, causing any havoc they could. It was also their lookout tower to watch the girls. They did not allow the girls to come up there, but we tried to when they were not around. Rarely did our family, or the neighbors, use the church as a place of worship.

The white families that attended regularly would drive in and out, and you would not see them again until the following Sunday. It was like whitecaps coming into shore. They would come and disappear inside the buildings, then roll back out and fade away. Not long after, they stopped coming altogether. We assumed they had found suburban church homes nearer their new neighborhoods. Father Cunningham and the nuns started making their rounds to introduce themselves and the church to the new Negro families, presumably when the tithes and offerings began to shrink measurably. But the new Negro families had all moved in with their own religions intact: Baptists, Lutherans, Muslims, and Methodists. We were Methodists. We never took the time to learn the tenets of the Catholic religion. The church bells were reverent, but those Latin verses and stoic hymnals were not rapturous enough to replace the resonance of gospel music. It just did not call us in. My momma said we were southern Methodists and we did not belong in a Catholic church, and that was pretty much that. We did attend an occasional Easter service when she didn't want to take all of us on the bus — all the way to the east side to attend The Church of the Messiah. She figured it was easier. And there was no way we were getting out of church on Easter.

Every black family disappeared to their own separate church homes on Sunday mornings. We played together, but did not pray together. If we did all attend the same neighborhood church, and if the kids got into a fight, then normally, everybody would know. Of course the preacher might find out, and nobody wanted to have the sermon directed at him or her. We did not have to fear a public "come to Jesus" confessional and forgiveness altar call to keep us in check. So if you did fight, and the parents did not resolve it, there was also no moral authority to publicly shame us. That meant the kids got away with a lot.

The Lyles were the only black family I can remember that attended St. Francis regularly. The rest of us went only to special events or classes hosted by the church as part of their mission. We visited for Vacation Bible School, summer arts programs, cooking classes, etiquette classes, and basketball tournaments. With the exception of basketball, all of these programs were informative, and you learned something new and interesting. But it felt like we learned more about how white people lived than about the love of God. We were grateful for the outreach and the new things we learned that we liked. But because they were so different and white, we were cautiously and culturally inaccessible. We were not going to convert to Catholicism, and they were not coming over for dinner.

I loved it when my momma would take a break from us and get dressed up for church or some ladies' event. She'd soak in the tub with her Avon's Skin-So-Soft or Calgon, always calling me in to scrub her back. She had the silkiest skin. Then she would start her makeup by applying a thin layer of Noxzema, rubbing it in good as a base. Then Flori Roberts powder foundation (one of the only two cosmetic companies that made makeup for black hues). She would be careful not to disturb the Noxzema, to get that satiny unblemished doll-baby face. She would do a light green, pale blue, or white eye shadow and apply rosy rouge in a circle on her cheeks. The eyelashes would be glued on and then she would do crimson lipstick to accent her perfectly full cushiony lips. Red was her favorite color. I would have to polish her beautiful elongated finger- and toenails. She just had the most perfect hands and toes. It was always a production ending with someone zipping up her dress that she wore over a girdle, which had an opening for going to the ladies' room. Her stockings would be snapped at the thigh. We always laughed about the "flesh tone" stockings that were always too light for brown legs, but we wore them to fit in. At least we had Afro-Sheen. But wigs would be what would top it all off. My mom's hair was very thin and super soft, so it never held a style. She wore wigs a lot.

She would catch the bus, or the jitney, whichever came first, and would not come home for hours, usually carrying two big tote bags. We would see her walking down the street and run to help her carry them. It was usually one from Kresge's department store, with a smaller Woolworth's bag in it and one from Sander's Bakery. There would be something new to wear for us younger kids in the Kresge's bag; and that famous caramel cake from Sander's was to die for. I never knew what was in the Woolworth's bags.

My mom was the best cook. Everyone always said that Florestine could burn! She could even make rice taste gourmet, and it didn't matter how many times per week we ate it. Monday: What's for dinner Momma? Chicken, rice and gravy. Tuesday: What's for dinner Momma? Rice, gravy and chicken. Wednesday: What's for dinner Momma? Gravy, chicken and rice. Dr. King, there wasn't anything a person didn't love that came out of our kitchen, touched by her hands. I'd like to think the phrase "you put your thumb in it," which meant it was exceptional, was created in reference to her. I always smelled onions on her hands when she combed my fro. Her desserts were just as good. Her homemade sweet-potato pies, cinnamon rolls, rice pudding and pound cakes were wanted by everybody. She would sell some on occasion, but she never tried to replicate that Sander's caramel cake. There was just no substitute. Downtown was where we had to go to get it. For shopping we usually went to Greenfield and Grand River. The best was going downtown, especially for the holidays and the Christmas displays at JL Hudson's, because you knew on those occasions Sander's would also be visited.

There was one corner store across from the church office that sold convenience goods and prescription drugs, plus fresh fruit in the summer. A Jewish family, the Riches, owned it. Mr. Rich was the pharmacist. They had two sons, Stephen and Larry, who played with us from time to time when they had to help out in the store. They were a bit older than me and spent more time with my older brothers, Tony and Ron. What I remember about the family: Mr. Rich's gentleness with us. I don't think he ever raised his voice while we were playing around behind his store. And Mrs. Rich's silent demeanor and her super long, down-to-her-butt, black hair, and the silver, ragtop Corvette convertible they owned. I also remember Stephen's unicycle and Larry's kinky-curly hair, or vice-versa. The other thing is that they hired a black female clerk to work the register in front. For the first time, it registered to me, that white folks would hire blacks to handle their money. (It did not occur to me that my father's employer was most likely white.) Mr. Rich would extend credit to my momma by allowing us to get milk, Wonder Bread, bologna, Miracle Whip, Lays potato chips, and Faygo pop when we ran out of money before the end of the month. He would do it privately, he himself shopping from her list, written in cursive, usually on a ripped piece of brown paper bag stained by cooking oil or hair grease from the hot comb. He would fill the bag, ring it all up, and hand us the bag away from the register so that we would not feel bad if others did not see an exchange of money. Thank you Mr. Rich, I think there was always a silent love for you and your family by ours.

We liked our neighborhood, and it served us for the brief time we were there. The remaining two white families I'm sure felt abandoned. I only remember that one family was blondes and the other brunettes. They never played with us, and used to stare out their front windows like we were in a fish bowl or zoo and they were the visitors. They finally moved away a year or so later.

One of my last remembered interactions with white people on our street was with the insurance man. He sold my mother, and probably most of the neighbors, bogus, under-funded, over-charged insurance policies, taking full advantage of our inexperience with business, and underwriting policies that pretty much just covered funeral costs. Something else black people then had to learn the hard way.

The other was with the swim-mobile guy. For about two or three summers, the city created a program to take swimming to the neighborhoods that did not have access to public pools. Or maybe it was really a way to keep us from going to the suburbs to swim. I do not know what the politics were, but Mayor Coleman Young (Detroit's first black mayor), was doing a lot of out-of-the-box thinking. The swim-mobiles were galvanized steel tubs about twelve or fifteen feet long, mounted on the chassis of an eighteen-wheeler. When it came to your block, cones and construction ponies would block the traffic. The driver had both a trucker's license and a lifeguard certification apparently. He would park the truck near the fire hydrant, unscrew the cap, tie on the hose, and fill the pool up with water. Something like a fire escape ladder came down for us to climb. There was a protruding narrow catwalk, with a guardrail, that ran the length of the pool. The depth was three feet on the back of the truck, to five feet at the opposite end near the cabin. The driver would go into the cabin clothed, and come out on the passenger side like Superman wearing a Speedo. He perched himself atop the cabin in a rickety metal and nylon cross-latched folding chair and let the kids climb in. He'd finger-paint a hunk of zinc on his nose and shoulders, throw on his mirrored sunglasses, and let us have at it, breaking all the crowd-capacity rules. We were like a school of black goldfish in a giant tank bobbing up to the surface for feeding time.

It felt like a private pool party because it was on our block. But kids from all the surrounding blocks would run over and climb in too, and we could not stop them. There was no room to actually swim. We would climb in and splash and bob, waving our arms and yelling over to our parents sitting on the porches that we were swimming. I guess we thought they had x-ray vision like Superman, watching us through the steel. The moment you tried to swim you would get pushed or banged by someone's butt or knee. The boys quickly learned that it was a good time to cop a feel and have their frisky way with bikini-clad girls who did not fight back. I was too young and flat for that, plus I was the baby girl in the Lee clan. I did not have anything to worry about. Willie C and the rest of my brothers were never too far away, and every boy in the neighborhood knew it.

The swim-mobile was a fun novelty, but it was just as silly as it was new. We lived just four blocks from a huge park that had a large community pool and ice-skating rink in it, Butzell Field. We were not necessarily the intended underprivileged recipients; but we enjoyed it. The best part was getting knocked down by the force of water gushing out of the drainage hole when it was time to empty it. We would push and cut in line. Those boys discovered another opportunity with the bikini girls. They would run up behind a girl, one would grab her wrists, another would grab her ankles, and they'd carry her to the front of the flow just long enough for the water to rip off her top, and then drop her on the ground and run. Our parents would just laugh because, after the first time, everyone knew what would happen, so they just figured that the girls wanted it to happen. But some of the parents did not like the water flow at all. Many of them were from the south, and it evoked very fluid memories of a very painful and recent past.

No "I" in Black

Dear Dr. King,

You should have seen my school; you would have been so proud! Edgar A. Guest Elementary, in Northwest Detroit, was awesome. This school was more than wonderful. We were a middle-class elementary school. But the sad truth is, maybe the part you did not foresee, was that by the time I was enrolled, most of the white people had already flown to the burbs, and there were just a handful of white students and teachers left.

Anyway, the principal, Erma K. Greene was black. She was a beautiful and powerful queen: tall, elegant, proper, graceful, sharp, smart, and strong. She was a true leader. She had an understudy, Vice-Principal, Mr. Richardson I think, who did not even come close. This was the first time I had seen a white man under the power of a black woman, and it was something to behold. She was not domineering in the arrogant and competitive sense; she was just good at what she did (running her educational institution), and he could not touch her. Even his posture conveyed his awareness of this relationship, and he never seemed to challenge her at any level. I did not consciously understand this as a child, but even as a child, I got the sense that she was undeniably in charge. And I am sure it registered subconsciously in me as some sort of equity factor.

You also would have loved Mr. Clarence T. Eichelberger. He was the science teacher and surrogate father to everyone (I need to say, I don't remember any of my classmates who were from single parents, so perhaps uncle is a better assignment). He was the best science teacher, so smart and so demanding. He was handsome, charismatic, and did not tolerate any drama. And his paddle was the biggest. (Oh yeah, corporal punishment was allowed in the Detroit public school system throughout my entire tenure at Guest. I believe the laws were changed in the late '70s.) Mr. Eichelberger was strong too, and he was not someone you wanted a paddle from. He, Mr. Banks, Mrs. Edwards, and Mrs. Allen—they were all quick to paddle. But we still had it all because our teachers were like parents, and they truly cared. One or two were questionable, but the majority did excellent work. They brought great honor to the role of teacher. We loved Mrs. Edwards, librarian; Mr. Styles, math; Mrs. Allen, English; Mr. Jeter, vocal; Ms. Nkwoicha, music; Ms. Jujuan Taylor (she was the hippest, and we loved her!), drama; Ms. Snap, civics; Ms. Armstrong, art; Mr. Varatio, PE. We even had a father of a local celebrity, Mr. Banks, economics. His son, Ron Banks, was a singer in *The Dramatics.*

Our history teacher was white, as were our PE and art teachers, but he was the scariest one of the bunch. It was rumored that he moonlighted as a vampire host for a locally broadcasted TV show called *Sir Graves Ghastly* on the VHF or UHF channel. It featured weekend horror movies like *Frankenstein* and *Dracula*. It didn't help that he was clumsy because of one leg being longer than the other. He would limp along, lopping one leg in front of the other, breathing with forced gasps of air, and sweating irregularly. You could always hear him coming before you saw him. He was notorious for getting angry and slamming books on his desk for attention. He was unfortunately, one of the least-respected teachers. Not because he was white (everyone loved and behaved for Ms. Armstrong and Mr. Varatio), but mostly because he was, in our eyes, crazy as hell.

Our school lessons were layered with warnings of doing our best in order to prove we were "good enough" in the legend of "out there." Out there was the "white man's" world that did not want us to be equals—educated or not. Not next to them, not working "with" them, and certainly not befriending, dating, or marrying them. It was preached, day after day, class after class, by teacher after teacher. *Our* pledge of allegiance was first and then the US Pledge of Allegiance. The preaching instilled, embedded— and even occasionally inspired—that the only way to survive was to be smarter and better than them. If we could not accomplish that "out there," we would individually be responsible for casting shame on the race collectively. Because then, in these United States of America, there was no "I" in black. What went for one went for all. It was "Be your best," because you would be held to a much higher standard. Even if you met that standard, the most you could hope for was toleration. And with that toleration you could expect to be met with indignation and disregard. That was the set-up.

We were educated to fight for acceptance against real and proverbial resistance. A permanent state of underclass citizenship, or didn't our teachers know that? Like we did not have the freedom just to grow up and go out in the world; we had to be weighted down with the mental yoke of a fulltime and full-circle guarded existence. Kinda like what you preached, but it was so enigmatic. Burdensome. The very thing they were trying to accomplish for us would also be the thing that straddled us down in the lower position seeking approval and acceptance. But they did what they knew to do and thought it was with our best interest at heart. These lectures would be accompanied by special events that showcased the black struggle and the rise against all odds, or talent showcases, and history, history, history! We did not have Black History Month. Every day was black history. We would have musicals like *Porgy & Bess*, and *West Side Story*. Plays that included contemporary dances, poetry readings, and famous speeches and literature by you Dr. King, Frederick Douglass, Paul Lawrence Dunbar, James Baldwin, Paul Robeson, and Gwendolyn Brooks. It was a very intentional and rigorously scheduled school, where excellence was demanded. And for the most part, we delivered.

However, everything changed in 1976. The southern busing laws had finally rolled north into the Motor City, and Guest went from being one of the best elementary schools in Detroit to a questionable middle school overnight. Dr. King, by the time desegregation laws were broadly implemented, most of the white people had already moved out of the city. I can recall just a handful of white students left at Guest: Rayna, Rico, and Benjamin. We did not hold them necessarily as white kids. For us, they were more like misfits than another race. No one bothered them too much; and they were our friends.

So that fall, when the yellow school buses pulled up curbside, a bunch of 6th, 7th, and 8th grade black hoodlums, from I don't know what side of town, got off. They were mad, already poised to be rejected by mutually angry whites (a few were armed with switchblades and brass knuckles). They came in like a first battalion ready to kick-ass, and kick-ass they did. Dr. King, we could not believe the anger they showed us–their own people! We were caught off guard and actually felt terrorized by some of them. This was socio-economic warfare, the genesis of black-on-black crime, I'm sure. Well maybe not, but it felt like it. We did not know where these kids came from, and we did not like them. Class was introduced in a very contentious and painful way, and it was a tough lesson. We went from being young, gifted, and black, to being young, jilted, and black-eyed.

There was one specific incident when we went on a field trip in the spring of '77. We were walking along the trails of Kensington Park. Each time we encountered some white people, the kids started to beat them up. They just started swinging without any provocation. One of the white boys yelled for them to stop and asked, "What are you beating me up for?" One of our kids yelled back, "Didn't you see *Roots*?" Okay, all of us can recognize the anger that surfaced watching that mini-series. It was one thing to read about slavery, but an entirely life-altering thing to actually see it enacted so realistically and dramatically on television, so I understood how it made us all feel less than what we were. Seeing what we had previously read reinjured already undiagnosed, untreated, and unhealed wounds. I think many of us wanted to go out and start slinging and whipping. *Roots* was a powerful and indelible show. But those crazy boys were beating up white people in the suburbs, far away from home! We ditched them and ran back to find the teachers before the cavalry came back to retaliate, or haul our black-power asses off to jail. Dr. King, we were not operating on the high plane of dignity and discipline, we were shameful. I think we did not tell on them because we were relieved we were not the victims — and the fact that we had to get back on the bus with them. It took a long while before the clash of the classes adjusted to normal, or did it? My best friends and I were graduating in the summer and off to Cass Technical High School. I worried though about my little brother's fate in our newly economically desegregated middle school.

50 Shades of Black

Dear Dr. King,

Cass Technical High School—The Green Machine. It was one of the best, some would argue *the* best, high school in Detroit then, and you had to have a great GPA as well as high-test scores to be accepted. Detroit's finest, 3,200+ kids milled around in that downtown, 7-story learning factory. Freshman year consisted of the core curriculum plus one or two electives. We were there from 8:00-4:00pm, and I had to catch the city bus, with all the downtown workers, rain or shine—or snow. It took nearly an hour each way, and sometimes I would have to stand for the entire ride. Nonetheless it was a welcomed trip!

The kids in the school were so pretty and so handsome, and smart, and talented, and even worldly. I had thought all black people were middle-class, kinda homely, and normal, like us, and like the bussed kids. But there were all kinds of kids here. Some were rich and had parents who went to college. Some of them wore designer clothes and drove their own cars and spoke other languages. Dr. King, did you see schools like this in your dream? There were so many varieties of black boys and girls that you felt like you had the option to shop and select what personality or values you wanted for yourself. Like you were not bound by your family's background or traditions. You had funny, silly, argumentative, troublesome, diplomatic, dramatic, charismatic, sassy, sexy, cool, demure, sweet, mature, sophisticated, serious, stern, stoic, smart, scientific, artistic, and so much more to mimic. These traits had not been so prevalent in elementary and middle school (maybe a few), but the differences at Cass hit you like the latest fleet of Cadillacs, or the newest hits from Motown. You had to stop and pay attention. For those seven or eight hours at school, you could be anyone you wanted, and your family had nothing to say about it. Because you reappeared as your ordinary self by the time you got back home — if you were smart! But your new friends and teachers knew you as the wondrous creation you chose for yourself. It was better than an alter ego; it was more like being a superhero. It was sinfully delicious!

I fashioned myself as a hybrid between a girl named Dee, one of her friends, Cam, the Spanish teacher, Ms. Carter, and this boy whose name I cannot remember. But he carried a really cool art portfolio and could draw his butt off! I wanted to be most like Dee I think, with a sprinkle of the other three. Dee was tall like me, around 5'9", about the same shade of brown, but much more sophisticated. She was mature and ladylike. Because of my athletic family upbringing, and my six brothers, I was a tomboy with secret aspirations of being a sexy lady. But not as sexy as my older sister, so Dee was a safe in-between.

Dee's hair was always, always perfect, and my sweaty un-coiffed "do" was always in a state of disrepair, much like my house. She was pretty, but did not seem to use that pretty to sexually advance herself with the boys. I think she had strong moral fortitude and did not "put it out there" the way so many girls had started to. Plus, she had designer handbags and shoes and perfume, and dressed sharply, but not overdone. Although she wore heels a lot, which I both admired and was jealous of, I was not as comfortable as she seemed to be with her height. So walking with confidence at six feet tall in heels was not among the accomplishments I could boast. Besides, my feet were already a size eleven, so heels, or any ladylike shoes were hard to come by. She did not seem to have that problem. She had all kinds of shoes, which also meant that her folks had money. Pretty much in my household you got a pair of galoshes, and three pairs of new shoes: school shoes, black or brown suede Hush Puppies; or church shoes, Mary Janes (black patent leather in fall and winter, or white patent leather in spring and summer); and a pair of gym shoes, PF Fliers or Chuck Taylors from Cancellation Shoes (discounted overruns and irregular shoes). My CTs always had uneven lace holes, or the rubber-toe front unmatched and misaligned. They would come from the store wrapped like a gift in brown butcher paper concealing any brands. Maybe to spare you shame. But at least they were new. I would squeeze my feet into size 10s, trying to fit in where I truly did not belong, trying to be cute. This not only gave me ugly corns and bunions, I suffered stupidly in the name of style. The flamboyant disco and black-power styles had relaxed by the late '70s, and our school had become prep. This meant penny-loafers, pencil-legged jeans, (designer preferably) were in. It was such a relief to me because I could now be stylish in flat shoes with rounded toes, so the toe jamming and pinching were deferred, and my feet had a couple semesters off.

There were white students at Cass, but they were in the minority, outnumbered at least 7 to 1. I cannot recall a single racial incident at Cass. The whites may just as well have been ghosts, or invisible, because no one seemed to care. The atmosphere was truly academic, artistic, industrious, and progressive. I do not even remember any fights. It seemed that was all left behind in middle school, for kids. These teens were serious about being smart. They had ambition. We had it too, but the number of kids with it there was astounding. One of the 33 of us who came from Guest had wanted to be a pediatrician from the time we were in second or third grade. Cassandra Adams was my academic hero. That girl was smart as hell and tough too. She was also heavy-handed. You discovered that by playing Tag, or Duck, Duck, Goose, or Dodgeball. With any of the games that had incidental body contact or demonstrations of strength, once she hit you, you knew not to even think about trying to fight her. She would knock your ass out with one blow. I was intimated by her for that, but tried to compete academically. True to her excellence, she primarily outscored me most of the time because of her unbreakable determination, and because she did not live in my house. She aced practically everything and studied more than most of us. I do not know where she got the goal of pediatrician, but I always hoped that she would be my kids' doctor when I had them.

The boys were smart too. I remember Major Taylor (loved saying that name repeatedly and real fast) and Darryl Willis as being two of the brightest. I do not know what they wanted to be. You just knew they were going to be somebody. They were boys no doubt, but they were gentlemen too. You never felt threatened by them and your friendship was genuine. Plus, they'd challenge you academically all the time especially in science. We were a proud and accomplished graduating class from Guest. And we loved Cass even more. It was going to be a great first year, and it was, until I got some bad news at home.

Dr. King, my mom was diagnosed with colon cancer right before winter. I had no idea what a colon or cancer was, until she showed me the colostomy bag and the fleshy pink intestinal stump that was serving as her anus. It was so gruesome and shocking to see on so many levels. My family rarely ever went to the doctor, and the illnesses I remember growing up involved seasonal colds and flu, teeth extraction followed by infections, chicken pox, and injuries. All usually fixed by Mercurochrome, Pepto-Bismol, Calamine Lotion, rubbing alcohol, and Campbell's Chicken Noodle Soup. But from this moment on, I knew I never wanted to see that plastic bag again.

I knew she hated it, and felt shame about it, and I felt guilty because I had scared and grossed-out feelings about it. That's probably why, even today, I have such a funky, disturbed, and I have to admit, unnatural reaction to seeing people walking dogs and carrying the dog's poop in a plastic bag!

But Dr. King, my momma was my biggest fan and loudest cheerleader. I was at Cass because of her. She would always be on the phone to her friends bragging about me. Nothing made me happier than knowing how proud she was, but I was afraid to get too close and hug her in her last days, due to my ignorance. I starting smoking weed to stop thinking about it, but it only made me silly and hungry. Physically and mentally it did take me away for a bit, but the results would be the same: shame and guilt, guilt and shame, upon my return. My eldest sister Pat stepped in to care for her daily, as none of us were strong like her. I was grateful for the strength and care she showed our mom. She was there when my momma needed her the most. Nobody really talked about it much either. At a time when we should have pulled closer together, it seemed everyone retreated to the craziness of their own world. My mom's health declined rapidly after the surgery. The cancer had metastasized to her liver, and it was just a matter of time.

My fragile self-esteem and her fragile health plummeted alarmingly, at about the same rate, and she was gone before the end of my freshman year. I think my younger brother Doug and I were the last of the kids to see her alive. We visited the hospital with our Aunt Gertrude and Cousin Rochelle. We could not do anything but just stand at the foot of the bed and sob. Momma didn't seem to be able to even look at us. No sooner than she tried to look our way did her eyes roll up into her head, and she grimaced with immense pain. We must have cried loudly then, because my cousin rushed back in and ushered us out. In our grief, nobody spoke on our way back home. That next morning, shortly after dawn, my sister or cousin received the death call. I think they told my brother Ron first. He yelled out in disbelief, cursed the walls, and ran out the door, slamming it behind him. I knew what it meant without anyone telling me. All I remember after that were agonizing waves of screams and howls. I don't even know how many of us were home. Grief had paralyzed us like an ice storm freezes the streets, leaving layers of heavy snow and rigid icicles stuck together on rain-gutters and telephone lines, waiting for a warm-up to melt our frozen pain away. Each of us falling at our own designated time, without the notion of who to turn to or how to pack together again. We separated. I lost interest in school and spent the summer session and sophomore year doing just enough grades-wise to get by. My main things were defending my fear of sex, my frequent checkouts with weed, and oddly enough growing up on Motown, I listened to rock n' roll. It seemed angry and desperate, matching my mood swings. Every time I got sad, I wanted to smoke a joint and to hear "Stairway to Heaven." That was my respite.

This behavior resulted in my academic removal from Cass Tech, and I was relegated to my neighborhood school, my third oldest brother's (Warren Jr.) neighborhood school, Redford High. His household doubled. It went from six (his wife and four kids), and one on the way, to all of them plus me, my brothers Ron and Doug, my sister Debbie, and her two sons Lorenzo, Lamont, and another son (Marcus) on the way. So in a matter of months, fourteen people lived in a three-bedroom, two-bath, two-story, single-family residence. Thank God there was a basement, but still, that was way too many people. Warren's heart was surely in the right place; he did everything, and I mean everything—he could to try and keep us together and happy, and at the tender age of 26. But he just manned up, way up, and did it. A lesser man, especially a lesser black man, would have hit the bricks and run as far and as fast as he could. But he never paled, Dr. King, and for that I will be forever grateful!

Having increased his family to fourteen, he began the search for a bigger house to accommodate us all. We moved right outside of Sherwood Forest in an area called Green Acres. This resulted in another school transfer for me to Mumford High. The thing that saved me finally was basketball. I had tried out for the girls' varsity team in my sophomore year at Cass. I did not make it because too many upper-class girls were in all eleven positions of the first and second strings. The only opening would be for one of them to get injured, quit, or graduate. My self-assessed skill and ego did not allow me to play junior varsity. I felt I was just too good, so I declined the offer. However, when I transferred to Redford and then Mumford, I was accepted right away for each varsity team. Mumford was nearly all black. That season, we reached advanced in the regionals and had to play an all-white basketball team from the suburbs. I had never played basketball against an all-white team before. Those girls had a certain precision about them. Every play seemed to come straight from the playbook, like no room for improvisation. It was weird, Dr. King, because I'm not sure if that was my prejudice, or just what I experienced in that game. It was like we were playing robots with sweeping ponytails that slapped you in the face whenever they turned their heads. When the ponytails became wet from sweat and water they were heavier. The ones that were braided, when they hit you, it felt like you were being whipped. And that sensation was more than physical. So I do not remember the name of the team, but I'm pretty sure we lost. I know I was psyched out before halftime and never recovered.

However, basketball at Mumford did a lot for me. It gave me something else to think about and something more to do that just academics, housework, and babysitting. (It seemed like I reared my eight nieces and nephews.) Their mommas were quick to take advantage of the new live-in babysitter, short-order cook, laundress, and hair stylist. Well, basketball kept me distanced from all that chaos and dysfunction at my brother's house, and allowed me to acquire and become fast friends each time I changed schools.

All in all, at each of these new schools, and for the most part, in each new neighborhood, I lived a childhood relatively free of racial incidents. In my senior year, my head coach was white, and my team members said she was a lesbian. Being that in the late '70s and early '80s made her an outcast, so essentially her whiteness was stripped away, and she was just one of us. No one really cared about her whiteness or her being a lesbian. She was just coach.

I guess why all this about my school years matters, and what I want you to know about it, is this: You were right, Dr. King. Even our parents said we were "freer" up north, but in truth that freedom existed in a big black bubble. With no whites in the neighborhood, except those in positions of authority, ownership, or at school, work, and public arenas, where the cultural lines were clearly understood, our reference points on how they really were came mostly from television and movies. Having TV as the primary source, white folks were summed up by us in categories defined by these shows: *All in the Family*, with Archie Bunker, was what we thought all white blue-collar families in urban cities were like; *The Brady Bunch* was the way suburban white-collar families were. (I wanted to be an architect like Michael Brady. I actually purchased a drafting table and took drafting classes in high school until the boys harassed me so bad I quit); *The Waltons*, rural and country families; The *Mary Tyler Moore Show*, professional white people without families. And this was our cultural lens. All of the other comedic and dramatic shows were abstractions and not the norm. These shows taught us we were not included, that we existed on the peripherals, and we were not wanted. But it was done in a way that infused the archetypal American way(s) of life, which we would have to eventually assimilate into.

It was a big deal, Dr. King, when they brought a black family into the show to live near Archie Bunker. George Jefferson was Archie's new neighbor, and Archie was not happy about that. But those two were cast as opposites of the same coin, as George did not like Archie any more than Archie liked him. Both were equally bigoted. This show truly was art imitating life, as many of us had already experienced what it was like to be the new Negro family in the white neighborhood. It became really popular, so popular in fact that it spawned off a new show. George got his own sitcom, *The Jeffersons*, which began by his "moving on up" to an upper-middle-class area of NY as a successful franchise business owner. Our family and most of our friends watched all the shows religiously. We were hooked. Admittedly it was fun to see George score and outsmart his white rivals—something we all wanted to do regularly with our bosses, teachers, and co-workers, but we knew it would create more drama and financial hardships than we were willing to risk. So we channeled our angst through the TV screen and lived vicariously through George. More and more black shows were starting to pop up. As one caught on with the viewers, another one would be created, slowly easing us into the mainstream with humor.

But it also did three more things: it occupied our minds—you could even say programmed us to thinking we were all like that; it delivered a subliminal edict of how we could or could NOT be; and it kept us off the streets. If it was a popular show you could almost guarantee what we would all be doing for that particular day, for those particular timeslots. I didn't know any black person who did not watch *Soul Train* on Saturday mornings, unless they had to work. While the networks were programming shows, we were being programmed how to spend our time and what to focus on.

On the flip side, white people also used TV as their compass for who we were too. Many of them did not engage with us voluntarily. This became problematic as the images of educated, intelligent, hard-working and "serious" black people (like many of my relatives, neighbors, and teachers), on TV were not produced for primetime. We essentially became dancing, slaphappy, last-hired, first-fired, second-class citizens all over again. We were told to celebrate poverty in the slums or projects and that we could become business owners if our businesses were in service to whites: something like dry cleaners, junkyard dealers, deejays, or cab drivers. It was all very subversive, intentional or not.

Yes, Dr. King, we were experiencing something new, perhaps "freer" in Detroit, but it was a freedom laced with fear. Black people were not just moving into newer neighborhoods, we were beginning to move into Hollywood as well. While the small screens were consistently depicting us one way, the big screen gave a much riskier rendition. There was a mad rush of black movies dominating the movie influx right alongside the imported drugs creeping into our neighborhoods. And too, the musical recording artists were making songs about the drug rise. There were so many new films made that they created a brand-new genre called "Blaxploitation" movies. We were big-money-making, sexy, powerful, and illegal pimps, whores, drug dealers, drug addicts, murderers, and thieves. In just over 15 years after your preaching about who we were (and your tragic sacrifice), the film industry went crazy imaging us as everything but. And we loved it! Bought it—hook, line, and sinker.

This deviant lifestyle became so glamorized that it was adopted and replicated as the way for us to get ahead in the white man's world. My two eldest brothers, "Super Fly and The Mac," we had dubbed them by now, certainly bought in, and it would be the further undoing of our family. Our family was already unraveling with the loss of our father, then our mother nine short years later, but cocaine and heroin ultimately destroyed what unity we did have, and we have not fully recovered to this day.

The drugs poured into every major city with large populations of blacks and destroyed generations of black youth trying to make quick money or to get high. Dr. King, I don't think you could have understood how badly and quickly the devastation wrangled the black family. Talk about "weapons of mass destruction," all the love and joy we had for each other that was reflected in the

Motown music was replaced by hardcore anger, fear, and disdain for each other due to the maniacal forces of drugs. Large segments of the black community turned on each other, robbed, conspired against, and even killed for those drugs. Those with any means moved as far away as possible as quickly as they could. It was the fastest most powerful brain-drain and separation of our people since we were snatched from the motherland. Black flight, and then black blight. It was worse than any military war, because its destructive and nefarious forces lingered on for two and three generations, and the family values were deeply buried underneath the carnage of our youth. Black-on-black crime had been forged into our collective consciousness, and we became, sadly, AFRAID OF EACH OTHER! Divided and marginally conquered. Criminals everywhere, making all kinds of illegal money, replicating those lifestyles we saw on film. We were freed from slavery, but now imprisoned by the collateral damages of drugs and the criminal justice system. Dr. King, you did not see that coming. Nobody did. And nobody predicted the hold it would have for generations. It was war for real, but one with substances versus people per se.

I know you rolled over in your grave when you saw the morals of our people beginning to corrupt for a set-up of fast and illegal money. I'm not saying that all of us were like that, not by any means. There were many, many folks doing great and wonderful things and even prospering. But those who were that way, got the majority of the press, and those images were being "programmed" on every media mode and channel defining us as a race of deviants—all over the world! A serious TKO. Dr. King, images of serious and intelligent black people like you, Medgar, Jessie, Ralph and Stokely were hardly ever broadcasted. If you were, you were marginally vilified. And shows like *I Spy*, *Julia*, and *Room 222*, that portrayed positive smart normal black people, were also limited or eliminated. Between those negative images of the movies and the growing succession of black sitcoms with formulas of fat praying mommas, barely working, overworked, and underpaid fathers, sass and loud-talking characters you mostly laughed at or felt sorry for—it was widely broadcast that THIS WAS HOW WE WERE! And not only did we begin to believe the stereotypes in all those shows, white people believed them too! Because that was probably the only reference most of them had about us.

Those influences were so pervasive! In my own house, I would see cakes of heroin baking in the oven. My brothers were having serious drug dealings, drug parties, and sex orgies in the basement of my momma's house. And she was dying from colon cancer upstairs! They had lost their natural minds! None of us knew what to do about it, because we were a bit scared of them, but more afraid of their druggie friends. They had guns. And we were not sure that the drugs wouldn't cause them to use those guns on us.

My brother, Willie C, tried to break his addiction after my mom died in '78, but he did not remove himself from bad company. He went through periods of withdrawal neurosis and fatigue. We would see him talking and laughing to himself and running through the house trying to hug everyone. His laugh was haunting. He scared us. His talking was incessant, muddled, and he would be sweating profusely. At times he would strip down naked and run around the block over and over until someone could catch him and bring him back inside.

One time Dr. King, on a rainy day, he stripped down and ran outside, and stretched his arms out across that old cross on the chapel like Jesus. He stood there, head bowed, and laughed and cried as if to offer himself to God in repentance. Or praying for help! I did not know what he was saying. Lord knows that freaked me out more than any other episode so I just ran away from the door. My older siblings grabbed a jacket and went to bring him back in. They put him in the bed, and I do not recall what happened next. Sometime later, maybe days, or it could have been a few weeks; we got a call from my eldest brother, telling us that Willie was dead. He had died from a heroin overdose in his big brother's house. This happened just one year after the death of Momma, it was too much for any of us to bear. That was August 1979. We left that house right after the funeral to get some mental and physical distance from the painful memories. When we returned a week or so later, the house had been stripped of practically everything we owned, even the ugly shag carpet, the kitchen cabinets and sink. Our furniture — gone! The prized pool table — gone! The tables, chairs, built-ins — gone! Even my momma's famed and loved rose bushes were uprooted out of the ground! Our neighbors apparently thought we were gone for good and decided to have a "free for all." They had rummaged through everything, and left only pictures, papers, files, clothing, broken dishes, and the roaches! It was horrible! Death had consumed all of the tormented life in that house. That is why we moved in with my brother, plus, we lost the mortgage. But nobody wanted to stay there anymore anyway.

There were some pretty rough times, and even rougher realities to contend with, but somehow I managed to survive it all with my integrity and sanity intact. You might even say, God had a better plan for me. I have to tell you, with all honesty, Dr. King, in spite of all the trauma and tragedies, there were pretty good times in that neighborhood before the drugs crept in. I had so many wonderful friends, and good times playing, traveling all over the city on our bikes and on buses. There are a lot of treasured memories. We all knew the most intimate details about each other's families. Shared some of the same hopes and dreams, and those parts were beautiful. (But, I have always wondered from time-to-time what Father Cunningham and the Sisters really thought about us all. They had to have been in a very long and deep culture shock).

Our house was foreclosed on before the end of 1979. Believe it or not, another black family occupied it for a few years before they completely wore it out and left it in shambles. It was abandoned for a long while, before it was demolished. I went home in 1991 and got the last picture of it in its boarded-up ruin. The church began to sell off sections of the fortress the year before busing was implemented. They sold the school to the city of Detroit. That was when Guest became a middle school only. The chapel was sold to Wayne County Department of Corrections and made into a halfway house. Sometime in the late '80s, early '90s, I believe, Mr. Rich had sold the pharmacy and relocated to the burbs. I was surprised that he stayed there so long.

Is it possible that you saw ahead to something like this happening? We were so focused on integration as freedom that no one really considered that the black family movement never had a plan for advancement beyond legislation and labor. I guess we will never know because you were not given the chance to consider these things with your selfless heart and great mind.

THE LABOR, 1980s

(The Afro-American Years)
Living Blackness, Understanding Whiteness

So you can say
I was sheltered
with(in) the city limits
and
lived a surreal existence…
Learning about
the world at-large
and
how it related to ME
was indeed laborious!

For some time, upon hearing the term Afro-American, I thought, until I didn't, that it strictly meant those who could wear an Afro and used Afro-Sheen…and that included everyone in my family.

The Outer Limits

Dear Dr. King,

I enrolled at HFCC (Henry Ford Community College) by default. I had wanted to attend Michigan State University, since the 10th grade, but after my mom's death, my being kicked out of Cass Tech, and my poor two-year academics, I knew I would not be getting an acceptance letter in the mail, so I did not even try. One of my best friends, Melayne, was going to HFCC, so I just followed in her footsteps. I was excited however, to go to school in the suburbs. It was adventurous. No one in my family had been there, so it was a retreat. They did not have college experience to tell me what to do, or how to behave. No one would come looking for me there, and I had a legitimate excuse to be away, far, far away from the craziness at home. It felt great to be on a college campus, to be eighteen and grown, and to have my new tan leather backpack. When I saw my dot-matrix, printed schedule of classes, it was official. I was a college student. I belonged to an elite class of scholarly people (and yes I know it was community college).

I liked having college in common with my white counterparts. I was "in," having taken my first adult step to assimilate into the world at large. I felt privileged in those moments. Getting fresh new textbooks from the college bookstore instead of having your teacher give out used ones was just a thrill. I was shopping for knowledge on those shelves. Very different than having it handed to you. My excitement was short-lived, however. Business 101 was first on my schedule, in a classroom not a lecture hall, and I was one of three black females in the class of roughly forty students.

Professor Benedict (name change) was elderly (that could have been 50 in my uninformed assessment). He took command of the room five minutes after the hour by closing the door and nodding his head as he walked across the front row of desks one-by-one, a well-rehearsed ritual. He laid a pre-counted stack of papers on the first desk of each row while announcing he was handing out the syllabus. He introduced himself, gave his credentials, and stated the name of the course to make sure the students were in the right room. Then he said he would first call roll before diving into the syllabus. He grinned when he said, "diving into the syllabus" as if he coined the phrase, like a teen that swears for the first time. After calling the first full name on the list, he paused and asked each student if they knew the origin of their surname. Surname, I thought, what's a surname? He repeated the boy's last name and asked if his family was English. The answer was yes. It took a couple of rounds for me to figure out that surname meant the country of origin of your family's name and ancestry. I was glad he had not gotten to the Ls yet, but simultaneously horrified. I was the first black student to have to answer. I sat there, painfully, with a swell of anger building up—at both Mr. Benedict and my parents and teachers for not preparing me for this. Yes, I had seen *Roots*, but it did not give most of us a strong desire for Pan-Africanism. It did leave us with a deeper and profound sense of separation and inherent (sometimes dormant, sometimes overt) mistrust of white people. Africa was a continent, not a country, and I could not recall Kunta Kinte's "country of origin!" I also didn't think there were any Lees in Africa. If I answered Chinese, out of sarcasm, I would be laughed right out of class. I did not even know any Chinese people, but I was always curious why my mother had purchased red Chinese lanterns on her trip to Las Vegas. So with anger suppressed and imminent embarrassment lingering, I saw Mr. Benedict grinning my way as he read my name and asked the social death-blow of a question, on the first day of my first class–in college! "So Wanda Lee, where is your family from?" My throat tightened, but a stream of air managed to escape enough to murmur a wimpy, "I don't know."

"Really," he asked to turn the knife, "your family has not done the research to learn what part of Africa you're from? Didn't you see '*Roots*?'" That mutha' didn't just ask me that! Every racist term I had ever heard flashed across my brain from Cracka' to Pecka'wood, and I wanted to kill him. But being just a student and taught to respect my elders, especially those in authority, and out of my sheltered Detroit world, I just burned the most evil look (trying to hold back the tears). I was sure my gaze would burn a hole right through his throat. He shrugged his shoulders with a lipless smirk on his ghostly, colorless face and proceeded to stroke his ego with the remaining English, Polish, Irish, German, Scottish, Swedish, Italian, French, and Jewish (not a nationality) students, while sadistically basking in questioning the remaining two black students. But it did not end with the individual points of humiliation, no. He announced in a reverberating summation, like a southern lawyer in a trial to win a case to hang a black man, how surprised he was that out of the three black females in the class "none" of *them* knew where their families came from. Racist bastard! That was a preemptive strike, and it mortally wounded me. It would have hurt less if he had called us "dumb-ass niggers." At least then we would have been able to justifiably retaliate against such an overt act of aggression. Like kick his ass in the parking lot. But we were unprepared, and there was no denying our lack of knowledge about our ancestry. The most we could do was hate him and Africa more. Welcome to college!

Instantly, I did not care about Business 101 or showing Benedict how smart I was. I had always sought to please my teachers with good performances. I no longer cared about being at Henry Ford or being equal to, or better than, my white peers. He had won the battle in that first attack, and from that moment, college, or at least HFCC, became a place to dread. But it remained the source of my survivor income from SSI and VA.

Dr. King, that professor was not even interested in the content of my character. I didn't know I was so unprepared. All that elementary school preaching did not come with a play-by-play, how-to book. Beyond a physical altercation, I did not know what to do. I crumbled. I didn't make any new friends, because a few of my friends from Cass Tech attended HFCC too, so I just hung out with them. I did not trust anyone in the administration building because they all looked like Benedict, and my siblings would be of no use. They would just cuss him out, threaten to hurt him, or actually hurt him. None of which would provide any benefit to me on campus. So I only told my friends.

Dr. King, I know that your generation, and all of my ancestors, suffered so, so much worse pain and degradation, but I was not ready for the wider world. I was blindsided. I had essentially forgotten about racism and the blows that could be thrown at me for my entire high school career. And I did not have a plan. I had to maintain fulltime (12 units) status to receive my benefits. This was my modus operandi for the next two semesters. I attended class everyday (high on weed most of the time), and would withdraw after the government reporting-period elapsed. That was fortunately, right before you could withdraw without an F. My sole goal was to keep my money coming in, until I figured out what I wanted to do with my life.

I See White People

Dear Dr. King,

The summer following my last semester at HFCC, I got a job at an amusement park called Boblo-Island. It was an island near the mouth of the Detroit River that flowed into Lake Erie. Detroiters, Canadians, and tourists from neighboring towns and states visited by the tens of thousands from Memorial Day to Labor Day. There were two large ferryboats, which could hold up to 2,500 passengers each, taking them to the island from the dock in downtown Detroit. I grew up visiting Boblo-Island, but I had only known what it was like to be a rider. Now, I was an official service worker and was going to learn how they made the boat magic. Each summer they hired 10-15 college students per boat to be ticket-takers, concession-stand workers, and video game coin-changers. We had a blast. We got to spend all summer on the river in a boat, without getting seasick, and work from 7am – 12am on rotation five days a week.

I was assigned the SS Columbia, and she had about four deckhands, the purser (who also doubled as the medic), and the Captain who lived on the boat. Who knew? I thought only cruise ships had live-in crews with sleeping quarters. This ferry was much bigger than the eye could tell, and was glorious in all its ferry rights. They had sleeping quarters in the hull and a couple of cooks in the galley who prepared three meals a day for them all summer. We were allowed lunch down there as well. That part of it made me feel like I was a sailor. There were twelve of us on each ship. Our crew had three or four blacks and the rest were white, and that was a pretty good ratio for us. I am sure there was some political design at play here. Mayor Coleman Young had a lot to say about Detroit's youth and jobs; he was pretty tough when he set his mind to something.

It was our practice to rotate assignments all summer in case someone got sick. Everyone had to know how to do all the jobs. So we sold and collected the tickets on dock, counted the folks as they loaded up, reconciled the count with ticket sales, prepared and sold concession-stand food: pretzels, hotdogs, chips, candy, nachos, popcorn, and soda, powered up all the video games, and managed the souvenir display and sales. We also learned how to pour three-second shots of whisky, vodka, gin, and rum for our basic soda and one-shot well drinks. We learned how to calibrate the soda tanks, beer kegs, and pour the beer on a tilt to avoid a half-glass of foam. Those of us who practiced, namely the guys, quickly made a sport of pouring two perfect glasses at a time, with just an inch of foam.

We'd begin each day by onboarding passengers promptly at 8:00am, to a maximum of 2,500. We set sail (or started the engine) by 8:30, and headed down the Detroit River for a ninety-minute sail each way. The passengers would hit the deck running to their pre-planned points of interest. Most would end up in the stern area of the second deck where you could view the dance floor, as well the port and starboard sides. Kids loved to get out on the polished oak floor and slide in their socks, shaking it up to the pop songs of the '80s. On occasion, Captain Boblo would come down and join them doing a trademarked rendition of the *Hokey Pokey*, in which they would all rally around him. His uniform was decked-out (pun intended) and way too colorful with red, navy, and gold embellishments. In addition to the naval stripes, he had tassels and frays around the embroidered striped and embroidered appliqués. He also wore a decorated sailor's cap. It was a wacky routine, but the kids loved it. It was a very fun or relaxing ninety-minute cruise to the island.

When the passengers disembarked, we made the rounds to check for stowaways. Each of us manned our designated areas. Once the boat was cleared, we took off and sailed back to get the next group amassing in Detroit. Since Boblo Island was also on the Canadian side of the Detroit River, there appeared to be some international clause or treaty that required the boat to touch Canadian soil before returning to the US. It was hard for me to think of Canada as another sovereign country, because it was just a bridge, the Ambassador Bridge, or a tunnel ride away, ten minutes in normal freeway traffic from Detroit to Windsor, Ontario. The Columbia would sail east and then detour north to literally slow down and touch the padded dock in Canada and continue southeast across the river to the Detroit docks. During this time we would do our cash and inventory counting, restocking, and depositing the cash-drawer overages with our supervisor. We would also clean up by sweeping, reorganizing the chairs, wiping down the counters and soda fountains, and emptying the trashcans from all the stands and the bathrooms, delivering them to the deckhands for disposal. Lastly, the girls would freshen up our makeup for the next round of on-boarders. It took us about a week to get this part of the first run-down to an efficient science. We quickly learned that the sooner we cleaned and got organized, the more time we had to do whatever we wanted on the one and only dry-run during the day. No alcohol was served on the first run coming or going, so everyone who came at that time of day typically wanted to spend as much time as possible on the island. The SS Columbia was first to leave and therefore had the benefit to the crew of no passengers to attend to on the return. That made the Columbia the premier boat to work on, and we vied for it. As much fun as it was to be on a boat all summer, we enjoyed the down time when we did not have to wait on passengers. We could do our thing. Our thing consisted of playing cards (they introduced me to Euchre, Hearts, and Pinnacle); reading, talking, sleeping, and sunbathing of course—but I did not do the latter.

So here I was with my first peer-to-peer experience with whites, where I had the chance to actually learn about them as individuals. Real white people — not the ones abandoned to fend for themselves in the city. (Yes there were real too, but as I explained earlier, they were more like outcasts to us than a race of people.) Here in this controlled environment on the boat, I could safely presume that it was also their first genuine exchange with black people. I was friendly with them all and had an honest curiosity. I learned early on that most were there to earn money for college, a car, or to travel. I hadn't thought much about any of that, since my first college experience was lackluster. Everyone I had ever known lived near me — except my granddad, who lived in Oklahoma City. One visit down there was enough for me, even though I loved him dearly. I didn't need a car because I had inherited my brother's 1971 yellow, Volkswagen Beetle when I moved in with him after my mother's death. I had also carved out a corner of the basement as my own apartment, so I did not have any of my fellow employees' goals. I was just happy to have a job. I was impressed by their determination and fortitude. Their views also appeared worldlier. I was intrigued.

They all struck me as serious whether they were or not. I am sure there was some psychosis of the legacy of slavery playing here. The way we were taught to think that all white people had always been and would always be smart and educated and have command over their futures. How they seemed to have all resources readily available. The late '70s' massive drug infestation and subsequent serial decline of the black family created so much doubt, frustration, and abatement about who we were. Who I was. You can understand why I believed more in their capabilities and ambitions than in my own.

Our experiences in school were similar. After all, I was "accepted" and did attend Cass Tech, so I was just as smart, but I did not have any real plans for life. They had some ideas and support and direction, it seemed, from their parents, older siblings, and peers. I think my family assumed I would go to college, but it was not a topic we frequented. I made no mention of my older siblings to match their stories, hiding behind the embarrassment that none had graduated yet from college. So there was nothing grandiose or unprecedented that I could exchange for validation.

Playing cards was the most popular activity on the dry runs. A few of the crew were content to just sunbathe or read. Not me. I enjoyed learning the new card games. I was a quick study and started beating them at their own games within a short while. I had grown up playing Bid Whist, Spades, Tunk, War, Solitaire and Canasta. As a kid I had played almost every board game that was available. Winters were long at times, and TV and games were the primary sources of entertainment. Our crew games typically took place on the stern side of the third outer deck, right below the Captain's Quarters on the partial fourth deck. We would arrange the tables and chairs to seat six and get it going.

Most of us were in our late teens or early twenties. But there were two who were somewhat older. I think John (name changed), who was in his mid-to-late twenties and another woman whose name I cannot recall. She seemed more mature and experienced, bringing carefully prepared and appetizing, balanced lunches for herself, versus our paper-bag versions of thrown-together bologna or peanut butter and jelly sandwiches with some chips. She also made the best fruit-infused, iced tea drinks. I have always wondered if Snapple got their idea from her. Or if she became an investor, a partner, or was even the founder!

A couple of team members figured out how to beat the exchange rate system and earn a little bump to our weekly checks. As I stated earlier, Boblo was partially in Canadian waters, but we were employed in MI. For some international, economic trade reason, both the Canadian dollar and US dollar were accepted as par on the ships. During the early '80s Canada's exchange rate value was roughly 70% of the US dollar. Joe (name change) told us that we should cash the checks in Detroit. Then go to the border currency exchange and switch our dollars to the *Loonies,* (nickname of Canadian dollar). Then bring the *Loonies* back to the boat and exchange them bill-for-bill from the daily cash intake. We could get $30 to $40 more per check this way. He spelled it out in these terms: take $100 US dollars to the border and exchange them for $130 Canadian dollars. Then at the end of the day, counting the daily intake, switch the $130 Canadian dollars back to $130 US dollars.

I wasn't so sure this was not an international crime, and wondered if Jackson Prison could become my future residence, so I just watched and waited. I'm not sure if everyone applied this economic stimulus to their weekly banking ritual, but for eager college students with plans, it was a very attractive idea. The customers (presumably from Canada) did it all day long. They would buy something for $3 with a $20 *Loonie* and get back $17 US dollars on request. It began to make sense. There were always two boatloads of cash, figuratively and literally. Credit cards or checks were not yet the mainstream for that kind of entertainment. Everyone paid in cash. And with a minimum of ten thousand passengers on an average a day (per boat), spending an average of $10 each on concessions—well Dr. King, you can do the math. After about the second or third trip, and all their bragging, I decided not to be left out. I figured if whites did it and got away with it, it must be safe. I really did not like the feeling, but would numb it out in the evening with our beer and burger runs to a local dive we frequented on payday.

I had never known a white hustler (aside from a much-older shifty insurance man), so I was fascinated by Joe (a future Wall Street broker no doubt). The next thing he enlightened us about involved inventory counting. He realized that the hand count of soda, beer, and wine cups, that we had to do after each run, was flawed. We used these same cups for tap water requests, or as extras for people to share their drinks, or popcorn, or if their ice cream fell off the stick. There was no system in place to account for those uses, just the damaged cups. We would lump them all together. So a decent percentage of the cups would be written off as losses, without any questions. Joe had calculated for the bar workers (I was included) and three others that if we each took (or should I say, leave out of the inventory count) and sold one box of beer cups each (50 count), we could each earn an extra $75 dollars per week. Okay, now this was downright stealing, and I was sure to go to hell for this, but white people made it okay, and I joined the conspiracy. I had already joined the previous scheme, so Joe knew he could talk me into it. He made that theft an "all for one" deal. Talk about bad company corrupting good character, Dr. King; I had eaten the forbidden fruit and for the summer it became sweet. I would repent later.

I had become pretty good friends with Krista and Kathleen. They were white, but they seemed authentically interested in me. I think they lived in Grosse Pointe, a suburb northeast of Detroit. The only thing I knew about Grosse Pointe was the Eastland Mall that I had visited once or twice to shop for my prom dress. These girls were not involved in this operation, and I never told them I participated. I'm not even sure if they knew about it. I guess Joe was good at reading people and knowing whom he could entice and whom he could not. I suppose I should have been mad at him for assuming I was easy prey because I was black, but that thought did not occur to me then. I was, however, the only black in that group. Actually, it could have just been that I was the only other employee of age allowed to bartend. Because we had to do inventory together, I had to be enrolled, so I would not report the shortages.

So there it was—my first deal with "the dark side of white people." I had crossed the line. I had already routinely listened to rock and then pop music, and Michael Jackson made being friends with whites okay with the "Ebony and Ivory" hit single he made with Paul McCartney. I was doing my part to try to create racial harmony in real life.

On the bright side of summer, my bond with the group was strengthened by a weekend party that Krista had at her family's cabin on Lake Huron. I think it was around mid-summer after the 4th of July, and somehow we had time off, but in shifts. Krista invited all of us, and the plan was to keep the party going from Friday evening 'til Sunday morning so that everyone could attend. I don't remember how we pulled it off, but Krista, myself, and two others were there the entire weekend.

Okay, so some people have a house *and* a summer cabin to live in when school was out. I did not know people did that. I knew white people went to summer camp. I had seen the movie *Little Darlings*, but I had never heard of them owning their own cabins. This was a trip; surely, if I had made it to their homes and their summer retreats, I was getting to join the ranks of the privileged. No black people I knew had a cabin on the lake. No black people I knew went to any of the Great Lakes except Lake Erie, and that was by default.

Krista's cabin had two (might have been three) bedrooms, one bathroom, a kitchen and living area. It was functionally decorated with furniture that was sturdy and dark or patterned to hide dirt.

A few of the walls were paneled, and the floors were linoleum for easy cleanup with woven rugs to provide some warmth and cushion in front of the brick fireplace. The finer details, I actually do not remember much, as my eyes were mostly closed asleep when I was inside, which was only about ten total hours the entire weekend. It gave you the overall feeling that you could relax there and not have to clean up so much. That no one would yell if you put your feet on the coffee table, or let your chilled glass of iced-lemonade (or in our case, beer) sweat a circle on the dining table. I guess you could say it was the "recreational comforts" of the privileged. And amazingly, here I was.

We spent every possible hour outside, and I loved every single minute of it. I do not remember what we ate, or how we prepared it, I just remember how massive, yet calm, the lake was. But two things immediately confronted me. I had not swum in open waters before. And never had to swim amongst whites that were my new friends. I felt like I had to pretend that I was accustomed to this form of fun. My prior swimming experiences were only in pools, the afore-mentioned swim-mobile, and the occasional dip in Metropolitan Beach. But even when we went there, we spent water time in the pool and only picnicked and made sandcastles on the beach. I never swam in Belle-Isle beach either, because it was too close to where my brothers fished, and I was afraid of fish touching me. So there I was now fronting like my family did this every summer too. (Like me and the Great Lakes go back a long way.) I was not sure how I would handle it, or if I could actually tread in open waters long enough, if they swam out too far and I got tired, without a ledge for me to grab. Nothing would embarrass me more if I got out there and ran out of energy and started to sink. I would probably rather drown than be rescued and be the black girl who could not swim.

After we unpacked and had something to eat, Krista wanted to go out to the lake in the canoe. Damn, they had their own canoe too—this was living! Yeah, I know it wasn't a yacht, but I had never been in a canoe, so I was just as impressed. I was happy to go and learn how to row. It was pretty easy and I only leaned too far to one side once or twice, but managed not to tip the canoe over. I think we were out about 500 feet before I noticed I could not see the shoreline—in any direction. Reading about the Great Lakes and being on one are very different things. A slight panic crept in, but just then Krista turned it back around and headed back. She stopped about 100 feet away from shore and jumped in for a swim. The water was pretty calm so there was no need to anchor. My fear had subsided. I had my camera so I took some pictures.

Krista motioned for me to come in and I jumped. It wasn't that cold and the level was not too deep where we were. We splashed around a bit and then she went to the canoe and grabbed some Prell and began washing her hair. Okay, that, I did not understand. The water was fine to swim in, but washing your hair? I mean, how clean could that be? She said her hair was feeling oily and she only wanted it to feel cleaner, that she would wash it again later when she showered. Now that was new. If they did not put oil in their hair, how did it become oily? Hmmm, my hair had been permed so I was fine with the swimming and did not worry about my natural look being exposed. I just swam a bit more, away from the suds she was making, before I got back in the boat. And I managed all of the swimming and getting in and out of the canoe without one tip-over. God was looking out for me and sheltered me from any supernatural challenges. I did not even see any fish to be afraid of.

Krista took pictures of me when we got back in the canoe. Before we got all the way to the shoreline, a couple of little boys in swimming trunks were running across the properties. They saw me in the boat and started yelling, "Black-O," "Hey, Black-O..." and I could not hear what else before they picked up speed and ran away to a cabin in the distance. Krista was mortified. She did not know what to do or say, and I could tell it was her first experience of this. I shrugged my shoulders and shook my head in slight disapproval trying to ease her discomfort, and chose not to say anything. She just said something like "stupid kids" and we just continued rowing to shore. Nothing more was ever said about it and I was actually glad. I did not want this to be a racial experience, at least not in conversation. We headed back to the cabin to greet more of the gang as they started showing up.

We drank a lot of beer. There was a lot of talk about the beer types too. The brands. The darkness. The barley. The hops. The bitterness. Oktoberfest. Germany. It was like they had all took courses and studied beer. At home, people just drank it. It was either too warm, or deliciously cold and refreshing. Those were the only two distinctions I can recall in conversations about beer, that and the cost. I didn't really care for beer. To me it all seemed the same. But it only took a couple of weeks to acquire a taste for it. I know I only started to fit in. We ate a lot, but I don't remember what. It was likely hot dogs, burgers, potato chips and corn. We listened to a lot of music too. Someone had made a cassette of the latest pop songs, but most of the group preferred the popular rock radio stations. They loved Bob Seger, Van Halen, and the Stones. Some of it I liked. Some I tolerated. And some I did not get at all. I think it was songs by AC/DC, or Metallica, which actually irritated me. I had not known music to do that before. It was like sandpaper rubbing out my senses. I made no connection whatsoever. I didn't really know what to expect and did not bring any of my own music. I was surprised that no one tried to appease or make me feel more included by playing a little Stevie Wonder, or the Jackson 5, or Smokey. They were too much into what they had brought. Probably the first time in a while that they could feel grown-up and play the music as loud as they wanted and act as crazy as they wanted without a parent telling them to quiet down or turn it off. I could relate to that, and eventually found my own groove to their tunes.

The first night after everyone was done eating and drinking, someone suggested we go back into the lake to skinny dip. Skinny dip? Oh snap. Dr. King, they wanted me to take off my clothes and swim in the fish-water butt-naked! Now, I was the only black thing there and not sure I wanted them to see all my African glory. But I was also afraid to appear prudish or cowardly if I did not, and I was not sure if something more threatening would take place. I was also stunned that this is what they did for entertainment, but I didn't want to be left out. I needed to know what it all meant. What it was all for. So I agreed and waited until I got closer to the shoreline away from the cabin lights before I undressed. I didn't know who had eyes for whom then, but I was sure none of them had better not try a damn thing with me because beer and nakedness be damned if I was going to cross-over that far. I mean they were not fascinating in that way to me. Besides, I knew my family would kick my ass if I brought someone home, talking about my white boyfriend. Lord, Dr. King, my brothers would have gone nuts! *Guess Who's Coming to Dinner 2* would not have been pretty. But fortunately, there were no passes made, so I did not have to deal with all the cultural abomination drama that would have definitely ensued.

We all got in, I, cloaked in the darkness and they, glowing like wingless fireflies with human silhouettes under the moonlight circling around. There was a quick second of fear, but then ease once I was immersed and feeling the water trace every inch of my body from the neck down. It moved over to make room for me and soothed me at the same time. Everyone was awkwardly quiet at first, and then someone started making conversation. It was really kinda cool and freeing. However, within just a few minutes those sensations were sharply interrupted by a scream. One of the girl's felt something hit her leg and she was certain it was Jaws (in fresh water), the Loch Ness monster, or its offspring (in Lake Huron instead of in Scotland), or Big Foot (now amphibious and waiting under the surface of the lake for would-be skinny dippers to hit that very spot instead of hiding in the woods). It was a hoot, Dr. King. Everyone took off running at lightning speed screaming and yelling and laughing and splashing everywhere. Our yells were echoing and skipping across the water like stones, and you could see a couple of cabin lights turn on and off in the distance. We all scooped up our discarded clothes and ran to separate spots for cover. I cannot say I didn't enjoy every minute of it. It was thrilling, funny, and fun! It was the first time my naked butt had been kissed by a fresh water lake. It was something I knew none of my black friends had done yet, and many wouldn't dare.

Dr. King, as I look back, that entire experience was innocuously pleasurable and I can't deny that. It may have been un-Christian like, and my family would have not approved. But I remember thinking about the laundry list of fears about the world I had inherited from my family, friends, teachers, ancestors, and the world at large. How much more of *my* life would I allow myself to explore in this unadulterated manner? Not necessarily naked, but new and different. I did not know what would be next. Whether it would be something tamer, or even more risqué, but I was determined to at least try to go beyond the trappings of my fears. To some degree, I was born again in that lake—to a new sense of freedom. Thank you Krista!

At the risk, or safety, of sounding like Malcolm X after his trip to Mecca, I began to see each of those white people as individuals, instead of a giant white blob of hate and oppression. Their physical features of eye color, hair color, texture, freckles, skin hues of olive tones, alabaster, tan and blush were unfolding and suddenly distinguishable. Their cultural heritages and ethnicities were more apparent, and the various European countries became more recognizable than the maps in school, and more understandable than when my former business professor exalted them. I learned that they had their own pride and prejudices against their fellow continental cohorts, and that it had nothing to do with Africa. And they didn't necessarily hold the Irish, Polish, and Jewish people (from any country) in the highest regard. It was eye-opening to hear them battle politics and tout loyalties, but mostly reciting what they memorized of their parents' logic for loving JFK, or hating Ronald Reagan, or vice-versa, and all feeling unabashedly ashamed of Jimmy Carter. That was most interesting. This was better than any history books I had read.

I was also surprised (understatement) to learn that they did not necessarily like each other—did not prefer the company of each other over people like me. It did not occur to me that they would call one another a jerk, idiot, or asshole, and in the same breath point out endearing qualities about me. I thought there was a code of solidarity that they all had to uphold the way we black people felt we did. So to hear them speak ill of their own kind in the presence of someone not white was bizarre, yet selfishly encouraging and relieving. I did not feel like I had to pretend to like any of them I didn't, simply because they were white and because I was seemingly a part of their inner circle. I could call a spade a spade—or whatever the white equivalent to that expression. We returned from the weekend-long party somewhat bonded. Suddenly, maybe inexplicably, I had some *real* white friends, or some white *real* friends. The three of us girls talked for days about how cool the party was and dreamed up other parties and maybe traveling abroad together.

Dr. King, in the honeymoon of my newly consummated relationship with white individuals, I got stupid. Or in my brother's words, I got put back in my place. Slapped right back into my unequal blackness. Annulled. You see, what had happened was...we had four security guards on the boats of which two were black. They alternated schedules and boats. One day, one of the white guards came to the bar during cleanup, when no passengers were around, and asked one of the white bartenders for a little hit of booze to go with his pop. The supervisor was in earshot near the backside of the bar facing the half-door. In seconds, his request was granted, and he continued to stroll the deck—drinking before drinking hours, while on duty. Witnessing this, I just shrugged my shoulders. The very next day, as if ordered by the Gods of Temptation to test me, the black security guard repeated the same request, during the same time period, but to me. Seeing the "no harm-no foul" events of the previous day, I thought nothing of it, and granted his request right away. This time however, well...Dr. King, you know I don't even need to finish the story!

Anyway, no sooner than I had started pouring the rum, did the supervisor walk into the bar area, and catch me right in mid-pour. The supervisor frowned, I mean, that had to be the longest three-second shot ever, for all the images that flashed before me. Enough for a full-length, feature film. What could I say? I just waited and avoided eye contact with anyone. He gestured us to his office (the Purser's office). To his credit, the Security Guard tried to save my job by saying he would have reached behind the counter anyway and taken it by himself, but thought it would be okay for me to pour. For a second, I felt hope, but the manager was not buying that. He stated it was against the rules and that we left him no choice. I said nothing. I was wrong. Period.

He drafted up a document for us to sign, and then asked us to go get our things. I went back to the bar holding back tears—wearing a new layer of cross-cultural infamy and left. The security guard tried to claim indignation as we off-boarded across the broad creaking planks, that seemed to be lowered just for our dishonorable departure, but I did not have any fight in me. It was due me. I stole the cups and then I stole some booze. Justice was served. I had not only lost my job, but also my new white friends. I was now their black friend who got fired for stealing. I was certain they would not want that social baggage. I didn't even want to find out. About a week later I had a brief surge of wanting retaliation—claiming a double standard against blacks—and actually called and threatened to sue for discrimination. But two wrongs don't make a right. Thankfully, my anger waned with the last days of the summer. By then, I had decided to try another round of college.

Despite the bad ending of the summer, a new seed had been planted. I had been inspired by my former co-workers and became determined, not to get left so far behind on educational pursuits. I enrolled at Oakland Community College in Farmington Hills. I still had a fleeting fantasy of trying to find and join my white "friends" who were planning to backpack through Europe. A part of me really wanted to go. I made that desire public to my brother Warren, and he had thought I had lost my mind.

He cussed me out for even thinking the thought, and asked me who did I think I was? "Do-you-think-you-can-go-across-the-ocean-and-not-speak-any-foreign-languages-and-not-get-strung-up-and-killed-by-those-racist-Europeans? That's-where-all-that-slavery-shit-started!" His anger initially shocked me, and I got mad at him for not thinking it was a cool idea. But he scared me when he reminded me of some of the historical facts. Though a part of me still really wanted to go, I did not have the chutzpah to make the break.

So I retreated to my private and traditional segregated aspirations, and charted new territory to explore.

It Takes All Kinds

Dear Dr. King,

This was a completely different experience; this time I enrolled in commercial art, at Oakland Community College. I really wanted to do fine art instead, but it seemed then that fine artist was synonymous with starving artist, and I needed to make money. My benefits from SSI and VA had been significantly cut due to new "trickle-down" policies. Mr. 666 himself (the nickname given to President Ronald Wilson Reagan by my most-religious relatives, due to his three names with six letters each, the mark of the Devil) had dealt that blow in the name of reduced federal spending. I took a direct hit. Right when I finally got somewhat serious about going to college, I would lose most of my financial support. I was glad I had saved a little from Boblo, but now my benefits were cut in half. Art supplies were expensive alongside books, car repairs (more frequent in the winter), insurance, and gas. I was able to pay, but it took everything I had. And so it was.

I loved my new college, the curriculum, and especially the culinary arts department. We had the opportunity to have freshly prepared soon-to-be-gourmet food by the students daily. It was an absolute treat to enjoy that level of lunch at college. I stayed there for three full semesters, and really enjoyed all the great art techniques I learned. I was one of maybe a handful of blacks in my courses, and all the instructors were white. I have no recollection of even one racial incident there. Maybe because in the humanities people are more human and more interested in artistic expression rather than what you look like. Or maybe I was in a bubble. I do not know, but I was able to do really well and maintain a GPA over 3.0. It was just the prescription to boost my confidence and provide some direction for my future. It also gave me a new lease on white professors. I did not hold them in disdain, and was not waiting for racist hoods to be revealed in the form of contempt, exclusion, and belittlement anymore. I was able to have enriched educational relationships, and that made me feel as though the playing field was level. That, and the fact my work was as good as the next person(s) in my classes. I was no longer afraid, and felt if anything happened again, I would be able to handle it maturely with an educated, yet brutal and swift administrative retaliation that would not diminish me, or my newly rebuilt character.

California — A Different, Different World

Dear Dr. King,

Just as I was gaining my sea legs at college and looking forward to earning some fulltime money with a summer job in the summer of '85, I got a call from my brother Ron. He had graduated from Oklahoma Christian College the year before and was married right afterward. He and his wife were lucky to both be recruited to management-in-training jobs at a reputable bank that would also put them in driving distance from her family in California. I was needed that first summer — as a babysitter for my newly born niece. I left Detroit happily — especially for the money they promised.

Within a couple hours of landing in San Francisco, I was riding in the back seat to Stockton in shock and awe at the gorgeous mountains, the non-stop traffic, and all the people. I knew California would be my next home. Actually, I kinda knew I was not going back to Detroit before I left, but I only packed a couple small bags of summer clothes.

The very first thing I saw when we pulled up to the apartment complex off Benjamin Holt

Boulevard, was a teenage-looking blonde female walking through the parking lot barefoot. The bottoms of her feet were black as coal and scaly. I did not understand how she tolerated the sweltering pavement. It had to be 95 degrees that afternoon. My next thought: white people are crazy and nasty to walk around like that collecting God knows what from dog pee and poo to human piss and vomit and blood on their feet. It seemed all-wrong to me, but at the same time, I intuited that she was somehow free. If I tried that at home, my momma would have slapped me upside my head for fear of me cutting my feet (like I did when I stepped on a nail when I was six), and then taken me to emergency, and the cost would drain whatever leftover money she might have been able to squeeze out of a dollar. Where was this white girl's momma? Why did she let her do that? Her feet were so black you knew that was more than one day's worth of dirt. But she was walking around that apartment building like it was all hers.

Stockton was a quaint suburban town northeast of SF, and was technically a part of the Central Valley, not included in what is known as the Bay Area. It was a typical town born from the military during the gold rush. My sole source of entertainment was with the three of them, and although my niece was beautiful and full of life, babysitting got boring after a month, and I needed to step out and begin to develop my own new life. I was bored—but I was also by nature adventurous. So after settling in and learning a few streets driving around, I felt okay and a little more excited about being there. I spent many hours writing my friends I had abandoned for the summer about the wonderful life I was discovering in California. I also made a few long distance calls, but was soon to find out from my brother that I was running up their phone bill, and they could not afford to keep paying for my long distance. I asked them to take it out of what they were paying me for babysitting. That's when I realized that no babysitting money was coming. I decided to make the best of it.

You see, Dr. King, I was rather proud of my brother for moving: first to Oklahoma to go to a "Christian" college; momma and daddy would have been proud of him too. He was the first college graduate and white-collar worker in our family. That's right, Dr. King, he graduated and the first job out of college was in a bank, handling money — mostly white peoples' money. He was also the first sibling to get married and *then* have children, in that order.

One day after he and his wife came home from work, I took the car and decided to go swimming. I think it was 102 degrees that day. I had never seen steam float from pavement before. Man, it was hot. Part of me wanted to see if I could fry an egg on the hood of my brother's car, but I knew he would kill me if I tried. I headed to the local YMCA. I was going to go to the pool at the complex but "Blackfoot" made me think there was more of her around and that they all jumped in the pool without cleaning and scaling their feet, so I went ahead and paid for the use of the pool at the Y. At least, you had to pass through the shower area before you got to the pool. Hopefully, this was not an irresistible invitation to dirty visitors.

I was quick to undress, shower and get to the pool. It was decent sized—about twenty-five yards—the size of the pool in high school, and I think the depth went to at least eight feet. There were about ten other swimmers. I found an empty lounger, rested my towel, keys and flip-flops, and jumped right into the middle. My favorite thing to do was to fold my arms around my legs, sink to the bottom, and squirm for full immersion. I came up, brushed the water from my face, and stretched out to stroke to the deep end. I swam the length of the pool several times before stopping to rest by holding on to the edge and letting my legs float behind me. I was feeling good, remembering the swim team practices at Cass Tech before I quit the team. Yeah, I was a real good swimmer and also very fast. I am tall for my generation and have the longest arms of any female I had known, as well as the biggest hands and feet. So my gorilla-length arms and finlike feet propelled me in racing. When my short career as a would-be, freestyle Olympic champion had ended, it was because of my hair. Swimming just made it too much work. I was feeling unlucky with boys, and I needed to be cute for them. So I stopped. I also stopped because no one in my family seemed to care that I was even on the swim team. My three eldest brothers were all excellent swimmers too, but after they stopped, I guess it was not that interesting anymore.

I caught my breath, turned around to see that everyone else had left the pool. I did not think anything of it. (Though, that in itself should've said something!) I decided to slow it down and do a couple of breaststroke laps. A man came and stood on the side of the pool with a white plastic jug. I looked over at him a couple of times and watched as he started pouring the contents into the water. I turned over on my back and began to float for a while. I did not think about what he was pouring; I don't know why. I probably dismissed it as routine. I swam for another ten or fifteen minutes before I decided to leave my private pool party and go home. As I passed by the mirror into the shower area, I was horrified to discover the grey ashy hue all over me. My skin was the color of a sundried worm on the pavement after a rainstorm. My eyes were bloodshot. They were stinging in the water, but I thought it was just because I swam too long. Later I realized what actually happened. I was so humiliated and angry I did not know what to do. I hadn't paid attention to what he looked like; I knew only that he was white. I had no evidence, because I had washed and oiled it all away. I had no witnesses. I'm not sure that I even told my brother. I had crazy thoughts to contact PUSH, and ask Rev. Jesse Jackson personally, thinking he needed a cause after losing the Presidential run, or Rev. Al Sharpton. Seemed like they would come fight for me. But I knew that was crazy. I even wanted to blow the pool up. But in fact, all I did was just not go back there. Fortunately, we moved in September to Fairfield to be closer to my sister-in-law's parents. California was bigger than the pool incident, so it didn't make me want to leave the state, but I was now aware that I had experienced my first physical act of racial aggression—I had been burned—literally. For years after that, I could not go swimming without wondering how many people would leave the pool—or attempt something worse—just because I showed up. The new me: guarded…or maybe aware?

My First White Roommate

Dear Dr. King,

Soon after the move to Fairfield, I was told I needed to get my own apartment. I had taken a job at the brand new Macy's Department store in town. It was a beautiful three-story, 40,000 square-foot retail heaven of my new material-girl dreams. I was hired as a sales associate in the Juniors' section. This store was a pilot attempt at full-commission sales in every department, and that excited me. I had big dreams of sales, sales, sales, and found quickly that my salesmanship was not limited to just my department. I could escort my eager shoppers all over the store and up-sale them to hundreds and even thousands of dollars on back-to-school weeks, or during Christmas season. And I soon learned that any time of the year, if I considered customers' entire households, I could entice them to fill up every room with newly gotten goods. This did not happen as often as a decent salesperson would like, but it happened often enough to give you the shark reputation if you accomplished it. Plus, it was more fun than just hanging out in your department. But this is all backstory.

Dr. King, this was the first time I worked with a multi-cultural group of competitors. My first job at the movie theater in Detroit had been with all black workers and an Armenian manager. My second job there was at JL Hudson's in Southfield, MI, with primarily black clerks and white managers, and my last home job was at the amusement park. Up until now, my employment history was characterized by a handful of us, and mostly white co-workers and bosses. Being in daily, direct contact with this new group of diverse women was really quite different.

So now, there's me, a Mexican, a Filipino, an Irish girl, a Russian older lady, a Scot, English, and German managers, initially. Of course, since my first day of college, since Mr. Benedict's public hanging of my classmates and me, I had begun to develop a practice of matching surnames to countries. And there were people from all over the globe throughout the store. A commercial microcosm of Jessie Jackson's Rainbow Coalition maybe? I came to understand that Fairfield was right outside of Travis Air Force Base, and not too far from Mare Island Naval Base, about ten miles west, and yet another naval base in Concord, which was about 15 miles east. So the military was responsible for the diversity in this region.

I needed to get my own place, and I had no clue how I was to afford it, or even what affordable meant. Of course, across town was a brand new apartment development and it had me at hello. There was a two-bedroom, two-bath dream apartment, and all I needed was a roommate to split the rent. I think it was about

$450.00, per month. My salary was slightly short of $4 per hour, plus a 6-8% commission. My employee number was 489174. I remember because you had to punch that number in on every single transaction. I would remain an employee for three years with a six-month hiatus due to grandiose sales promises at a nearby furniture store, and then returned to Macy's for an additional two years before finally leaving to find my corporate America white-collar office, nine-to-fiver. However, I became friends with everyone, as we had to work together to keep our department in the top sales performers' column. We were lucky not to be stuck in men's ties in a military town. My Irish co-worker told me that her older sister needed to move out of their parents' house, and she was looking for a roommate. This sister just happened to be a store manager in the same mall.

Eleanor (name change) seemed nice enough. In those days "nice enough for somebody white" meant not threatening or outwardly racist. She ran her store very well by my assessment, so we agreed that we would share the new apartment. Spending a party weekend with whites was an adventure, but I was taking a giant leap of faith by becoming long-term roommates with one. I had internal betrayal (sell-out) conversations, but did not let it deter me. I had had a string of successful or seemingly harmless encounters with some whites so far at work, so I was willing to give Eleanor a try. Something told me her thoughts and experiences mirrored mine.

We were happy to declare our independence from the day-to-day strongholds of familial obligations and expectations, so it felt great. I can't remember why I let Eleanor have the room with the private bath. I honestly do not remember if we tossed a coin, or reasoned, or if she actually paid more for it, but she was designated to have the master bedroom. Anyone on the outside could easily read "oppression" or "legacy of slavery" in that first arrangement, but it was not something I thought about initially. I was too excited about the freedom.

Eleanor's parents seemed happy to get her, and all her dowry items, plus twelve years of school memorabilia out of their house. They had no problem helping her move in. This briefly created a slight twinge of envy. First, because she had two parents and they were there. Secondly, she actually had memories she could see and touch. I had none of that. Just a couple of ragged suitcases with my shoes, clothes, toiletries and my art portfolio consisting of some drawing supplies to complete my Incomplete grade in my former art rendering class. I had no real prized belongings, as I had just moved to CA for a few weeks in the summer. My brother had not yet sent my things after several requests. And it would only be more of the same. I had one piece of jewelry from my mom, a silver and diamond band that I had lost the previous winter on my way to Kathleen's house for a party. Before getting out of my car, I had stopped to put lotion on my hands placing my mom's ring in my lap. I hopped out of the car afterward, and it likely rolled into the two-foot snow bank curbside. That night it snowed again. The next morning the snowplows cleared the streets, and the homeowners had cleared their sidewalks, piling more snow on top of what was already there. I didn't even try to go back and search for it, realizing it was lost and getting Kathleen's post-weather report. I felt so bad for a very long time about that.

It took an afternoon for my roommate to move in. By the time they were done, her room was two-thirds piled up with boxes nearly floor to ceiling. Her bed covered the remaining floor space minus a path to the bathroom. I could not imagine what could be in all of those boxes. I briefly had my own bedroom after my mom died, so I never had a storage closet or area to manage and preserve keepsakes. We used a buffet bureau for our school report cards, and photo albums. Beyond that, I had only a shoebox of school trinkets and old coins that eventually got confiscated and tossed out by someone thinking it was trash. Everything else I possessed at this time was something that had immediate use or function. She had twenty-one years of memorabilia.

Soon after moving in, I declared I would furnish the living area. Having my furniture in my apartment, would give me more power over what happened there—or so I thought. After making that announcement, I had to represent, so I decided to buy everything brand new, to match my newly declared power. It was the natural thing to do. Everything had to match. After window shopping and realizing the true prices of all these items, I decided I needed another part-time job to afford everything, and Eleanor was eager to hire me part-time at her store. Cool, easy gig. With this extra money, I purchased a living room set, a dinette set, a bedroom set, dishes, flatware, linens, towels, and pots and pans — the latter items all coming from Macy's. I applied my 20% discount on White Flower-Day sales to lower my costs. Our apartment was fully furnished in probably two months. It was official, and we were certified grownups. We even had a fireplace and patio! And I had materially represented me, my family, and my race, as smart, savvy, educated, capable and professional. I was on my way and could stand up to any white standard. We were having a blast impressing our friends and having parties, (mostly Princess House Crystal). But I did not pay cash for everything as I bought it, some of it I purchased on credit. Hindsight.

The guest bathroom was attached to my bedroom and had two access doors; one from my room, and one from the living area. This was to become a point of contention for me, as guests mostly used my bathroom. So I had to keep it clean all the time, but also had to clean up after her friends. Hindsight once again. With the constant cleaning, I was beginning to feel like Florence the maid from *The Jeffersons*. It got old very fast. And it had a gradual shredding effect on my self-esteem.

I discovered many things about women with blonde hair, and euro-suburban activities and the status quo of teens, twenty-somethings, and housewives of the '80s during our tenure. Some of it was typical; much was so different from how we did things at home. The first thing was Princess House Crystal. My mom had real china, and real silverware. She even had a single crystal punchbowl. My grandmother had real china, real silverware, real silver buffet platters, and coffee service, but no one I knew had crystal pitchers, and glasses, and bowls, and serving platters, and cake plates, and wine glasses, and salad plates, and lots of other crystal items (olive bowls?), which I did not know were necessary or even had a function in my customary soul-food meals.

This was intriguing because I learned of the PH parties where you could earn such items by hosting them, and it was apparently the law of the land for these young suburban ladies. They were diligently preparing for their dowries (that was the first time I knew someone personally to do that, and mostly thought it was a TV thing). I didn't have a plan for a dowry or a trunk to store it in. And what exactly do you put in it? Who decides that? This was a European-imported tradition, American made. The way I grew up, people just got married (if they got married). My brothers taught me that I was the gift! The bride was the prize possession; she did not come with a conjugal "make house a home" fund and secret treasures. Why should she? So I purchased and was gifted a few items, not to be a total outcast, that I stored in the cupboards. The others, I gave to co-workers as wedding presents. I could not align with the whole dowry thing; it was too much work. Besides, they all had years of a head start, I did not want to compete. It was just too much baggage for me to hoard around.

Dr. King, it was hard not to feel like something was wrong with me for not wanting to build a "crystal-clear" future. Honestly, it was hard to reject many of these Eurocentric ideas and lifestyle choices, because they represented freedom and affluence that we were told to go after. I mean, how do you assimilate and be who you are, if who you are is defined by external trappings of another culture, material goods and accomplishments that were systemized and predetermined without any input from your origins? How does a person find their own true freedom? How can you reject a system and co-exist in it without compromising access and fair and equal treatment?

Our relationship was pretty surface-level. We never had deep discussions about life, race, parents, boyfriends, or work. They were typically about who was coming over, what to cook for dinner, what the weekend plans were, and our crazy customer interfacing at work. I was surprised to learn that white women obsessed about their hair almost as much as black women did. It had never occurred to me before. Partly because we were so busy straightening ours so that it could move like theirs. And partly because TV made you think maintenance and basic care was wash and go. She had thick, "healthy-looking," shoulder-length hair. But a fair share of her paycheck was spent on the maintenance. She said once, likely on a day when she was not feeling her best, that her hair was her strongest asset. Wow! That tripped me out. Did she not know she was white! Wasn't that asset enough?

But I suppose she stacked herself against other would-be blonde bombshells and did not feel like she ranked all that well.

I remember another point of contention for us outside of my bathroom. Eleanor had ordered the phone from Pacific Bell, and it was in her name. That was our one and only phone. I seemed to answer more times than she did when her parents would call in the am. My morning voice is less than attractive, and likely had an urban twang to it. Her parents were very cheerful and ended each sentence with one of those happy intonations at the end. I on the other hand was flat and short with my responses. Not rude, just straight to the point without much interest in cordiality. I guess after a few unsuccessful attempts to make me cheery in the am, they gave up and complained to Eleanor. She actually asked me to be happier when I answered the phone – that her parents felt I was rude. I did not go Detroit on her with that request, but I did assert something to the effect that this was my house and I did not move in to be controlled by her parents. I told my brother about it. He laughed and teased that I had too much black in my voice for them; that they needed me to sound more like them. I think I called the phone company to order a second line for myself. I honestly don't remember if there were other contentious points in our cultural exchange, but she moved out at the end of our lease. I stayed and found another roommate. I have no idea what her assessment and report would be of me, and black people. But I do not think I got a passing grade.

20,000 White People & Me

Dear Dr. King,

Before Eleanor's departure, we had one adventurous event. One weekend, she wanted me to accompany her to the Beach Boys and ZZ Top concerts. The Beach Boys were playing in Chico, a small college town, northeast of Fairfield, and ZZ Top was headlining an all-day Mountain Aire '86 rock n' roll music festival in Angels Camp; another small town southeast of Fairfield, but closer to Stockton. I had only a small concept of college towns or rural towns then. Not many of "us" lived in them, and our safety was in "our" numbers. The closest reference would have been Ann Arbor, MI, but I only visited U of M's football stadium once as a preteen on a school trip. Stockton would be my other real-life, small-town reference—and that was more of a drive-by.

Chico was known to be an infamous college "party" town, home to Chico State University. What I had heard about Angels Camp was a giant bullfrog (imported from Africa) leaping contest, and the Hell's Angels. If I had paused and thought about what kind of people jump frogs as a source of entertainment, I probably would have associated a negative redneck stereotype, and deemed it too risky. And I certainly would have backed away at a deeper reflection of "hell" in Hell's Angels. But I did not, so it was not enough to scare me away, partially because I didn't put two and two together. It was also because I was bored and had nothing else going on and was therefore seeking adventure to report back home. Maybe subconsciously it registered as a privileged sense of security, because her two regional bosses were accompanying us like, "she's okay, she's with us."

We caravanned for the three-hour trip on Friday evening, and the plans were to stop in an even smaller town named Corning, to overnight it at the parents' home of one of her bosses — an older-than-us white guy who took the opportunity to visit his aging parents. I thought this move was pretty bold, because I did not know anyone very well, but I just trusted that my associations thus far were safe. After all, they were working-class people and apparently educated. I didn't have the typical southern KKK fears that I know my brother at home would, and many AAs would have. You always question when visiting small suburban and rural communities whether blacks are one of three things: unwelcomed, an anomaly and culturally sanitized, or easy prey for incarceration or death. Every historically based TV show, movie, or documentary about the plight of African-Americans in this country, from *To Kill a Mockingbird* to *The Color Purple*, depicts some hyper-racial crime, or mistreatment — in small suburban or rural towns. If that was subliminal programming it worked on me. So I normally entered sagaciously. Or at least exited before sundown. However, I do not know why I trusted this group so much. Perhaps it was simply that they were people who were taught to honor all people, or that it was a California brand of whites whose socialization was not rooted in black/white racism, so there was no perception of a threat. I did not know but so far, it was all good. My fears were mostly about being accepted as an equal, not as some exotic visiting animal to interrogate about the state of black America.

They were friendly enough, greeted me warmly and seemingly the same as the other two white strangers their son had brought over for a quick night in. You got the feeling this was not the first time. Of course I wondered if I was the first AA, but I was not intending to touch that subject, and they must have felt the same way, as there was never any references to race or culture. I wondered how hard that was for them. They made dinner for us, but I have absolutely no memory of what was served. The house was a ranch style, with three or four bedrooms, and had as many baths I believe. It smelled of furniture polish and was comfortably decorated all over, and there was a lot of oak furniture. I later learned that they owned the local furniture store.

The most memorable thing about that night was the guest bathroom. It was pretty spacious, but the entire fourth wall, which faced the backyard, was completely paned glass. It included a French paned door. The wood was painted evergreen. This door opened to a concrete shower stall outside that bordered the pool. This was the coolest thing I had ever seen. The thought of an open bathroom, with an outside, enclosed shower was just completely awesome. I did not know people lived like that. In Detroit, fear of feeling like a sitting duck, or being constantly robbed, would prevent that type of freedom. Plus the fact that the shower and pipes could freeze in winter would not encourage that type of installation. But I would burn this memory in my head so that I could build a bathroom like this in my dream house. In fact, Dr. King, no one I currently knew had displayed this level of freedom. We were always shutting curtains, closing blinds, and locking screen doors so we would not be targeted or appear vulnerable. I guess that was lost in the south by one too many bricks thrown through the windows of our homes by racial terrorists. That plus all the: "don't let the crack-heads see what valuables you have in your house and hide everything" rationale of the north. We are still in psychological prison even after the great migration up north.

Dr. King, I considered this to be my first official white concert. I had seen Boy George and the B-52s while in Detroit, but they were concerts of queer (in the strange sense) people in my assessment. Their personas and music did not fall into the known categories of white peoples' music; rock n' roll, country, classical, or polka (Hamtramack, MI). Their music was part of the New Wave that was filed under the new genre of Pop, so it didn't count. Many of my black friends liked Boy George, B-52s, Cyndi Lauper, George

Michael, and the Eurythmics, and we even mimicked some of their outrageously flamboyant clothing styles. Yet, some of us routinely listened to Phil Collins, Journey, Elton John, Blondie, Joe Jackson, Pat Benatar, and Supertramp. I had even ventured into listening to the Doors, Led Zeppelin, and Patty Smyth during my Detroit, high school, pot-smoking days. But no one I knew had ever purchased or listened to the Beach Boys, not even my white Boblo friends, nor had they ever mentioned ZZ Top. So I was really out of my element. The one and only song I knew from ZZ was the song "Legs." We had TVs and video tracks at Macy's in the Juniors' department to attract the teens. Those videos were most of Billboard's top pop songs. That summer "Legs" had crossed over. That meant that whites as well as blacks were buying those songs.

Dr. King, all kinds of music exploded in the '80s. The crime and poverty generated by the drug offensive produced a fallout of music that was called rap and hip-hop. This music was the highly emotional, political and cultural voices of the disenfranchised youth. They channeled their anger through musical protests to the world at large. These kids, primarily our young African-American males, voiced their anger at the system, the racism, the poverty, the crime, the abandonment, the injustices, the women, and the streets. It was hard, fast, highly rhythmic, passionate, racist, sexist, funny, funky, and aggressive, and it caught on like wildfire and flowed into pop culture like thunder. Rap and hip-hop crossed-over to mainstream too. Shaking up the youth to jump on board, shaking up the adults to get their world, and shaking up the music industry making fortunes for many, for something that just came off the block. I do not think you would have approved the language and the misogynistic antics, but you certainly would have understood the anger and the passion. The cries for change, maybe even help. I had collected a few rap songs in my repertoire, but I had not attended a rap concert yet, and here I was in sunny northern California about to partake of happy beachcombers music from the '60s. Worlds apart. How does this happen?

The Beach Boys concert was pretty uneventful. Aside from my group singing "Help Me Rhonda" as "Help Me Wanda" to poke fun at me, I don't remember much about the performances. The temperature was mid-80s and the attendees were pretty much like the music, easy-going and rhythmically happy. This concert was okay, but I would not become a fan, and had no urges to begin to listen to any more of their music. The day ended without incident and the next morning we would hit the road to Angels Camp.

We followed the guys in Eleanor's car the entire time but after about two hours into our 166-mile drive, she noticed she was low on gas. I had no idea of her mileage endurance and for that matter, no idea where we were going. So there we were, me and blondie, on the two-lane, rural and golden, hilly State Highway 49, in ninety plus-degree weather. We had lost the visual of the guys, with no way of letting them know our circumstances. Naturally, panic set in. We had no sight of farmhouses, gas stations, or civilization at one point. We decided to just slow down and cruise as much as possible to preserve what gas we had left. My thoughts were of doom and that my brother had no way of knowing where I was. I do not think I'd even told him that I was going away for the weekend. I did not think that Eleanor would be much of a defense partner, because she was white, short, and did not seem to have ever had a fist fight, so we would become like the girls in the old Chuck Conner's movie, *Nightmare in Badham County. Two female college roommates, one black, one white, plan a trip to drive across country to California for the summer. They experience car trouble and get approached by a sadistic, racist, and sexist sheriff. He makes advances toward them, they reject him, and he arranges for their arrest on trumped up charges. They are imprisoned and separated in different cells. He of course torments them, does not allow calls, and has his way with each of them night after night, until they try to escape. They actually break out of the jail after careful planning, but separate for distraction and he shoots down the black escapee, while she tries to run away.* I kept my homicidal worries to myself and had begun to feel immensely thirsty. This of course deepened my fear. Now, we would also roast under the hot sun without assistance from any passersby. Road kill, dehydrated, and petrified by the sun.

As God would have it, and I'm clear He had the gas fumes carry us as far as we needed, there was an exit sign approaching along with the gas symbol, less than a mile away. Our spirits revived and we had been saved. By now, however, we were in the Twilight Zone. This gas station had been lost in a time warp, and had the oldest mechanical analog gas pumps either of us had ever seen outside of a museum. And to top it all off, there were two elder, sun-aged statue-like men in sombreros, perched on a bench near the door staring at us, while licking and smacking their lips as we entered the store. I was sure we would be accosted in the store, that it was not really a gas station at all, but an ambush for dumb female travelers. We were equally alarmed by the look and gestures of these men and just wanted to pay for our gas, buy some drinks and snacks, and be on our way to hopefully catch-up with the guys—and pissed that they had not done a better job of looking out for us.

We finally did arrive at the concert location about thirty miles after the station and cruised the parking lot until we found them, waiting, at their car already in communion with two half-naked female concert attendees. I let Eleanor tell about our near-death episode, as I was upset by it all and did not know them as well. They laughed it off, and Eleanor let it go, so I decided to as well.

The lot was filling up, and I began to notice the crowd. Although I had let go of all my earlier created drama, I instantly began to create a new kind. Unlike the Beach Boys concertgoers, who were all happy, perky and light, these folks had another presence that gave me a sensation that I can best describe as primal fear. I looked around as we entered through the gates, and scanned and scanned, and so far, there was not one other black person in sight. This horrified me, because these white people looked scary. I had never seen such a high concentration of white men with beards, and tattoos, and motorcycle vests, and tattoos, and shaved heads and tattoos. The women were primarily in string bikinis, and tattoos, and hot pants and tattoos. They were all tattooed at a time when it was in fashion only for the deviants of pop culture. Every other person appeared to be glazed over in the eyes, and I did not know if the drug of choice was acid, weed, coke, or something much more ominous. I was already paranoid from the highway incident, realizing my brother could not rescue me. But this fear took it to a whole new level. I was at a concert with the biggest and most notorious motorcycle gang, and I attached every stereotype to that realization. This would certainly be my end. I would be beat up, raped, cut, and hung, and Eleanor (and her two bosses, Fred and Barney) would not be able to do a damned thing to stop it. All I had was my brown with metallic gold dots, one-piece bathing suit, my white short-sleeve button-up, and my white boxer shorts. What the hell was I thinking? I should have known better than to go somewhere without any knowledge of the land or the people, and without letting anyone know my whereabouts. I would deserve whatever happened for being so damned stupid. I had abandoned all of my Detroit sensibilities about the dangers of white people, and I was really sure that this time I would meet my end. Eleanor suggested we get some beer and I followed her to the beer tent. That line was of course a mile long, and after observing a few of the served rockers walk by us with trays of four cups of beer, I decided I would order the same. I thought if I were to be hung, at least by getting drunk, I would not feel as much pain.

The music had started and the first band in a huge line-up of performers got the crowd excited. People were cheering and dancing all around us. Before the end of the first song, and about ten people ahead of us, the crowd began to part like the Red Sea, and we were shoved to one side. There were a few screams and then a slight break in the frantic group ahead when a-six foot, tattooed, man appeared with blood running down from his forehead, his nose and lips, a ripped tank undershirt, and fists balled. Another equally tall, muscular man was escorting him away. Eleanor and I were disturbed, but following the lead of everyone else, we got back in line. A normal occurrence apparently and nothing more was made of it. Oh God please spare me!

At last, we made it to the front and I ordered my tray of beers, twelve ounces in each glass. Eleanor asked if I were ordering for the guys (wherever they were), but I said no, that I was really hot and thirsty and did not want to have to come back again for more. She giggled and decided to order two cups for herself. As we carefully walked to locate a place to park ourselves for the best view, I guzzled one down right away. We searched a bit for the guys, but they were nowhere to be found, so we settled ourselves on a twenty-degree grassy hillside close to a rail. Some time passed and it was beginning to really heat up. There were said to be 20,000 attendees to Mountain Aire '86—19,999 white people (or just non-black), and me. I had managed to avoid eye contact with anyone, because I didn't want my mania to add to my feeling of being personally threatened. I was fine with my own self-imposed threat. At this point I guzzled down another beer. Another band had begun and got the crowd really happy. Eleanor was enjoying it and was anxious to hear a band called Night Ranger as well as the headliner. But I didn't know any of the music, so it made me no difference. In fact, the music had been consistent for a while, but I really hadn't heard any of it. My mind was primarily on my looming death, the now-present exhaustive heat, and my remaining two beers. People around me were bouncing up and down dancing, clapping, cheering, kissing, groping, smoking, snorting, and just having a good time. At this point, I began to feel the buzz from my beers strongly. I also felt a sudden urge to pee, but did not want to leave my remaining beers with Eleanor to babysit, nor did I want to take them into the restroom. I decided to chug and cut to the bathroom. I downed them within ten minutes.

As I was walking to the bathrooms, I began to feel really hot so I opened my loose white shirt. I noticed that some of the attendees were wearing wet wraps over their heads. At closer glance, it was their t-shirts and some towels they had soaked in water to keep them cool under the sun. I would be sure to do the same when I reached the restroom or water fountain. It had to be over 100 degrees and the arid air was beginning to suck my drunken energy into another unknown state. As I continued my walk downhill, a man squirted me with his water bottle, and I was slightly refreshed at first. Then unnerved, as I was not sure if he was trying to help me, make a pass, or do something more aggressive. I just told myself to smile nicely and keep walking.

Predictably, but not in my immediate pre-thought, was the insane length of the women's restroom line as I got closer. I soon realized my bladder was in trouble. I found the end, about two blocks along, on a slight incline of the hillside, and tried to focus on the music through my haze. Shifting my weight from leg to leg began to feel like I was squeezing my bladder. So I tried to stand still and observe more of the crowd. My lips were parched. I felt like a burnt-black baked biscuit. The line was inching, and I felt I had been waiting for an hour and had just progressed three or four feet. I noticed the water fountain about twenty feet away. Seeing this made me feel better, and I feverishly, both figuratively and literally, asked the woman behind me if she would please hold my spot while I went to the fountain. She agreed.

Walking removed some of my bladder tension but did not lower my body temperature. I was sure to spontaneously combust, and even Eleanor didn't know where I was at this point. I was getting closer to the front of the line of the fountain while standing in the muddy puddle with three or four people in front of me. It was like each of them read the same playbook, suck down as much water as you can, wet your hair as much as you can, soak your t-shirt dripping wet, and fill your cups or bottle. Okay, I was not prepared for that. At least I had my shirt to soak, but I'd left my cups with Eleanor. I was not going to wet my hair. I had washed and gelled it the night before and was not sure if the water would turn brown and gross everyone out from the gel, so I was content with the turban approach.

Hallelujah, I had made it to the fountain of survival. I don't think I have ever gulped down so much water in my life. I'm not sure if it was well water or pumped in from some treatment plant, but it was the best damn water I had ever tasted! I must have been there for at least two minutes before I sensed the person behind me shifting around to see if I was coming up. I stood back and took off my shirt. Attempting to avoid dipping it in the pool of the fountain that had not yet drained. I asked the woman behind if she could hold the nozzle while I used both hands to soak my shirt. She was happy to assist to hurry me along. After it was soaked, I followed the lead of the others and rang it over my head loving every cascading drop roll down my face, neck, shoulders and upper body. Talk about refreshing, I was coming alive again.

I had the presence of mind not to wring it out completely so I would have some cooling reserves for later. Then I gently twisted it the long way in preparation for wrapping it on my head. I started walking back to my place in line and as I was doing this, the roll loosened and slipped somewhat. I jerked my arms and body to catch it, the sudden movement reintroduced my drunkenness, and I lost my balance and fell over into a puddle of mud. Oh no I didn't! Upon landing, my bladder decided it also needed a break and at least a quart of pee gushed out before I could squeeze enough to stop it. I was so humiliated. Ain't nothing worse than a pissy drunk, and even though every other person was stoned, it did not matter. Shame. Shame. Shame. All over me. Literally. I do not remember if people laughed or were concerned, because no one assisted me and I heard no comments in my direction. I hoisted up what was left of my pride and went straight into the bathroom in front of everyone with urine and muddy water streaming down my legs into my sneakers.

Dr. King, If I ever needed the Lord before I sho' did need Him now. But I would not have dared asked Him in that state. Walking around half-naked, in no-black man's land, wasted, fearing death, sweaty, pissy, and stanky. And not a soul there to protect me. I began to brush the mud and water off the back of my shorts, trying to resurrect a shred of self-respect, and turned into the cheap foggy mirror to see what I could see. If the pee wasn't bad enough, the mud stains on my shorts were located in the perfect spots to look like poop. I was a hot mess in every sense of the phrase. I went to the sink first to wash my hands, and then as soon as a stall door opened, I bee-lined in front of the other women. Relieved, I had to figure out what to do about my impending stench. I took off my unraveling makeshift turban, rolled my swimsuit and shorts off, put the shirt back on, and went to the sink to wash my body, bathing suit, shorts and shoes.

The sinks were a disaster area. They were clogged up with sand, lipstick, cigarette butts, gum, and strips of paper-towels over the drain with murky water. The floors were wet and silty and everything smelled like pee, or was it just me? I took my shorts and laid them by the side of the sink, rinsed my swimsuit first. The soap dispensers were only spewing bubbles so it would just be water rinses. I rinsed about three more times before it was clean enough. Then I soaked it two more times to shower my body. I did not know what those other women were thinking, but I didn't care. There was no way, intoxicated or not, that I was going to stop.

My shorts, oh my goodness, my shorts! I began to rinse and rub, rinse and rub, but the brown was not coming out. I repeated the process, this time removing the soap dispenser off its mounted holder adding water in it to capture any dried soap lining the insides, shaking until I got a soapy blend. I scrubbed harder and harder those stains just held on for dear life. Worn out and irritated as hell, I just tossed them in the trash. There was no way I was going to put them back on and be the tall black woman, in a brown sparkly one-piece, with poop stains on white shorts and a white turban on her head. Was this the look of assimilation? Why had I really come here? What was I trying to prove? Why did I boldly go where no black woman had gone before? I rinsed out my shoes one at a time, managing a circus tightrope, balancing act.

When I returned to where Eleanor was, she had finished her beers and was basking in the sun enjoying the music. She took one look at me and broke out laughing wondering what the hell happened to my shorts. I told her, and she could not stop laughing. I soon joined her and just decided it was no big deal. Somehow at the same time, my fears of being hung went by the way side along with my shorts. But I swore her to secrecy with the guys. They were in fact our bosses, and whatever was left of a cool reputation that we thought we had, she and I had to preserve it.

I also decided to try and hear the music. Dr. King, the music seemed to be the thing that would bridge an introduction to a relationship with other people outside our race. We went from the soulful sounds of Motown to a genre of music that blended soul with rock n' roll. It was called pop music, and popular it was. There were rhythms and elements of pop that spoke to people whatever your political and racial disposition. Music artists also started making short videos of their music and performances, and that attracted fans and listeners even more. It was one thing to hear the sounds, but to see them perform without having to wait for a TV special or go to a live concert, was something special. The music and the influences of the recorded visuals accompanying the words infused more cultural acceptance and put new thoughts on our minds. However, there were some genres of music that did not break the color barrier, and clearly this ZZ Top genre was one of them.

I sat with Eleanor for the remainder of the concert trying to enjoy the balance of it. I even had the gumption to wonder why out of 20,000 people, with presumably half of them men, not one (well…maybe the water-squirting guy), but not one man made an attempt to smile, talk, or make a pass in any way toward me. Did my fear exude an aura of "don't-mess-with-me" and they intuitively knew it, or was it that I was black? I mean, here I was now, sitting and standing in a bathing suit with shapely swimmer athletic legs as long as they come for women, decent-sized breasts and a beautiful smile. I thought everyone liked biscuits, baked or burnt, and yet, I was not approached.

In Detroit, you would barely make it to the concert from the parking lot without being asked out, or at least seriously checked out. What was it? I mean, Dr. King, I did not go there looking for a date, boyfriend, or lover, but I was a woman, and by all previous worldly accounts of beauty (black and white), up there on the ranking. So what was it? Surely I was not going to ask anyone. I didn't even ask Eleanor. For the record, she wasn't getting much action either. Okay, that was my ego talking there. But what the heck! Was I invisible? I think I understood Ralph Ellison's *Invisible Man* on a much deeper level now. But damn, this should have been a numerical impossibility! Truthfully, it was sobering. And I would need a trip back home to Detroit or Oakland for some brotherly accolades and acknowledgment to regain my womanly confidence.

We survived the rest of the heat, the longest concert I will ever attend, and drove home that evening. The bosses were curious about the shorts, and I snidely responded that I had lost them. Thank God they didn't know me enough to impose further questioning. I left both concerts mostly unscathed, except for the self-imposed humiliation. I tried to be in the moment, but could only be in my inner dialogue, and yes there was more than one voice, about how much I felt out of place: Was I ugly? When would I die? Who would find my remains? Would Eleanor care? What would my brother tell the family, and what would they say at my funeral? Crazy.

Yo Hablo Español

Dear Dr. King,

One of my closest competitors at Macy's was a spunky Mexican girl named Nora (name change). We never stated it out loud, but we knew that we were competing against each other, not just the other girls in the department. She was primarily known for being the "sharkiest" of all of the sharks, but I was very close behind, and many times matched—and sometimes exceeded—her monthly sales. Because of our aggressive salesmanship, we developed a mutual respect for our hustling spirits and quickly became really good friends. We were matched in our eagerness to make as much money as possible.

Oftentimes we would plan activities to hang out with her and her sister and do various things around town and around Northern California to have fun spending the money we were making. I befriended her older sister Bianca (name change), who was also tall, a retail queen, and liked to party as much as the rest of us. She and I were the same height, but she was a year older than me. I was two years older than Nora. We continued our friendship for quite a while, and I would actually stand up for Nora when other associates would try to put her down because she was being aggressive on the sales floor. I told them, "No, it's anybody's game. If you want to hang out and not approach the customer, then wait. You know she'll do it. So if you want to win you have to play a little harder." Knowing this she would invite me over to her house because she figured if I spoke out on her behalf then I would be someone she could trust. I met the rest of her family and spent a lot of afternoons and evenings visiting and eating with them. They had a big family too, which reminded me of home. It was four girls and two boys. However, they were first-generation Mexican, and they mostly spoke Spanish at home.

At first it bothered me because I thought they were being rude. But then I realized that her mom and dad were not that fluent in English, especially her mom. However her sisters would also speak Spanish, and there were times when I knew they were saying something not so nice about me. I pretended that it did not upset me. I also decided to take Spanish at the community college so I could understand what the heck they were talking about. I would use them to help me with my homework and the pronunciations. They would often laugh at my attempts to sound authentic. But I was getting the hang of it and began to sound better. I learned that they spoke Spanish but did not necessarily know how to read and write it. It never occurred to me that they had left their homeland to be in ours, and instead of learning Spanish grammar in school, they were only taught English. So I had some skills that they did not have in terms of grammar and spelling. I never really caught everything they would talk about and had to ask them to pause and repeat quite a bit. The Queen's Spanish and Mexican slang were not exactly the same. I kept at it, and I think that an affinity grew toward me because I was trying to get their world. It was also a relief from trying to fit into my own world. I grew really close to this family. I would help out in the kitchen with their mom. I met her aunt from Guatemala, who would come and spend months in the summer with the family. I would also help babysit their niece and nephews. This was a really tightknit family, and I learned that they were very smart and business-minded.

Their father was a laborer and retired from the Southern Pacific railways, and their mother was a homemaker. They moved over here when Nora was little. I believe they all were born in Mexico. I figured out that like black people, they had a segregated belief about who they were in the world. They had placed themselves here, had not been brought over like the blacks, but they also did not see themselves as "typical" Hispanics — but as a "superior" class of Hispanics, more European. It also seemed they had a shallow disregard for other ethnicities, especially Filipinos. I never understood why, but perhaps it was the American way to find a group of people to hold under you in order to feel confident enough to be accepted. More collateral damage from the legacy of slavery. I think too, it was primarily because they identified their aspirations and wealth gain as upper-class white. However they were very close to each other and strictly loyal to their family values and did not take on all of the culturally white mores.

I had heard the N-word once in their house from her brother while they were watching a boxing match. He shouted at the TV, "Hit that N!" wanting Roberto Duran to beat Iran Barkley in the middleweight championship. I was in the room around the corner and they were so into it when we came in, they did not see me. Nora was embarrassed and shouted something very quickly in Spanish and then apologized too. He was embarrassed and also apologized, but I understood. Sports and boxing matches especially, had a way of dividing fans into national or racial solidarity. And with boxing's very violent nature comes jabs of vulgarity; even prejudice surfaces. I would be lying if I said I didn't wonder what they said about me while not around. Or when they were sure I didn't understand, but I did not dwell in it. Her brother was not my friend, she was, so I let it be.

It was shocking to me to find out that Nora and her sister, both in their 20s, not only shared a room in their parents' house, but they also shared the queen-sized bed in the room. Now mind you, both were working and making in the neighborhood of $25,000 a year each. Not a fortune but a lot of money for young people living at home. Definitely enough for the two of them to afford their own place. But they were also a Catholic family and their father was very domineering; he had plans for them. The rules of the house were, you go to school or get a job. If you went to school, meaning college, he would pay for it. If you went to work, you brought home half your paycheck to him and he would put it away. Because of their religion, he did not allow them to move out of the house until they were married. This really stunned me. Grown people, making their own money, living under those conditions. This was truly a cultural shock. I hadn't known any person over 18 who wanted to stay at home. Especially, if they had the money to leave. But they all fell right in line. Not one sibling deviated. One of the older sisters married at 18 or 19 and was first to leave right after high school.

Their business plan began to unfold when I discovered that Nora's money was being saved in order to buy a house. I think she gave her father half of her paycheck on a weekly basis, and he had been tucking it away in a savings account until there was a large enough deposit to purchase a California home in Fairfield. When she made that determined amount, he matched it with his own savings, and they purchased her first home. Cool I thought, now Nora can move out into her own place, but that was not the plan. After the home closed escrow, Nora's father told her to list it as a rental and she did. The other siblings working at home did the same thing with their money, and they all followed the same home-acquisition plan. This went on year after year until someone got married. This was in the late '80s and early '90s so California suburban properties were still somewhat reasonably priced, circa $80-150k.

Once the value grew in the first house that Nora purchased, her father instructed her to pull out enough equity to purchase a second home. She pulled out just enough in order to maintain the rent value to match the mortgage payment. This was the process they created for the wealth generated in their family. When the third home was purchased, it was most interesting because now she was engaged, and this was to be the home they would move into when they were married. But they had decided that they needed a custom one instead. The siblings would team up and go into homes together, kind of like you would go in on a pizza or dinner with a roommate. They would say something like "Hey, I saw this house on so and so, it's $150k? Would you like to go in half with me?" Somebody would respond yes, and within weeks the purchase was made. I was amazed at how quickly and easily they made it work. I don't know if they were part of a secret Mexican cartel, with a national strategy to regain ownership of California via individual family land acquisition, or not, but they were for sure well on their way and represented Mexico respectfully. All it took was a plan, some discipline, patience, and willingness to execute it.

Dr. King, no one I knew had done, or thought to do things this way. Growing up in Detroit, our older siblings barely got married before having babies. The ones that did were not homeowners when they were starting out. They were so happy to be "grown" that they immediately got their own places as renters. So anxious to have a place where no one could tell them what to do. They wanted to be free to have as many people over as possible, for as long as they wanted, and to party and have all the premarital sex they wanted too. We were so focused on just getting in, and not being denied jobs, that working on those jobs, for a paycheck, and saving what you could from that, was the extent of how financial planning went for most of us. Wealth building was not on the forefront. Some saw fame as the road to wealth, a few had big business ideas, others had the "lottery," and the most notorious had drug sales. In my family, we were unknowing heirs to acres of oil and timberland in southern Alabama, but my father died before we knew anything about it. By the time we learned details of it, it had already been acquisitioned by greedy oil companies and equally greedy and scheming lawyers through leases that can be renewed in perpetuity. Dr. King much of the land that black folks owned down south from sharecropping was oil and resource rich and likely stolen, sold for pennies, and leased forever. I'm trying to remember; did you ever address this historical fact in your talks about your vision for the future?

By the time Nora was 30, she already owned three or four California homes. Her sister had three of her own. And two other sisters and her brother probably had three or four as well. This self-made record of success had far outpaced any white person's successes that I had known to date. They were not born here, but had already gained in ten years what generations of us Americans (black and white) were still "dreaming" about. Meanwhile back at my ranch, I was struggling to keep up with rental payments on my newly furnished apartment. I wanted to replicate what I had learned from them with my brother. Pool our money, pay off all bills, and begin to save, but I did not want to move back in with him, and I'm pretty sure he did not want me to move back either. So no sacrifices were made for the sake of gaining wealth. I even thought about asking Nora if we could go in on a house together, if she could assist me with my budgeting and help me so that I had a real savings plan. But she had already categorized me as a lost cause. Instead of doing any of that, I addressed only immediate concerns. I purchased her old Ford after selling my Honda Aero Moped that gave no rain protection. I had bought the "scooter" during one of the wettest CA winters on record. Buying that Ford EXP on credit, which anyone would rightfully call an "experiment," deepened my debt and thus I began my life as a serial debtor. Something the Bible warns strictly against. But Dr. King, if I'm to confess, which I'm sure you've guessed by now, I had not incorporated strict Christian principles into my life, barely read the Bible, and had no one to enforce better behavior. Just my flighty emotional choices, my wandering sense of self and belonging, my blind ambitions of upward mobility, and my need for immediate gratification of material needs to give me a false sense of accomplishment and relevance; to fill the void of having a displaced and distant family love and life. But even this instability was not enough to make me move back to what had now been dubbed "Destroy," MI. "Que' vida!"

Happy Black Housewives

Dear Dr. King,

My sister-in-law's mother was a very sweet southern woman, who seemed to live straight out of the Bible. Her life's mission was to be a loving wife, mother, grandmother, homemaker and Christian—not necessarily in that order. She loved serving and helping people and had the second cleanest house I knew of. Her husband was a retired Navy veteran also from the south. He spent most of his time fixing and repairing things for others and caring for and admiring his newly expanding family. They displayed a very loving and nurturing relationship. They had endured some hard times, but always met them with a demonstrative force of faith, action, and servitude. I came to know them through their frequent visits and ours, to their beautiful home.

She attended faithfully, a non-denominational church in Fairfield, and had a set of loyal friends and families. She led a very modest but comfortable life and established a rigorous yet satisfying routine attending to family matters, church matters, and housekeeping. She was petite physically, but had a very large and jovial personality and a very generous spirit. I don't think I ever heard the word "no" come out of her mouth; and requests to her for things were frequent. She loved to poke fun and make you laugh. They had been married close to thirty years when I first met them. Next to God, her husband, kids and grandkids, her house was a place of pride. She was a bit OCD (but in a good way) and kept everything in meticulous order. She had taking care of her family and home down to a science. Even though the house seemed so much bigger than she was, it was no match for her energy and orderly concerns. It was hard to compare her to my mom, or my closest friends from Detroit, because all of them had at least double the kids, and my mom was a widow. So this woman's energy was the first noticeably stark difference. I don't think she was ever tired.

One of her closest friends was another woman from New Orleans who also had a Navy veteran husband. I'm not sure if their husbands served together their entire careers, or met sometime during or afterward, but they were fellow comrades and enjoyed combining the families for feasts, holidays and fun activities. They had had the same number of children as well. This woman was very soft spoken with big beautiful peering eyes. Her voice was sweet and soft like cotton candy, and she had a slower yet deliberate way about her, including her walk. Her husband worked a little longer at his civilian post at the Carquinez Bridge before he retired. She was also a Bible-living and loving Christian, and they attended the same church. Lastly, there was another family. They were the cousins of my sister-in-law. Her father's sister and her military husband had also relocated to Fairfield and had three children. It had seemed that three was the magic number to black family happiness.

What impressed me about these couples was that they were black, but appeared to have no visible stress. Dr. King, these women were happy! And happy being housewives. The mothers in my neighborhood did not have this display of joy about them. They laughed and even sometimes played but it was in specific moments, when something obscure happened, or if their kids did something silly. It was a release, or situational bouts of joy or ceremony. They did not display ongoing happiness and inner peace like these black California women. The women in Fairfield were not sullen and weighted down with the troubles of household finances, the political state of black people, the craziness of their kids, the pressures of work, or trying to hold on to their husbands. They did not seem to have a care in the world beyond what dishes to use for the next church gathering, Bible study, or Tupperware party. I was just in awe. It was TV-like, but white people TV, not black people. Maybe it was the military training, or just the blissful spiritual rewards of being hyper-religious and devout Christians. I don't know. But I mean, Dr. King, I thought I was in episodes of a black *Mayberry R.F.D.*, or the *Andy Griffith Show*. I think their impact on me was so profound because I fashioned them as how black people could have been as a community if there were never a thing called racism. I could not figure out what their secret sauce was. And maybe it was simply God. But you had God too, and they were also from the south like you, and just a few years younger than you. So how?

Their preoccupation seemed to be primarily wrapped around the duties of the church and serving the needs of the congregation. And this congregation, Church of Christ, in Fairfield, was not like congregations I had visited in Detroit. It was multi-cultural, and my sister-in-law's family was on first-name basis with all the members. They knew all the white kids and watched and scolded them for misbehaving in Sunday school, just like they did the black kids. Made fun of and joked with their parents, and did not seem indifferent to their white counterparts at all. They did not display any, even subtle, apprehension toward whites that you would expect black people to have in an outnumbered environment. It was so surreal. I loved these families. It was a beautiful thing to witness, but with all that love, I still completely felt like an outsider.

I was not baptized in a Church of Christ and I was told I would have to do it again because my church's name did not include the name of Christ in it (Hartford Memorial Church, Detroit, MI, by Dr. Charles Adams in the fall of 1984). I was single and had no suitor in line for marriage. I liked to go out with my single friends from Macy's, and I did not go to church with them three times a week. So I felt like the devil incarnate most of the time. My brother would try to make me hook up with anyone who was Christian and had "good teeth."

He joked a lot about that, and me being single, but I knew he usually meant what he said in a backhanded kinda way. He even suggested once that I was a lesbian, because he was getting impatient with me making excuses for me not being married. He never made me feel attractive enough, and I was always seeking his approval.

The culture here was — to get married! Yeah, go to college, but focus more on your "Mrs." degree. Then graduate — get married and make a family to serve your God, husband, and family in that order. Dr. King, I was not feeling that. I had periods of loneliness and being a wife wishful-ness, but it was more to fit in and not feel ostracized than it was to actually be someone's wife and a mother. Witnessing their lives, the only thing I knew I wanted was a nice and comfortable home. But everyone around me had the full dream package, so I was out of place yet again. I stayed in the Fairfield area for six years, learning suburban life and trying to get underneath my skin. I think the biggest lesson for me was that you could be black without being angry and feeling like you had to carry the weight of the entire race on your shoulders and simply focus on the education, experiences, and spirituality of your own family — a micro degree of self-determination.

EMANCIPATION, 1990s
(The African-American Years)
Black Is, Black Ain't

We had to memorize this poem at Guest Elementary for our English teacher Mrs. Allen. I can still recite by memory after all these years.

I, TOO
I, too, sing America.

I am the darker brother.
They send me to eat in the kitchen
When company comes,
But I laugh,
And eat well,
And grow strong.

Tomorrow,
I'll be at the table
When company comes.
Nobody'll dare
Say to me,
"Eat in the kitchen,"
Then.
Besides,
They'll see how beautiful I am
And be ashamed —

Langston Hughes

I Played the Race Card and Lost?

Dear Dr. King,

I enrolled at the University of San Francisco, College of Professional Studies (CPS) program to complete my bachelor's. I did this knowing that I wanted to get my degree as I had already been overlooked for many promotions and jobs because I did not have one, and I was just tired of that being the reason I had lost out. The program started in February of 1991, which was only one month into my last semester at the community college where I was earning my Spanish degree. I had fifteen units at the college, and the CPS program was fulltime as well, but one class at a time, at an accelerated rate. So it was tantamount to 12 additional units. For all practical or crazy reasons, I had 27 total units, a part-time job, an unreliable car, and miles to go in-between — in Bay-area traffic! I averaged 100 miles of driving every day. My job was at a collection agency in San Leandro, my community college classes were in Suisun, my CPS classes alternated between San Francisco and Pleasanton, and I lived in Fairfield. For those five months, I was a robot, and my life was hell, but it turned out to be a period of my greatest peril and greatest achievements.

There was much, much writing at USF in the CPS program. The first part of the program included a series of essays to challenge your breadth of knowledge in a discipline in order to qualify as having completed elective units of credit. The degree to which you demonstrated your subject matter expertise (per APA format) determined how many units you would earn, and what grade you got. Writing is more time consuming than rote work, so I had enjoyed the classwork at the community college more. However, I was beginning to get good at telling stories also. I was the only black in my cohort of fourteen. I believe everyone in the class with the exception of three including myself, had corporate reimbursement for their educational pursuits. Pacific Bell, and Chevron were footing the bill for most of them to attend this private Jesuit university, and those employees were taking full advantage. I used student loans to fund my tuition. Another woman stated she was paying her own way as her employer was CA State. The third was recently widowed (and it seemed had an inheritance), which she used to pay her tuition as she reinvented her life. The instructor questioned our motivations for returning to school and all of this came out. I do remember feeling a twinge of inferiority for having to student-loan fund my way in, and I think it slightly dampened my full potential. I wished he'd never asked the questions in a group setting.

Dr. King, I want you to know about this next chapter of my life because something happened that I now know is not only possible but even common among young adults who are determined to stay in school no matter what difficulties they find themselves in. I fell into circumstances that you will see why I didn't want exposed. I had to start living in my car. I had earned very little commissions for the past three months due to my workload at school, and was running out of money. While at work, it had become difficult to focus on just the job, as I was also using the job as research for my class project. So my paychecks had dipped, and I had two major car repairs that exhausted my savings. When I received my student loan check, I had just enough to pay the tuition due for that period, or pay rent and drop out, which would have resulted in my having to make immediate loan repayments.

I chose to stay at school. So, I packed up my things, told my landlord I could no longer pay the rent (fortunately it was month-to-month), and let him keep the deposit to cover my full-month notice period. After paying tuition, I took the remaining cash and went to the craft store. I found a cardboard storage container (with drawers), to use for my underwear, toiletries, and mail. I bought some round Velcro sticky tabs and a black fabric remnant for curtains. I went to Kmart and bought a baseball bat, and then to a moving company and purchased a large cardboard pseudo-closet so that I could hang up my work clothes. I rented a P.O. Box from the post office. I purchased the smallest rental storage unit and moved all my furnishings in it—the first month cost just $1, thank God! Lastly, I joined a health club, ironically called "Living Well Lady," for $25 per month so that I'd have a safe and clean place to shower. You can imagine I did not have time to actually exercise.

I positioned the sticky tabs on the ceiling of my car right above and behind my front bucket seats, and over the smaller half windows in the back. And attached the other half of the tabs to the fabric I cut into shape. Fortunately, I had black louvers over the back window and did not need additional covering for privacy. I kept three or four pairs of shoes, a flashlight, my purse and other valuables on the floor behind the seats. My Ford EXP hatchback had become my mobile home and "hatch-bed."

My routine was to drive to work, then to class, and then back to Fairfield, stopping at the storage unit to pick out my next day, or two, of work clothes then to the library until dusk. I would eat at Happy Hours, or Nora's, or my brother's, or other friends' by casually dropping by around dinnertime on the evenings I didn't have class. I never revealed that I had moved out of my apartment. Some nights I would stop at the health club to shower, or just change into my sweats. I would drive to the apartment complex parking lot on the opposite side of where I used to park when I lived there. I'd back into a parking space as close to the dumpster as I could, climb in the back where my palette of blankets and sheets were in position. My routine ended with taking my homemade curtains and sticking them up over the windows and behind the seats, lying down, saying my prayers, stretching out (diagonally so that I could sleep without bending my knees), hugging my baseball bat, and going to sleep.

The sunrise was my alarm, filtering through the louvers like a prism, but with all bands of light the same color. Or on occasion, someone would come out early and start their car, and that would wake me. I'd climb back into the driver's seat after peeking through the front curtain, remove the ones on the side window, and drive off. It was just three blocks down Fairfield's main road, N. Texas Street, to Living Well Lady. I'd shower, put on my clean work clothes and drive to work to begin each day over again.

I began to feel a vagrant sense of freedom, Dr. King. Can you understand that? It provided some sense (perhaps false) of security. I felt as long as no one knew I was in there, I had nothing to worry about. I did not fear anyone trying to steal the car, because it was a lemon and not on the short list of most attractive cars for thieves. I was saving money by not paying hundreds for rent and all the utilities. My grocery bill was lower, as I had no refrigerator to fill up. I basically only had to buy breakfast for myself, and a glass of coke or two for Happy Hour meals when I didn't get fed visiting others. My monthly storage was $32, my gas was the same as before, and my gym membership was $25, so I was able to save money right away. I would do it for as long as weather permitted and for as long as I needed to save up enough to pay rent again.

Dr. King, I did this for six weeks until my brother Ron found me. There were a couple of nights I actually felt homeless, but I didn't lament too much because I had no time. There was too much reading and homework to do. One Saturday while I was studying at the library, my brother Ron brought his family to visit the duck pond behind the library. Ron came in to return books. He happened upon (God sent him to) my table, saw me, and simply asked, "What's your new phone number?" I looked up, said hi, and then feverishly tried to think of something without telling him the truth. He had apparently been trying to reach me. I just stared without saying anything, and he repeated his question. I gave him the numbers and letters of my license plate. (What was I thinking?) He said what, and I repeated my response. Of course he figured out what I was doing.

He charged back with a bit of angst and confusion, "Are you sleeping in your car?" I casually said, "Yes," then put my head back down pretending to read my homework. He responded, "You're crazy!" then walked away. Okay...I thought...not the response I would have guessed. I shrugged and went back to my homework. About five minutes later, my sister-in-law came in, and asked, "Are you sleeping in your car?"

"Oh, hi...yeah."

"Why didn't you come to the house?"

"Because y'all live too far in the wrong direction, and I didn't want to bother anybody. I'm saving money, I'll be okay."

"Are you crazy? That is very dangerous."

"It's 'Square' field, not Detroit, I'm not worried." But the moment she mentioned danger, fear began to brew.

"Well you should be, because that's stupid. You're coming to the house."

"No I'm not! I don't have time, I can't add another twenty miles to my drive, I don't have time!"

"Yes, you are!"

"No, I'm not!"

"I don't care if it's not Detroit, you're a woman and it's still dangerous!"

And just like that, fear percolated and I started to cry. Basically I broke down with the realization that the freedom I had gained by living so cheaply could cost me something much more tragic. I also felt embarrassed. I agreed that I would come to the house when I finished my homework. She left. I stayed at the library for a while and then headed to their house in Dixon, CA, around dinnertime. By the time I had arrived, she had already contacted her mother in Fairfield (the happiest of the happy black housewives), and arranged for me to stay with them in one of their three vacant bedrooms for the remainder of school, rent-free. I was grateful for the comfortable shelter, financial relief, and no increase on my commute, but I would now have to render an unspoken payment of church attendance three times per week. Goodness gracious! So the five hours per week I hadn't had of "would-be-driving-time" to stay in Dixon, turned into five hours of prayer and worship. Have mercy!

I finished the semester with 27 units and a combined GPA over 3.0. I was happy that I did not drop out and was able to complete the scheduled USF coursework. My story of struggle had a happy ending, but I guess I told you this story because as I look back on it, I am struck with how many ways all people (not just black) can become suddenly marginalized in our "democratic" and "caring" country and end up in pretty bad situations. Of course, you always knew that, and always spoke on our behalf, but did you expect it to continue for so long and to come up on so many different levels?

I was able to hold my own with my seemingly more successful cohorts. They appeared to have accepted me as well. I can't remember one episode with this group where I felt racial isolation being intentionally perpetuated by them, but I did do something to cause my own racial humiliation. You see, I was writing one of the essays for the course and remembered some of the "intelligent sounding" verbiage I had heard my cohort's use that I did not know. In one of my essays, I was describing my mother's strength in having the nine of us to care for. I wrote how I could not fathom being a widowed mother of nine in today's world. However, "fathom" was a foreign and new word to me and not in the vernacular of anyone I had known up to that point. Nor in any books I had previously read. I read my essay out loud and I said fathom, mimicking what I had heard, but I wrote p-h-a-n-t-o-m in its place. I had known about the musical *The Phantom of the Opera*, so when I heard the word in class, I attached the closest phonetic I could think of, believing I knew the definition and the spelling and therefore never looking it up. When I received my graded essay back, the instructor just circled it and added a big red question mark. When I saw this, it may as well have been a "WTF?" I felt as if there was a bulletin board of my mistake, with me on it in a dunce cap, spread across the Bay Bridge for all white people to see and laugh at, and for all black people to repo my "black-educated" credential. I did not know if this was an inherent case of subconscious, post-traumatic racial stress syndrome (PTRSS— has this termed been coined before?) or not, but I certainly felt as if I had just walked off the plantation, and my stance and confidence diminished for the remainder of that writing class.

I was so degraded that I let go of a huge opportunity to earn more writing credits and save, literally, thousands of dollars. It's funny, in the peculiar sense, that when the PTRSS kicks-in, false pride takes over. I had the chance to have the instructor evaluate any essays for the remaining elective credits I needed. He offered his editorial service, post-class, for a nominal fee that would have pretty much guaranteed my success, but I did not check my pride and allow myself to do it. I turned my work in for credit evaluation without professional editing. I turned in six essays for a possible grand total of eighteen credits. I was that delusional, or cocky. When the review was complete, I received exactly three, and therefore not enough to complete the 120 required for graduation.

Many of my other cohorts used his services and earned the credits they needed to complete their requirements on time. So my paradoxical prideful cowardliness cost me another nine years of incomplete misery and confidence, and I remained in my hazy world of circumstantially delayed goals. "If only I had _____." Fill in the blank.

I was able to walk at graduation with my classmates and celebrate my partial success, with gown, mortarboard and tassel in tow. But I did not invite anyone except my roommate to attend, as I felt like a complete fraud. Somewhere in the video coffers owned by a woman named Judy (Hispanic married surname) is the recorded ceremony and post-ceremony celebration at her home. (I would love to see it if you are reading this Judy. I'd love to see if at least my acting was credentialed since I was not.)

I did finally finish nine years later in 2002, with husband, toddler daughter, baby boy in utero, and friends in attendance. However, I had to pay for four more courses to complete my electives to the tune of over eight thousand dollars; not including the class time, study time, homework time, driving time, and all the other intangibles (years of educational discontent, would-be-better jobs or promotions, and time away from my family) that made stupid even stupider. And all of that self-denial, success-blocking drama could have been avoided if I had taken a pride-eliminating pill or something and paid a measly fifty dollars per essay. The *phantom* will haunt me forever.

The other b/w thing that happened was when one of my classmates had everyone over to her place for a celebration. She lived in the exclusive, gated district of Danville, CA, called Blackhawk. I had never heard of it, but had passed the Danville signs on the I-680 corridor a few times so I knew the area. This was the first time I had to state my destination to a guardsman, sign-in, and show my ID to go to someone's house. I did not know that *regular* people could legally block entrances to their neighborhood, require invitation-only, and make you present identification before you could even drive on their streets. My first snapshot with real and present economic segregation. I thought that only happened on TV, and in areas where important government officials, dignitaries, celebrities, and millionaires lived. Certainly not for ordinary, middle-aged undergrad degree-seeking women. But for all I knew, she could have been a millionaire. I would have probably copped an attitude and declared my inalienable rights and liberties as a US citizen with the guard, but I knew that my others would have to pass the same scrutiny. Or would they? Was it just me? I was given my tourist visa with verbal driving directions and I was off. Down the street I drove. The reflections of the overarching trees on the hood of my car caught my eye, and I watched the shadows spread across my hood, up my windshield, then on my fingers, and then my arms. It was as if the shadows magically brushed the dust of working class off my car and body and transported me to Never-Never Land. The meticulously landscaped yards cautioned an orderly behavior along the way.

This area was so Anglo even the guardsman was. Oh yeah, Dr. King, sometime around the mid-80s, there was a shift in patrols, along with police and firemen; black people were allowed to get jobs as security guards, and policemen, although not in large numbers, and certainly not all at once. Which means they carried guns and had the right to use them. Imagine that! Black men sanctioning white men and women to enter an establishment or not. Something I wish you could have seen.

I do not remember much about the layout of the home, just that it was well furnished with European upholstered neutral and earth-toned, fabrics and lots of heavy oak and maple furniture. What I do remember is the feeling of *uber* orderly comfort, and modest luxury, that I had not experienced before. Her home hugged and caressed you like a full-length mink coat that you would try on at Saks Fifth Avenue for minute, for fun, but carefully put back because you knew it was out of reach. Every piece of furniture, tableware, linens, and decorative accents (lots of them) had a pre-planned and very specific purpose. Everything was in its place, and there was a place for everything. There was nothing that seemed dual-purpose, or multi-functional. I found this fascinating and exhausting at the same time. My mom had never had the time, or money, to collect and reflect on so many particular items. We had always lived in a "make-do" household, and almost everything had more than one purpose. You know how that living room sofa was also a sleeper bed and a trampoline for the kids (when mom wasn't looking). If you were ironing in the same room while watching the only television, the sleeper frame with just the legs extended would double as a hanging rod for those freshly starched, ironed shirts until the entire load was done. And if you could not find, or did not have a bottle opener, the corner of the frame would do. We even reused brown paper bags before recycling was in fashion. They served as bags to shake up the flour for frying chicken; it was the faux pan when my mom shucked corn, or snapped green beans, and if you snagged it before any of that, we could rip it into rectangles and roll it individually, like flat cigars, to use as hair rollers for overnight setting.

Here, our hostess had every tool you could think of, and many I could not. Plus, a proud collection of grandfather clocks that got everyone's attention. I couldn't recall anyone in my family or neighborhood ever having even the notion of a grandfather clock as a possession. It was not in our sphere of middle- or upper- class aspirations. Not because it was a luxury item, but because the practicality rendered it moot.

It was a pleasant evening and the group really enjoyed the non-class time. But with all the cuisine, cushions and comfort, I was not completely at ease. My brain was fixated in comparative analysis, over-analyzing everything. I even cataloged the varieties in their looks, European ancestries, and religions. But with all of those differences, the commonality they displayed was their right to be there, affirming luxury, totally at home with it, like a reunion with an old friend. Something that they seemed to carry as a guaranteed certainty to attain, with the right amount of focused time and attention, in pursuit of their happiness. My pursuit however, seemed to be outside of my capabilities, in the hands of others, of people like them, holding and providing the key to the door of opportunity — but only if I met their historically, pre-determined, instituted, and widespread matrices of measures. Or even something arbitrary, like knowing when and how to use a proper serving tool, or knowing and understanding that the Swiss made the best timepieces to date.

Their conversations, which I was mostly outside of, centered around their European relatives and ancestry, and their love of the goods, the quality and craftsmanship of various foods, recipes, household furnishings and accessories — from the old country. Not quite an anglophile, and uneducated in European cultural and social customs and art appreciation outside of what was satiated in high school and a few of my art classes, I chose to just listen, smile occasionally, and pretend I was interested. But feeling mostly inadequate. What could I share of equal association from the old country, my old country? Mainstream had not yet embraced African art, or African crafts collectibles as the staples of affluence and sophistication. And I had not forged my own personal alliance with any countries in Africa yet, nor owned anything representative, not even Kente cloth. I could school them on contemporary African-American art, but felt that I would sound too defensive and left it alone. They carried on and on, and I briefly pondered if any of them secretly wondered if I felt left out. But their conversation was so fluid and fast, it just ticked on with precision and chimes just like those clocks, minute by minute, without a pause for any untimely abstractions. Shortly thereafter, someone announced they had to go, and I jumped at the opportunity to make my exit as well. I turned in my temporary visa upon exiting, and that was the last time I visited Blackhawk. Somehow I'm bothered that its name was Blackhawk. And I still do not know why.

My First Black Boss

Dear Dr. King,

I worked at MCI right after completing my CPS program at USF. In fact, I was recruited from the campus job placement activities. I was one of ten or so new team members that MCI installed to focus on the sales from the small business sector. There were three blacks on the Territory Sales Reps (TSR), sales team. I found it curious that two of us were assigned the "territory" of Oakland. The TSR Sales Manager was also black, and she was to be the beta tester and fall guy for this new trial. I knew the success or failure of this new installation was going to make or break her career with MCI.

This was my first white-collar job, albeit I would spend more time in the field than in the office. However, I had the freedom to schedule my day, to come and go as I pleased, a cubicle, an easy quota, an expense account, and generic business cards. In retrospect, those should have been my first clue that this team installation was purely a pilot test, with no assurances for longevity or promotion; they were not willing to pay, even for personalized business cards. Some of us actually purchased name stamps and spent hours preparing cards with our names and titles. Others just hand-wrote their contact information. By this time, I already had over six years of retail sales experience under my belt, so I had no real fear of meeting people and asking them to buy from me. I did, however, have a bit of trouble asking for the decision makers. I guess I thought I was too young. I would talk to whoever was there and wait for them to tell me they could not make the decision. So I wasted a lot of time, but still managed to exceed my quotas regularly.

I befriended rather quickly one of my colleagues from Ohio. She was savvy, smart, and an Ohio State grad, who had moved to CA to get over a broken engagement. She and I became quite a dynamic duo. She was my first Jewish friend. Her territory was Walnut Creek (nicknamed WASPY Creek for its dominantly Anglo-white, upwardly mobile demographic) but that did not daunt Pam's enthusiasm for her territory one bit. She actually rented a condo there as well. We liked pairing up as much as possible to knock out our quotas before noon, so that we could play the rest of the day. She had those store clerks and owners eating out of her hand. They could not resist her genuine charm, and when they tried, she would flash her perfect teeth, green eyes, and super-long eyelashes, keep at them with her logic, and they would eventually surrender. That was interesting to watch. I always wondered how they would have reacted to me. Actually, now that I think back, most of the black business owners in Oakland had treated me the same way.

Surprisingly, the Chinese community did too. I would call ahead for appointments instead of showing up first, fearing rejection if my face was the first impression. Calling as Wanda "Lee" gave me the cultural inside edge, so I used it as much as possible before hitting the shops in Chinatown. When I showed up and announced my name, I would get laughter and disbelief. But invariably they would sign up, because calling China was expensive, and MCI was willing to give them up to $500 for the first month of free international long distance. I probably could have been an alien and they would have taken the deal.

Pam and I had a blast with this job, outside of the easy quotas and short days; we tried practically every restaurant in the east bay at least once. But we would not just eat, we would use the time to calculate our earnings, strategize and leverage our territories, and plan more fun. We also spent afternoons shopping and swimming. We made a couple odd crazy trips to Los Angeles, Las Vegas and Lake Tahoe. We were never short on fun. Once her twin came to visit, and we had to pick her up at the Oakland Airport. We arrived about thirty minutes early. As we were waiting for Shelley, I was at the phone bank calling into my voicemail and noticed groups of black people huddling throughout the area. My first thought, hmmm, there must be a convention in town. I can sell scores of accounts to them! I got off the phone and approached a man who was smiling a lot and talking to two women. He was short, but had a very tall presence. After excusing my interruption, I asked him if there was a convention or something, and he said yes. Ka-ching! The dollar signs began rolling in my head like a slot machine. I started adding up my commission check right away. He invited me to the International Black Summit's opening-night ceremony at the Oakland Convention Center. (He explained that the Black Summit was an international annual gathering of black graduates of the Landmark Forum to address issues of people of African descent around the world). Pam had already made extensive plans for us for the evening (she was well known for her planning skills) to welcome Shelley, so I knew I could not attend and told him so. He mentioned that I could attend another "introductory" meeting to be held on the following Tuesday night at Samuel Merritt College Hospital. I told him I would be there. He said that I could find out what the Summit was all about. The next day, I got ready for the event by making one hundred copies of the LOIs (Letters Of Intent) for my contracts — from my people.

On Tuesday evening, I arrived a bit early to scope it out. There were lots of classrooms in this facility. When I got to the classroom corridor, there were a few white people arranging nametags into rows on a table. I pretended I did not see them, walked past to the open door, and peeked in. There were two more white people arranging the chairs and no one else in the room. It had two sections of stackable chairs and a director's chair upfront with a music stand. The chair and stand were bordered by chalkboards with pre-written statements of the meeting outcomes, and inspirational statements done by hand but very neatly, and even in a straight line — hard to master on a chalkboard. I stepped back out, surmising that I was in the wrong place and began to walk away when a man asked if he could help me. I said no, knowing that I was searching for black people. He continued in an assuring tone that he could help and asked who was I looking for. I paused and then glanced at the card the airport man had given me and said Maurice. He smiled and said, "Yes, Maurice will be here, you have the right location." Not completely trusting that, I asked if this was where the International Black Summit met. He responded that Maurice was in the IBS and would explain when he arrived. He suggested I take a seat after asking my name and handing me a nametag. I decided to go in and took a seat on the far end close to the back rows.

There were only a few others seated at this point, and they seemed preoccupied with notebooks. A matronly white woman came in and made her way right to me smiling. She sat next to me and turned to say hello in a too-friendly way. I wondered why she chose to sit next to me with a practically empty room. She adjusted herself in the seat and turned back at me to talk further. I responded in kind. She asked who invited me. I told her. She smiled bigger and said how great Maurice was and rambled on about the contributions he was making to the group. I had no idea what she was talking about, but continued nodding. Just as I was about to ask her if she used long distance much and give her my MCI spiel, I noticed that more people were pouring in, and within ten minutes the room was practically full. I looked toward the door, and there came Maurice. He was smiling broadly, and I stood up. Our eyes met and he came over to greet me and ushered me to sit where he usually sat. He asked if I found the place okay and then explained that the session would start shortly with a brief introduction for about thirty minutes. Following that would be a breakout session for the rest of the evening where the guests (meaning me) would go to find out more about the program. He said he would stay in the main room and meet me at the end. I just wanted to know what time I would be able to make my sales pitch, and where all the black people from the Summit were hiding. There were only a few black people in the room; we were clearly not the majority. I did not understand what kind of Black Summit this could possibly be. But I was willing to stay and wait it out. The jackpot of a month's worth of sales quota met in one night was too attractive, so I hung in there.

Just as Maurice finished, everyone started to stand and clap for this skinny brunette who looked like a cross between the actress Pam Dawber, of *Mork & Mindy* and Morgan Fairchild, of *Falcon Crest*. She thanked everyone and began the event. She explained what the evening would be about and how long we would be in session. Then she asked the participants to introduce their guests. Maurice was third, and he asked me to stand. He related how I had approached him at the airport for some reason, to the amusement of everyone there. He said he was thankful I accepted his invitation and then asked me if I wanted to say anything. Following the protocol of the previous introductions I stated my name, affirmed what Maurice had said, and then confessed that I had really come to sell long distance to a big group of black people. They laughed louder and thanked me for deciding to stay anyway. I sat down. Now they thought that was cute, charming, and funny, but I was serious. I intended to make my sales quota, and ushering me to another room was not going to prevent that.

The facilitator then introduced some people in the back whom she referred to as assistants. They all came up and waved and stated what room they would be in. Six of them were black, and I was glad to finally be going to the Summit. We went to a smaller room on the ground level where Mary Jane, Thornton, Donnie, Nicole, Norma Jean, Tyra, Barbara, and Rosaland took turns explaining principles and sharing personal details that were kind of interesting but mostly anecdotal. I listened keenly for the opportunity to make my pitch. An hour or so passed and I was beginning to get irritated. My intention had been thwarted. I did not get to make my purpose clear to anyone. And my monthly quota expectations were not going to be met. But I waited 'til the end, hope against hope. When they were done, I hit the exit as quickly as possible. I was on the street looking for my car when one of them called out my name. Tyra had followed me out to urge me to go back in and say goodbye to Maurice.

Maurice wanted to know if I was interested in taking the course. He said in order to participate in the IBS, I first had to complete the Forum. He then explained that the summit ended, that it was a weekend conference for graduates of the Landmark Forum of African descent. He went on to explain in order to participate in the next summit, the prerequisite was the program I was introduced to tonight. Feeling suckered, and annoyed that I had lost the sales bonanza opportunity, but trying to conceal it, I told him I was not sure. Then he flipped the script. He went into sales mode and convinced me to sign up. But I did not really understand what I was getting into—something about getting more juice from the lemon-y life I had—how to develop more meaningful relationships and regain vitality. These were touted as two of the many benefits you could gain by participating in the Landmark Forum course. Being more human with the emphasis on "being" versus doing and having, and being/living in the present and not in your past. It all sounded esoteric and counter-intuitive but I was more curious than disinterested. So I signed-up. Worst case scenario, it may help with my sales and give me lots of leads.

We were in a room with close to 200 adults dealing with issues ranging from being ignored as a child, to divorce, parenting issues, mid-life crisis, etc. The laundry list of human error. It turned out to be one of the most eye-opening experiences I have ever had—not just because they were from all over the world, but because they had a lot of the same issues as my friends and I did. It was shocking and inspiring and nurturing and healing all at the same time—almost like a church revival but without the music, praying and preaching. I saw not only white people, but people in general in a whole new light and began to understand in a very profound way that we had more things in common than we had in difference. Most of the psychological baggage was sad, traumatic, and very deeply felt by the attendees, including me. But I experienced a degree of emancipation to learn that white families, other nationalities, and ethnic families were just as fucked up as black families. Crack invasion or no crack invasion. I mean Dr. King, they had rapists, robbers, sexists, abusers, alcoholics, drug addicts, and as much emotional carnage, if not more, than any black family I had known. You might say it was an equalizer of sorts. Not only did I lose decades of mental and racial shame and guilt, I gained an inner peace and outer confidence I had not previously had. I really did not comprehend how a man from as far away as India could stand up and share parts of his life that mirrored my own story. There was something very surreal, yet quite loving, about what was said in that room, and it blew my mind. I had started this evening and the subsequent journey, wanting to sell long distance to a room full of black people. I completed the sessions discovering so much more about who I was as a woman, who I wanted to be as a woman. The biggest learning was that I had spent the last fifteen years grieving the death of my mother and was finally able to forgive both my parents for dying and to forgive God for taking them from me. And release the shame and guilt I had about myself for all of us (my family) being imperfect.

I also gave up my fear of what I thought people were like and that they were all after me. I allowed myself to take my mask off and allowed my vulnerabilities to be seen by others I did not know. I think I lost about 200 pounds of mental weight. This experience freed me up to be more of my authentic self without trying to be a certain way in order to be liked by white people—by all people really, but primarily whites—because like so many other black people, I was still mostly packed with the unspoken need to assimilate, how to assimilate, and why to assimilate. That had all precluded me from being who I genuinely was. An entirely new way was created for me to be and show up in the world, and I loved it. I no longer felt the need to apologize for being Black! Or that I needed to be more "white" to be liked, and accepted. This may sound odd being from Detroit and having the very healthy dose of ethnic and racial upbringing in the formidable years of my life, but society had done a number on my self-esteem that only magnified when I found myself truly in the world alone in CA, without the immediate support and proximity of family. I had become a societal ambiguous puppet, pretending to be like white, pretending to be not-all-the-way black, pretending to be a confident in-your-face black. Pretending. Trying to fit in anywhere and everywhere and be who or what the recipient of my presence needed me to be. And with the ensuing coursework, those layers came off. As I reflect on this, I feel somehow more convinced that this was not your dream of assimilation. Am I right, Dr. King?

Meanwhile, back at the office, many of my colleagues on the sales front were dropping like flies and I wanted to follow, but I did not have a plan. Tonya (name change), my boss, left (under ambiguous circumstances) and was replaced. The success of the program was marginal, and it appeared that the window for it was beginning to close. I could tell her separation was not really her first choice when she told us she was leaving. I felt bad for her. I think she put her heart into it, and sacrificed a lot of time away from her toddlers. But it appeared that her time to prove it viable had expired and she was being thrown out like spoiled chocolate milk. Only to be replaced by the "great white-hope," our new boss that we referred to as our new Jewish-American Princess, to save the program. I did not know if Tonya was not qualified enough, or if the expectation was too high. The general public was very loyal to AT&T (the only game in town) for decades, and we spent a lot of time educating our customers about how phones work to diffuse their fears of having no service by making the switch. So marketing did not do a good enough job in my opinion, and I felt she did not get enough time. But hopefully she was relieved from the stress of it all.

Soon after that, Pam, my hanging buddy, decided she had had enough and wanted to be a chiropractor instead. A decision like that for me would have required accumulating more debt and finding someplace super cheap, almost free, like couch surfing to get through it. She however was able to make a single phone call to discuss it with her father and he of course absolutely supported her decision and was able to financially support her as well, with her car, tuition, room and board, and anything else she needed to be successful, like any good father of means would do. I was happy for her. But I was also a bit unnerved. Because it was that easy. Maybe not truly easy, but it had the appearance of easiness and, to me, of distinguished parents of means and community economics.

The next day I pulled out my Yellow Pages phonebook and started calling down the list of medical professionals within Oakland, and looked for surnames that sounded black. It took me about three hours, but when I was done, I had switched my OB/GYN, Optometrist, Dentist, and MD to black doctors. Literally by calling the offices and asking if the doctor was black, and if he or she was accepting more clients. I told myself if my consumer choices could help another child go to college or to grad or medical school, full board, it would be a black child.

Pretty much after Pam left, it was no longer fun for me. The whole TSR program was beginning to feel like a joke. All the rah-rah team meetings, and the whack sales trainings. Still, I hung on for a few more months, eighteen months total, but then decided it was time to go.

Rather than give the customary and professional two-week notice, I took the low road and just did not go back. On the third day of my AWOL, responsibility and guilt kicked in and I walked into the office. The new manager called me immediately into her office and shut the door behind me. She stared at me a bit before speaking, long enough to strike a bit of fear. I'm not sure what I was afraid of, as I knew my job was over and I truly did not want it back. Nonetheless, I was worried. She queried me about my health, curious if I had been deathly ill, thus unable to call, and then listened to my languished explanation of why I pulled this disappearing act. Something I said pulled her into counsel mode and she sat with me the next three hours analyzing, coaching, and supporting me to make a "thoughtful" career decision. Wow, Dr. King, she was really trying to help me! I could not believe it! It went as far as her writing two columns on the board "Pros" and "Cons" of quitting vs. staying. What? I wasn't automatically being fired. Wow, was she doing this as a generous and decent act of support, or was she trying to save the program, or her ass? Either way, I could not have foreseen that, because when she replaced Tonya none of us liked her initially and we had collectively given her the cold shoulder on more than one occasion. She was to be avoided at all costs. So there I was being hand-held and helped seemingly for my benefit only. Well at the end, I had to make a choice. She was not going to let me sleep on it, by going home and coming back, nor take any additional time. She laid it out as follows: Choice 1) Stay and she would increase her management and require hourly reporting from me for a set period of time, in her words "ride my ass" to make sure I was selling well above quota; or Choice 2) Leave and submit my resignation notice, effective immediately, in writing. It was at this point that she left the office to give me ten minutes to think about it. I had created more Pros (many lofty) than

Cons on my board for leaving, and stared at it the whole time, weighing my options.

She had erased all prejudged Cons I had concocted about her. How could she have been so misunderstood? Not just by me, but the entire team it seemed. Upon her return I informed her that I was choosing to leave. She was disappointed. Again, that surprised me. Now if her next move didn't take the cake, nothing did, because she asked me, Dr. King, if I wanted to be fired or to quit, meaning on paper, for the records. Now part of this sounded like the southern Sheriff who opens the back door of his cruiser with a falsely arrested black man, releases his hand-cuffs, and tells him to get out and run, in which his jaunt would be met by a bullet through his back. I truly was expecting an ax to fall with this question, but she went on to explain to me that if I wanted to collect unemployment she would mark fired, if I felt I could use something coming in so that I would not have to cash in all of my stock to pay the rent. Or I could just quit with no chance of claiming unemployment. This was one of those life decisions I truly had no concrete plans for, nor any real safety net to fall on, and was again gambling with my livelihood, but I still felt I needed to go. So with that, I took the less financially damaging route and asked for her to check "fired" and thanked her for her time and the option. She agreed and assured me that if a future employer called, that MCI could only legally validate that I worked there, my title, and the dates of my employment, and that she would be a reference. She gave me pen and paper. Had me sign a couple of documents. Wished me well. Hugged me and ushered me out after I gathered my few belongings from my cubicle. Ring, ring…Wanda…new life calling.

Another White Housemate

Dear Dr. King,

As my fearlessness increased, I found myself looking for another place to live—having left my apartment in Oakland, due to my unemployment. As if the teaching fates would have it, there was another woman at the center where I had taken the coursework, looking for someone to share a house with, and she became another white housemate.

Sheila (name change) needed a roommate as soon as possible to split the rent. I needed a cheaper place to stay, so it worked out. I moved in within two or three days. It was more cabin than house in the high hills of Montclair, an upper-class district of Oakland. It was also a long climb from the bottom of the street. We nicknamed it the "treehouse" because of that and its run-down, primitive state. It had three bedrooms and one bathroom. She already occupied the master room with a sliding-door access to the patio, near the front of the kitchen. I had a room in the back, also with a sliding glass door, but it was ill planned, being built too close to the 60-degree hillside. The door was also fused shut. But it was great to be in a natural setting.

The kitchen was already stocked with Sheila's dishes, pots and pans, and spices, etc., so I just brought in a couple of place-settings as well as my favorite coffee mug and stuff. I put everything else I had brought under the house in the un-walled garage area. I really liked the fact that we were somewhat hidden from the street, because there were lots of trees and natural plants and vegetation—and I later found out—lots of native animals also. This became a bit unnerving because I was a city girl and not used to having creatures roaming around outside, and on a couple occasions, inside my house! However, it was very humorous for Sheila because she was like Ellie Mae Clampet *(The Beverly Hillbillies)* and loved any and all types of animals. She thought they were God's gift to humans and wanted me to treat them the same way. She had a cat who had freedom that I did not actually have. It seemed to me his rights were more important than mine. I had the habit of kicking (not literally) her cat out of the kitchen when I was cooking. She sternly informed me that Sylvester was here before me, that he had free range of the house before I arrived, and she saw no reason to change that whether or not I was paying half the rent. And she quickly reminded me that her name was on the lease and the landlord didn't even know I was there. Which I'm sure was a euphemism.

But we did work out more-or-less satisfactory living arrangements—she loved to cook, and I loved to eat. We shared the living room and television as much as we could. She had completed the seminar where we met, so we had that in common as well. We often used the course tools to coach one another whenever one of us was slipping from our newly committed behaviors. I really did like her and I loved living in the Oakland Hills and having that access to nature — even though I was somewhat afraid of it most of the time. The bottom line is, I was willing to be somebody new, so this deal worked out perfectly for me.

I learned something significant at this time. I did not know my 5'4" blonde roommate had so much fire in her. Animal love yes, but not fire. At a group gathering, one of the session coaches did something that really pissed her off. They decided to go into the storage room to talk it out and I followed. They were standing about 5 feet apart, began calmly enough, and then started yelling back and forth. The contention escalated. The other woman was Mexican and about the same size. They moved in on each other at one point, until they were only inches apart. They were face-to-face screaming and cussing each other out and holding strong to their positions. I had never seen anybody other than black people fight in person. I did nothing to try to break them apart because I wanted to see what would happen. I honestly wanted to see who was the tougher of the two. It got to the point where there was spit flying from their forced words, when one of them said something that broke the anger and just like that, they both started to calm down. Wait. What? How does that happen? Note to self: You can argue passionately without fighting. Who knew?

In Detroit there was no way that two people could be in each other's face without a slugfest. Dr. King, I know we are supposed to turn the other cheek, but the mere fact that you got that close was reason enough to start "swinging," in the street lingo. I did not know that people could express anger so emphatically and not try to knock each other's head off. This was new. If any of my middle-school bullies had been in this situation, they would have started throwing blows the moment the door closed. In fact, it likely would not have made it that far. Heck, in my own family, if I looked at my brother Ron, or asked the wrong question, he would be ready to whip my butt. This was really something different, and I thought it was just phenomenal. I even called my brother Doug to share the story because it was newsworthy. He laughed about it, but agreed that at home somebody would've been beaten up.

I learned a lot from Sheila too—about sitting at the table and eating with friends and family on a regular basis versus special occasions. She always loved to invite people over. She took the time to set the table and prepare appetizers as well as the main course and a little bit of dessert, and did the same for all meals—company or not. I had never thought about doing that for every meal, because we had too many people to feed growing up. If we took out the china or silver for dinner, it was primarily for show. But for Sheila there were no pretenses and no attempt to impress anyone with utilities; the impressions were reserved for the meal itself. And that distinction made all the difference in the world to me.

The other thing I had never thought about had happened one night while we were watching television. Sheila was scanning with the remote control for something to watch that we would be mutually interested in. She was surfing pretty quickly from channel to channel, and on one of the channels flashed a black actor in a scene. Now we did not have a lot of shows that represented "us." I mean *The Cosby Show* and *A Different World* were off the air, and not yet in syndication. Oh yeah Dr. King, the black sitcoms of the '70s had done such a bamboozling job of telling everyone we were marginal and comical at best, that when *The Cosby Show* came out with a black doctor and his black lawyer wife as the upwardly-mobile professional parents of five children, people went crazy. They were saying black people do not live like that and the show was unreal because none of the kids were strung out. Well fortunately that quieted down and people grew to adore the representation of us. Its spinoff of black kids in college at an HBCU (Historically Black Colleges & Universities) was brilliant. It reminded me a lot of Cass Tech, so it was my favorite. And after that more black actors started appearing as positive role models in various shows as doctors, firemen, policemen, businessmen, etc. So it was a good thing. But you would be surprised to hear that Diahann Carroll was playing the richest black woman in a very popular show called *Dynasty*. She was an oil tycoon. You may have not liked her telling Barbara Walters in an interview that she wanted to be the first black bitch on television. I had not known anyone to want to be that, on TV, or in person, so that was a tad bit too boorish for me. But nonetheless, TV had grown up somewhat for us.

So in our family household or in my own apartment, we would look specifically for people of color when we scanned. When I saw that she did not stop when the person of color flashed on the screen, it rattled me. It never occurred to me that she wouldn't be interested. (To this day, I surf all the channels to see what interests me, and usually on the basis of content. But I always—almost subconsciously—pause when I see a black face because I want to see what's going on.) At that time, I guess I thought everybody else did the same—especially due to the lack of black quality programming. I did not ask her about it, I was too embarrassed. And so caught off guard that I did not trust that I would not sound too pro-black if I asked. Could have been a great opportunity to have a cultural exchange, but I was reprimanded once for asking if she could keep her cat out of the kitchen, revealing my dislike of her beloved. So I did not want to push any unnecessary buttons with my name on nothing, and I was not ready to move yet.

Happy Black History Month!

Dear Dr. King,

By now, 1996, I had been working as a recruiter for two years and enjoying the work thus far. I had left my first job and found a new company two blocks away, across from the Pacific Stock Exchange on Sansome and Pine streets in San Francisco. It was a quaint and efficient office suite on the second floor of the building with windows that opened to the buzz of the city's financial district. The company was small, owned by a single Jewish woman, Rebecca, "Bec" (name change), who had successfully sold her IT placement agency to a bigger company that wanted to expand west.

When I interviewed with this company I was happy with what I heard. The vision, the opportunity for growth within a larger company, travel, and the pay were attractive. My base salary was $14K, more than what I made the previous year at my former employer, with an additional commission incentive. Even better, the commissions were a flat rate per hire. So I did not have to calculate and reconcile monthly tiers of percentages against hours billed to know how much I was to be paid, as I had before. Dr. King, we had become used to accepting whatever payment was offered for a job. At this point in my white-collar career, I had not known anyone black to ask for more money than what was initially offered. And as you know, that was born out of our inclination to be grateful that someone white let us in, and that someone white did not get the offer instead of you. We assumed all those holding the hiring power felt the same way. But I had learned a little about negotiations from my first recruiting job. Plus, I was confident that I was just as good, if not better, than the rank recruiter. So I just put on my big-girl panties and implemented a higher ask into my next offer. Besides, I was still working and they wanted me, so I had to allow myself the courage to negotiate. Fortunately it worked. I think I may have left some money on the table, but I told myself I would make that up in placements, because the more people I placed, the more money I made anyway.

Bec seemed very liberal and hip. I had made a good impression on her, but I still had to interview with the other three team members, two recruiters, and the office assistant. The first recruiter was a perky redhead, and she and I hit it off right away, and I was on to the next. As soon as he stepped in the door, my heart sank. He was black. I just knew they would not hire another black recruiter even though she had brought him in to meet me. I am pretty sure he was thinking the same thing, but he did not let it show. This was just one-month post OJ Simpson's acquittal. So most of my black friends were in low profile, invisible mode, fearing any backlash because the color divide was highly polarized during that whole trial (don't make any noise, complaints, be on time—everyday, don't ask for raises or promotions, and certainly do not group up at work). It was not a foreign anecdotal behavior; each of us had to do this individually as the moments presented themselves, but this was the first time in decades we felt a collective vulnerability. I mean most of the black folk I knew were happy when OJ was acquitted, although many of them had rejected him because he married someone white. But it was not like they were happy he was not convicted because they didn't think he did it; many of them did. They were happy because a black lawyer, Johnny Cochran, beat the legal system using the tricks of the same system that had been used to trap, vilify, and imprison us unjustly and historically for decades. He beat them at their own game. The game of the most high—the legal game! It was as significant racially as the Joe Louis/Max Schmeling World Heavyweight Championship rematch of 1938. Black folks felt Johnny Cochran's victory carried the same, if not more, political clout as Louis's first-round victory. The trial was quite a spectacle to watch. People followed that trial like it was the longest boxing match in history, with their entire existence dependent upon the outcome. But making your thoughts known outside the immediate company of black folk was risky, especially at work. So with all of that in the air, I just thought she was going through the motions so that I could not claim anything discriminatory during the interview. Dr.

King when will all this groupthink about e-v-e-r-y-t-h-i-n-g stop? I mean, it really was mental anguish. What is the cure? Anyway, Jamil was very professional, thorough, and knowledgeable and I decided to keep his card handy for future help or contacts in the industry. As it turned out and to my sincere and delighted surprise, I got the job. I was now one of three recruiters, and Bec was the sole account manager when I was brought on. We had one office assistant, and a seven-room office suite. Our primary accounts were in the retail, transportation, shipping, and financial industries.

It took a few weeks for me to feel racial trust (yes, I will admit a lot black people do expect to secretly bond). I do not know why we have to be so guarded and pretend desires of cultural bonding do not exist for us. They do. Especially in corporate America, but we always joke that being seen together too frequently might make it occur to the onlookers (overseers) that we are more focused on race than matriculating into the company as a whole. Less interested in upward mobility and more interested in social security. I mean, Jewish people, and Asian, East Indian, and Mexican nationalists are out-loud, proud, and very transparent about their bonding all the time and it appears to have no repercussions.

So there I was with this diverse group. Within months another local company was acquired and merged into our business operations. This brought around ten more employees. All white. They came in like a squall to prove their worth and vie for the top sales and top recruiter spots. The office dynamic shifted dramatically. They added even another office assistant to manage the increase. Syl (the perky redhead) left shortly after the merger, and a few more months later, Jamil did too. The new office assistant and I were the remaining black employees. But my colleague had let me know early on she was not black but "bi-racial" and preferred the company of her white cohorts. (It could have been a generational separation, as she was at least ten years my junior.)

My first outlier move came when the department manager Tony (name change) called a recruiter meeting to inform the four of us that his boss, Jerry (name change) wanted to reorganize the way accounts were assigned to recruiters. It was our practice at the time to discuss all openings as they arrived, and all recruiters worked on the requisitions simultaneously, putting forth their best candidates as soon as possible. We had to do it that way because the requisitions were not voluminous and everyone needed a fair shot at making quotas. This caused two things between us. It created a healthy competitive environment to train us to present the best possible candidate and it kept the recruiters current on the swift tide changes of technology. You learned more and more daily that way.

Jerry wanted us to be assigned a specific technology and for each of us to be specialist in those particular technologies. I saw this as a threat of getting locked into an older technology. Because I was the only black on the recruiting team, I didn't trust it. I felt I would be given the older tech specialties. I did not see any advantage in learning all there was to know about COBOL and compiling a client base of COBOL programmers (coding dinosaurs), and expect to make any money on commission long term. So I pushed back and rallied the other recruiters to join me. They did and I was amazed. That was my first attempt at enrolling white people to be on "my side" and protest against something I expressed as a bad idea—to management. I truly didn't think white people in corporate America would do that, always expecting to be blamed for something and tossed out. But then again, they had nothing to lose with me taking the lead. If it backfired, I would be first in line for whatever followed.

We won the charge, and it was decided to maintain the status quo. I did like that my points were well received and hard to counter. But I did not like having to stick my neck out. However, I knew I had to stop it. That move did not come without some consequence because I think Jerry didn't truly appreciate the public defeat, and that put me in the "to be dealt with later" category. But I continued to do good work in spite of the changes that occurred with the merger. It just so happened at the same time I had been dating a gentleman I'd met a while ago. We got engaged right before I started working there. So the high of preparing the wedding relaxed whatever paranoia may have surfaced.

The teams were beginning to settle in and productivity was good again in about three months. One of our VPs from headquarters was coming to town, and our regional VP decided to use his visit as a team reward and bonding event.

He had planned an elaborate meal at a well-known restaurant in Half Moon Bay. It was a great day, there was no foggy overcast, and the food was simply fabulous. I sat near one end of the long table, and at the opposite end was the administrator of our San Jose office. She was a cheery, blue-eyed blonde, who was dating one of the account managers. The group had already taken full advantage of rounds of appetizers and drinks. Whenever the company hosted events for us, they really poured it on. Midway through the main course, our beautiful CA blonde called out from all the way across the table, "Oh Wanda!" She raised her glass to me, "Happy Black History Month!" What seemed like the longest pregnant pause I'd experienced was actually only a couple of seconds, but everyone at the table froze. It seemed the waitresses froze, the patrons froze; even the waves in the distance and the ocean mist stopped moving for that moment. That bitch! Everyone had been broadsided, and no one knew what to do. I peered right at her, and the words just came. "Aww man! How did you know I was black? Who told you?"

Everyone laughed—relieved I had "broken the ice" and let them all off the hook. But I really wanted a riptide to crash the shore and pull her narrow happy ass out to sea. She looked dumbfounded (maybe she actually didn't know the size of her giant faux pas). My coworker next to me quickly started another conversation. Nothing by anyone was said about the incident; but they all seemed to gulp their drinks a little faster in unison, with me and the salmon blackened, in my seat at the table. The VP was there, we were all trying to impress, and I felt "minor" in that moment in spite of my quick thinking. Not that he could not see for himself that I was black, but the intonation of her voice carried an heir of superiority that left me adrift at sea, crestfallen, like I was no longer on the boat, but the dingy tied on and dragging behind. I did not know how the incident landed with him exactly, but I could see a trace of uneasiness. Surely, he had no practiced managerial retorts for such a comment. Like what executive management training course includes, How to Respond When Your White Subordinate Says Something Racially Stupid to Your Black Subordinate? I also realized because of his age and his position he probably had never worked with too many African-Americans himself. He was well into his fifties and the technology sector really only started integrating in the '70s when IBM and other large software manufacturers did a mad dash across the nation to HBCU's recruiting black engineering graduates so they could meet the Affirmative Action hiring mandates to secure the federal contracts for government business...Dr. King, that is a whole other story.

Later, back at the office, our administrator (the bi-racial one) came to my office to apologize for her San Jose counterpart's behavior declaring, "She didn't mean any harm and was just trying to be sweet." Basically lessening it to a "dumb blonde" moment. But the damage had already been done.

I'm not sure if my attitude shifted then, or if their attitudes were more guarded toward me. They seemed to go out for lunch and drinks more than before, and I was usually not included. In corporate America Dr. King, it is often true that hard work was rewarded, but it was also necessary to get along and fit in socially. After-hour socializing was absolutely required to be really seen as a committed member of the team for advancements and promotions, especially in small offices, and I was beginning to feel edged out. One time we were in the conference room waiting to start a team meeting when someone brought up the subject of Disney movies and the Princesses. I do not remember what precipitated this conversation, as it seemed completely out of context of our normal adult chatter. Sometime into it, I referenced the lack of black Disney movies and princesses, and the team manager laughed out loud. Like he guffawed! If that was not insult enough he went on to ask what "happy-ending" movie could Disney produce about Africa or an African princess? Famine in Ethiopia? Eating mud-pies? He followed that with a bit of hysteria. And then added something about a princess being eaten by the former, in-famed "alleged" cannibal King Idi Amin of Uganda, followed by a face-plant on the conference table. Yes, he was laughing so hard he dropped his head on the table, I think he was hung-over from the night before. He could not control himself. Wow, talk about slapping me upside my head! How could I even counter that? He was my boss! WTF? Anything audible remotely displaying my inner-rage would have had us in a brawl or my being walked/thrown out the door with my briefcase. I was simply outdone. I probably became the aphoristic "angry black woman" in that moment and could not find a way out of this conundrum. Dr. King, how do you not take moments like this personal? I mean he just threw down the gauntlet with that remark. He surmised and dismissed the entire continent of Africa as a place to mourn, a place without beauty, tradition, history, and royalty. I wanted to channel my inner Shaka Zulu and have his ignorant head. I should not have been surprised knowing that for all of American public education, and he was definitely a product of public education, African and African-America history were mis-taught that our existence began with slavery. I hate it when I let people push me to this point of rage, and I also hated feeling like I had to defend the whole of black people globally. And I really resent that white people seem to be free of this burden. They glorify their ancestry as if humanity and civility began with them. Is there no ownership or generational shame about the historical abuses, terrorism, theft, death, and destruction disseminated by his ancestors? Are they already so far removed that it doesn't hinder their freedom the way it periodically hinders mine? So it pisses me off, when I hear declarations like that. But I did the best I could do to keep it together and just walked out. He later came to my office with some half-ass, half-baked apology, but that was strictly a CYA move. With no real sincerity I'm sure.

By now, 1998, I was newlywed and had found out shortly before our first anniversary that I was with child. Not planned, but perfectly welcomed as I was happily married and ready for motherhood. I announced my pregnancy to the team at our weekly meeting and received questionable accolades. I had not yet begun to show as I was just 9 weeks. But I didn't want it to seem as if I was hiding it, not knowing how quickly I would expand, and not wanting to be routinely sequestered to the after-work watering holes anymore. A few weeks post announcement I began to feel pain and my fetus began to miscarry. When this was discovered my OB/GYN gave me two options. She said I could do nothing immediately and let nature take its course until she could schedule me in for a DNC, or go to ER and have it done right away by the attending physician. We chose the former, feeling deeply saddened and helpless and not wanting a stranger to perform such a tender procedure. It just did not feel right. When we got home I called the office and left a voicemail to my boss, and faxed the doctor's note stating my absence for the next two weeks. One week until procedure and a week to recover. I had guilt that the stress of the job, my daily four-hour commute, and remodeling our home had taken a toll on my body and thus the life of my baby. It was very difficult.

Upon my return, I was given flowers and "glad you're back" salutations from my colleagues. One of the female sales members came into the conference room where I was eating lunch and began to inquire about my loss. She started the conversation innocently enough about work, the missed office gossip, and then she began to pry into my private life that I had to make public. That was uncharacteristic of her, because she rarely spent time with me in any type of conversation long term and we were certainly not friends. She fired off about three questions that I answered before I realized she was sent in there by Tony to probe for some holes or evidence as if I lied about my time off. Like I really wasn't pregnant and was faking a miscarriage! Who does that? And why would she lower herself to such tactics?

The very next day, I had to meet with him. He had prepared a review of my work that included my attendance. He told me I was par on my candidate recruitment, but that I was sub-par on my attendance, and that combination put me below the other recruiters on total monthly hires headcount. Well...duh! Therefore, I would be put on attendance and performance probation. What! He calculated the times I was late and absent, not very frequent, but enough to make a case if you wanted to, and had the audacity to include the two weeks of my "earned" vacation for my wedding and honeymoon, and the two weeks of medical leave. I was fuming! What the hell? How is it legal to tally in state-sanctioned and legal "sick leave" and "earned vacation" as excessive absences? Now I truly felt picked on, singled out, and unjustly wronged. I cannot believe he had sent in that snoop to try and bait me as if I was lying. That was treacherous. I considered taking it to corporate and launching a formal complaint, the DOL, lawsuits, the works. But after I thought about my health, the commute, the now-hostile office climate, and my lack of trustworthy cohorts, I thought it best to seek employment closer to home in the San Jose area. But it became too hard to manage interviews, because I could not have any more time off, so I just quit. Screw it. I later secured an exclusive contract with a small software company that allowed me to work from home. My husband was relieved I no longer had to commute and elated that I had gotten a cool contract. Okay, I suppose at this point, Dr. King, I should back-up and tell you about my husband. And besides, I want you to know him!

My Big Black, Multi-Cultural Wedding

Dear Dr. King,

I didn't like him at first. He seemed to have an air about him that made me think his substance was just his status. He had pulled up to the training course I was taking in a charcoal, four-door, Mercedes sedan. C class with a sunroof. He was wearing a black turtleneck sweater, with his nose peering over the steering wheel as he drove by. I don't know why, but it reminded me of the Emperor's walk when he was strutting down the aisle in his "new" clothes. I went inside not impressed.

In one session there was a point when all of us had to go in front of the others (over three hundred people). We had to make our assigned statements shouting out loud and to take the rigorous, pointed coaching without complaint. When he got up there, he had a smirk on his face, like the exercise was a joke. Below him. I could tell he was just placating to get through it and move on to the next thing. Clowning us and our aspirations to be better than when we came in.

Who did he think he was? That confirmed my uppity-buppie assessment. I would not give him the time of day.

After the intense life-altering weekend, we all congregated at the crowd's favorite restaurant/pub, the Faultline, for comfort. Not together, but with our respective regional cohorts. I was with my San Francisco group. He was with the San Jose team. I did not notice him noticing me, but he later told me he did as soon as I came in. In his words, the earth stood still, and I illuminated the entire room. He said that watching me engaging whites and others was mesmerizing. He did not witness a subservient posture. That my affinity seemed authentic—powerful even. He said there was no trace of the inevitable "black only" comfort zone. Me? Worldly? Elegant? Hearing that lit me up! I saw him differently.

My group and I ended our faire, and we made our "until next times." My two friends and I almost closed it down. When we got to the nearly deserted parking lot, we discovered the keys were on the inside of the Honda. Locked. Perhaps the trunk would open for my friend to climb through, but there was no release there. Chester, with his "old-ish" name, appeared from the restaurant with his group still pumped from the weekend and loudly yammering. He excused himself from them. He would attempt to rescue us by engineering his way in the window with a confiscated wire hanger from the restaurant. It did not happen. We opted for AAA. He, being a southern gentleman, remained with us because the restaurant and lot was just about abandoned. He was concerned for our safety. Bonus point.

We exchanged war stories about broken-down cars and laughed a lot. The episode ended shortly thereafter. I was not sure whose affections he was aiming for, but the turtleneck was warmer now. His nose, now more sexy than judgmental. His hands, strong. His eyes, invasive. His smile big, bright, and forthcoming in every direction. We ladies were being equally summoned to his attention and grandiose anecdotes. For that night, who *she* was would remain to be seen. Each of us stunning and powerful in our own way. Three beautiful and available black women. Unfortunately, a typical ratio. I would not throw myself at him as if to compete. He would have to *clearly* choose me. *Only* me. I would not let my biological time-bomb force me into aggressive behavior.

Some weeks passed, and we were back in San Jose again for the final weekend of training. The northwest region of leaders had more going on now. Everyone was stronger. Faster. Better. And had let a ton of life's "ever-present sucks" go. Far away from our negative controlling psyches. Completely transformed.

The finale was explosive. We were on fire. Our lives would be different. We were not the same people who had started the program six months ago. Not even the same who came in on Friday to complete it. It was that impactful. Surely we would again cap the night off with merriments at the Faultline. This time Chester made his intentions known. Me. He joined our table almost as soon as we came in. He asked for my number and I gave it to him. And so it began.

He would drive from San Jose to Oakland or San Francisco during the week, and weekends, to woo, wine, and dine me. It was working. I had a man! He introduced me to his friends and SJ life. I didn't know he commanded an audience. You see Dr. King; he became "*my*" Dr. King. He was an advocate fighting for the public school rights of African-American children. I hadn't known anyone like him before. He picked up the cause for those less fortunate and made public stakes, which would later be personal sacrifices. He organized and made demands on the administration to do something different/better for the sake of our children. Even built a small company around it. Raised thousands. He had met with local and national politicians. Congressmen and Senators alike: Susan Hammer, Mike Honda, Zoe Lofgren, Dianne Feinstein. He did not care about their titles. Or how out-of-reach they were supposed to be. He was on a mission with the urgency of now. You would have been proud of him, Dr. King. I was.

At first I wasn't sure if it was ego or something more authentic, because he loved to talk and be the center of attention. And then I learned more of his southern history. The personal traumas and the abuse endured on the *frontlines* of desegregation. He was fixing his past. His heart was in it. His head could not come out. He did not want to see another black child feel slighted at the hands of uninformed or even malicious teachers. This was intoxicating. His diction so eloquent. His speeches moving. His passion so transparent. Real. Enrolling. People listened, applauded, supported, took action at his command. He was a different kind of risk-taker than what I was used to. He did not let his recent layoff from IBM—after 21 years being labeled a "troublemaker" for speaking out against discriminatory corporate practices and the personal hardships it created— deter him from what he knew was the right thing to do. How could I resist? I tried Dr. King, I really did. I tried to use the fact that he was divorced twice and fathered and had singularly "raised" a daughter from his first marriage be the things that would keep me at bay. The two deal breakers from my ever-present and evolving "must have" list constructed as a teen and fortified in my twenty-something years. But he kept coming back. Calling. Challenging. Opening up my little "me" world. I even tried letting his same height (although he would argue he was two inches taller), not-bigger foot size, and southern style be restraints. His charm would only grow bigger and taller each day eclipsing all that youthful wishing. And I could easily makeover his southern simplicity.

He "grow'd me up some" too. He even made me *want* to grow up more. Quicker. To be in front of the room "being the change I wanted to see" instead of in the single-mindedness of my own ambitions, or on the sidelines of others holding back. Hiding out. Spectating. He was teaching me to let go. To get in. And finally I did let go. Be damned my ignorant wish list of what a man needs to be. It was created from a very limited and unrealistic view. The likely culprits: Disney and *Essence, Jet, Ebony* and *Seventeen* magazines—along with a bunch of equally inexperienced teenagers, long gone and in my past. All saying the same "make-believe" things about what makes a man. All wrong. Mostly.

It started with a poem on our first date and was sealed with a patio tryst at my "treehouse" nine months later. Mother Nature and us. The leaves applauding in the wind while the birds crooned. Mag-i-cal. Simply the best! Nothing would compare. What else did I need him to prove?

We had fun. Unconventional and traditional. I would challenge him in every way I could think to test his resolve. Ask him to drive to see me in the middle of the night at a moment's notice, and then fall asleep before he got there and not answer the door. Invite him to stay the night and make him sleep on the sofa. Then turn the heat up on high to toast him in his sleep to make him sweat. See if he complained. Take his car after a disagreement, pretending to go to the bathroom, but slip out the door and drive away, leaving him at the bar with the tab, the damsels, and watered-down drinks. Being with me as a keeper, he had to prove he would stay around and not align with his track record. I was not to be more practice. Take him to an unknown corner of the city and have him figure out where we should go to eat, to be entertained, but only to my liking. Put him with my female friends as the lone male; see how he acted. He almost failed, but managed to catch himself before he crossed the line. After all they were beautiful alluring women. Go to his family's home and make demands that would not be within the norms of the family ritual. Watch what side he chose, or if he'd make a bridge. Tell him to tell his daughter to grow up like I thought I had done. Call the other women and tell them he was not to be contacted and no longer a possibility. Break some hearts.

Dr. King, none of this was really planned. It all happened organically, spontaneously, and honestly without much forethought. But as life can have it, and it did, it showed me that he was serious about me and that my precautions and juvenile assessments needed to be put to rest. I was in love. No doubt. This *man* really wanted to be with me! To take care of me. To be a family. He was going to make right all the familial wrongs of his past, and I was going to get to that place I had planned for and dreamed of for years. Married.

We had developed many, many friends with folks from the training. It had a way of getting people related beyond the shallow existence we typically carry on in our society. You would get underneath another's skin within a session or two, sometimes just hours, and become friends on a real human level. We could be vulnerable. Race didn't stifle that, as it normally would.

Our wedding we knew would be large. By the time the planning was done, we had eight bridesmaids and matching groomsmen, two candle-lighters, a ring bearer, a flower girl, two wedding singers, a piano player, photographer, an ad-hoc, makeshift videographer (thanks Pam!), a wedding coordinator, a jazz duet, a deejay, cake designer, two verse readers, and a seamstress. A virtual circus of love. Quite the display. They were all very happy, giving and supportive. Many had flown in from AZ, MI, OH, LA, GA, and OR. Over 200 guests. We felt really special.

The wedding party demographic was international. The groomsmen: African-American, Italian, East Indian, and English. The bridesmaids: African-American, English, Mexican, French-Irish. And the guests were all of that mix plus others. Dr. King we had our own United Kingdom. Who'd a' thunk? There was no way, given my traditional urban background, that I would have predicted this kind of wedding for myself in a million years. Let alone my husband, from the Jim Crow south! It was just NOT in the cards. Not for such an intimate event. I had been to many weddings of black friends, family and relatives, and in them, there may have been a guest or two who was not black, but to have not only white people, but a Mexican and East Indian to boot—in our wedding party! Man, we were just out there.

I am telling you this not because I'm bragging or feeling like we were so different or special, but because these people were not trophy nationalists to us. They were rooted in our lives on intimate levels, and we did not have to be afraid of a social or cultural betrayal with them the way we innately anticipate it. As an example, Michel (pronounced Michelle), who is French-Irish, worked with me at MCI. She was in IT Administration, and handled all the phone-order processing that determined the commissions from our sales. I do not remember what our initial attraction was to each other, as I typically wrote off short women (especially those with little-ass feet) because they made me feel like a giant Amazon, and not in a good way. She was 5'2", skinny as a rail, natural blonde (she would appreciate me saying natural) and wore size 5½ shoes, half my foot size. Plus, she was white. But she was a big personality. Most of the time you thought she was a lot taller. She spoke her mind and was a take-no-prisoners, don't-give-me-bullshit kinda woman. I respected that. She would have my back on getting all my orders in on time so that my commissions would never be delayed or miscalculated. We had Happy Hours together along with our other colleague Pam, and we had great times. We had wine-tasting trips that included spa treatments in Napa Valley, Ocean Beach campfires in San Francisco, and lots and lots of dining out. However, she really won me over for life when we were in Walnut Creek once at a popular singles bar/restaurant called Hannigans on Main Street. We were there just having a good time amongst ourselves with a few other co-workers, and I was the only black person with them. None of us were there to pick up anyone; we just wanted to celebrate the end of a crazy workweek. I don't remember there being any other blacks in the entire place. We were approached by a group of white guys, and you could tell and smell they had already drunk a round or two. They were making surface chatter when one of them decided to rag on my hair. I had a stylist I trusted and would try on different looks. This particular style was a low-maintenance one that was literally sculpted with gel and baked into place under the hooded dryer. It was pulled up in an elongated diagonal roll that crowned at the top into a fatter roll. The flat part of my hair was wavy from my natural wave pattern. So no motion. I did not truly love the style, but after three hours of sitting and $50 or $60 bucks, I needed to let it get its mileage until the next appointment. Anyway, Dr. King, Skippy (facetiously named) decided he needed to touch my hair and then he said something with a sarcastic tone like "how'd you get your hair to do that?" Before I could even swallow my sip and respond, Michel moved into position in front of me, got in his face (practically a foot higher than hers) pointing her finger, and cursed his ass out. I mean, she lit into him so fast he had no idea how to respond and could only back away. The other two trailed behind like he was the dog and they were the tail between his legs. Stunned was an understatement. Who knew? Michel had some guts. Who knew she would do that in defense of me? Who knew she would risk whatever he might try to do or say? She did not care. She was protecting me. It blew my mind. Again, one of those things that could not have been predicted. But she had me at, "You mf...!" We've been friends since.

Chester's groomsmen also had strong bonds with him. Arun from New Delhi was his college friend. He came to Louisiana to go to college and actually stayed with Chester's family for a while until he found housing elsewhere. You could imagine the shifting his whole family had to do to allow this foreigner into their sanctuary. I wished I could have been there to hear the conversations, but they became brothers as a result and had matching careers as computer engineers. Al (Italian) worked with him at IBM for many years and stood up for Chester once, to make sure he got properly credited for his invention—that resulted in an Innovation Award and bonus. Al went to bat for him. He risked personal isolation and career advancement, and he did not have to do that. Al's integrity was big enough to overpower his boss's alleged racial biases. He was also a very talented and recognized jazz drummer in the local and national jazz circuits, and had the opportunity to jam with some of the greats (Ella Fitzgerald, Vince Lombardi, and Johnny Mathis). Chester and Al are still jazz enthusiasts and friends.

So there we were, the whole-lot-of-us, representing three continents and several countries. We were slightly worried that our families would protest. But we also knew they would see a relatedness and love that would have them in wonder and that they would check their prejudices at the door—if not for the sheer surprise—for the respect of the day. I loved the entire group. I still love them. When will we be able to be free of feeling like we have to apologize or e-x-p-l-a-i-n for extending our love outside of our erroneously embedded borders? Dr. King, did you have the chance to love someone outside of our race? Did they allow themselves to get that close to you? Did you allow them to?

LIBERATION, 2000s
(The American Years)
I, Too, Sing America

January 29, 2013, Interview with Fox News, Bill O'Reilly, http://www.theblaze.com/stories/2013/01/29/colin-powell-reveals-why-he-voted-for-obama-twice-in-contentious-interview-with-bill-oreilly/

Former Secretary of Defense, Colin Powell, said on an interview once, in the context of the re-election of President Obama in 2012 and race, *"...I am an American!"*

Mr. Powell, I agree. I am an American too, born and raised. Generations deep. I will no longer annex my birthright with the hyphenation that declares me African first.

I am first an American, and my dominant ancestry is African. Thank you!

World Trade Center

Dear Dr. King,

On September 11, 2001, the U.S. was attacked on its soil. Four commercial airplanes were hijacked by middle-eastern, religious terrorists who flew them into designated targets that instantly changed the American way of life. Black Americans. White Americans. We were all equally terrorized. This was the first home invasion since WWII, and it was bad, a "coup de gras" that left Americans and the world in shock and awe. The Twin Towers of NY were hit first, sequentially; both buildings were leveled, killing thousands of workers and all the passengers on the commercial jets. As well as two more jets that targeted and crashed into The Pentagon; the fourth crashed in PA, before it reached its alleged target of The White House.

I do not remember anymore where I was when I received the news because the footage of the suicide strikes was so frequently repeated for days after the event; it was like it was the first time each time I saw it again. And then the death of one my nephews, two months later, stripped that shock and trumped my location memory. It was a very insecure time for me personally and my family, as well as many relatives and friends. You could say we all collectively felt a patriotic defenselessness that tested our resilience. And it ran deep.

I was pregnant with my son and attending USF to finally complete my bachelor's when it happened. My classmates were all also very saddened and stricken with this unfamiliar sense of national uncertainty, and yes, even fearful. So, Dr. King, for me it was the first time since I had been born that I felt ubiquitously aligned with my white countrymen. I grew up here, attended schools, lived in various neighborhoods, worked at various companies, shopped at stores, malls, paid taxes, sang the National Anthem, recited the Pledge of Allegiance, the Preamble, celebrated all the holidays, reveled in the July 4th parades and fireworks, cheered for the Olympic teams, etc., in all senses of the word, being an American, for close to forty years by this point. However, America until then had felt more like my address, not my true home. It was not until this happened that I truly felt American.

I guess for the first time white people were just as susceptible as blacks and everyone else here. So that incident provisionally squelched white privilege in my view. It was like we had diplomatic immunity from further racial apportion. Something I wish you had experienced. Not the terrorism part, just the immunity part. We shared the same vulnerability, and unlike Pearl Harbor, when we had to pull together when you were young, Jim Crow was not the rule of the land, so it was not in the way. This was something menacing for us all.

The new enemy of the state, Islamic terrorists, struck a chord of fear that whites could not immediately control, and the terrorists bore the target, not black people. It was a tragic trade-off, as I wouldn't wish racism on any people. I have to admit, having another group of people as the new menace to society was unfortunately a racial relief. But it was short-lived, because a black DC sniper surfaced, randomly killing ten people (whites and blacks), without any real notice. And many of us felt we were all back in the front of the firing line. He was the first "black sniper" in modern history.

Million Dollar House, No White Neighbors

Dear Dr. King,

We moved into our "close enough" dream-house in Feb 2004. It was 3,400+ sq. ft., 5 bedrooms, 4 baths and a 3-car garage. It cost a California mere, $650,000. (My readers from northern CA understand the sarcasm here.) Our down payment was 10 percent of the value, and we signed the now notorious 1/1 (1-year interest-only loan type). I remember the banker's pitch for this, saying "to make it easy on yourself the first year, until your wife goes back to work." That made logical sense to us, so my husband said yes and we were in like Flynn! Our monthly payment was just over $2,100 including PMI insurance. This would be comfortable for my husband to afford with his salary at the Silicon Valley OEM (Original Equipment Manufacturer, better known as computer or software company).

We loved our new location in the Bay Area. It was a hidden gem of a little city. Less than 30 minutes from most of our favorite bay area fun spots: Napa, Sausalito, Oakland, San Francisco, and Walnut Creek. The bonus: we were a block away from San Pablo Bay. Not the most eco-friendly body of water, but it ran into the San Francisco Bay, which ran into the Pacific Ocean. Both of us had always wanted what we called water property. Especially in California!

We now had the privilege (and it is a privilege) to decorate parts of our home to our tastes and preferences. To be the "original" owners. It was not custom by any means, but at least the model, the elevation, the floor coverings, the cabinet wood/color, counter tops, and tiles choices were ours. That felt special. We got to visit (many times) a "design center," hand-picked by the developer (probably his or his relatives' business), to make those choices. We had really "moved on up" to the East Bay. Black people visiting a white design center, in a white city, coached by a white design specialist on manmade tiles versus nature's granite or marble. And the aesthetic, density, and strength differences between oak, maple, and ash cabinetry was surely our passport to a place not yet affordable by the masses. No other human DNA had been impressed into the walls, floors, ceilings, and all parts that absorb light, sound, or vibration. No talking walls with layers of lives, loves, goods, or evils from the previous owners that needed to be prayed away, or smudged out with burning sage. No other family except ours. (Excluding the workers of course).

So after six months of planning, preparing, negotiations, and then four more months of rage and impatience with the mess-up of the original house we were supposed to move into, we moved in the middle of N. Shelter Bay. (I even loved the numbers and name of our new address.) We had to wait for the next phase because our lawyer only negotiated more upgrades, not a redo, and also did not include punitive damages in our settlement. I did not like having this gray mark on such a momentous triumph for the two of us. It may have proved to be an omen after all, but at the time we did not see it as such.

We began our ascent with a bottle of red wine and a toast in the kitchen on our Caesarstone counter with no other thing in the house except the contract, keys, and the beautiful bamboo-embossed crystal salad bowl. A "Welcome to Your New Home" gift from the developer.

And if we were not sure we had made it, the world famous, sky-blue Tiffany Box it came in was the "announcer" that made it clear:

"You have arrived! You have arrived!"

I'm sure we both heard it! We toasted more, walked back and forth from room to room, once, twice, or three times, rejoiced, kissed, and locked up to return to San Jose to finish our last bit of packing, confirm the renters for our San Jose home, and to hug the kids a bit tighter that night. Truly an American dream that had come to fruition. Not one house, Dr. King, two. And one of them a brand new house, in a brand new neighborhood, with brand new neighbors, by the water!

We were just one of the handful of families that had moved in. Most of the block was still under construction. We had neighbors on our right, left, and one or two across the street. This was February, and by the summer, I believe all 22 homes on our street were completed and occupied. We tallied the nationalities like any good American family would do. There were blacks, Africans (Nigerian, Ethiopian), Filipinos, Chinese, Koreans, Indians, Pakistanis, and Mexicans, and they were primarily immigrant families. I do believe all of the parents were born in their native countries; I would not swear to that, but I would bet on the odds. There were also my next-door neighbors, who were the only white (Italian & English) family. The other white family/man was married to a Chinese woman. A great display of your dream realized. A sort of racial Feng Shui.

Inspired by the newness and noticing that most had kids at or near our kids' ages, we decided (more like I decided and dragged my husband into it), to become the pillars of the neighborhood and get to know everyone as soon as possible. The thought of a truly international meal/feast at a long, extended table simply thrilled me to no end. Plus all the languages and native dialects my kids would get to experience. I would be that neighborhood mom whom everyone knew and whom all the kids loved. Our house would be that house everyone wanted to be at as frequently as possible. (I was going to be like my former super cool, neighborhood mom from Detroit, Bettie Joe Singleton.) Fortunately, our house was situated close to the middle of the block, so I had location in my favor. And my work began.

It was surprisingly difficult to befriend my non-American neighbors. I could tell they were leery at first, trying to clear the dense fog from their windows about *who* the media told them *we blacks* were. There was trepidation no doubt. Our Korean neighbor's son even went so far as to take his fear to the developer's office to question or complain as to why so many black families were allowed to move in. My husband was fuming when he heard this from the sales agent. She had ratted on him like she was plea-bargaining for a lighter sentence. *He's the bad guy, I'm not. What social points do I get for my good behavior?* My husband wanted to go over and raise Holy-Hell with them and blast the entire country of S. Korea (of course that is hyperbole). However, it did bother me that the Korean guy had not even been here long enough to learn to speak English fluently, but had already managed to usurp his nationality and ethnicity above that of the American black. We who are citizens generations deep, whose ancestors built and carved out the privileges he was afforded upon arrival. Without any regard for our history and ownership, he took it upon himself to occupy his mind with the attitude of the oppressor. I too wanted to kick his ass back to Seoul myself. Instead told my husband, "Never mind him, no worries, we'll kill them with kindness instead. He thinks he's white and hasn't been here long enough for them to inevitably inform him that he's not." I knew his

Mercedes chariot and shield would only protect him for a short while. The world would handle him in that regard, and there was not any immediate work for us.

We managed to befriend the white family, younger than we were. Their boys, slightly older than our kids, were still little enough not to care when it came to play. I guess it was hard for them to ignore us, because my kids would scream through the fence repeatedly asking them to play whenever they heard the balls bouncing or their voices. They loved their new home too, and we became friends because of *our American understanding* of how neighbors worked. We were not quite *Desperate Housewives* or the *Modern Family*, but somewhere in the middle.

Unlike my Detroit neighborhood where religion, drugs, and upward mobility had begun to chip away at what was once the monoculture of African-Americans, here we had one additional tier of broad nationalities to add to the mix. This meant a hodge-podge of religions, cultural mores, generational roles, and gender roles came that were not so easily recognizable. Our common bond, monster houses and the fallacy of "upper-middle-class-dom," in a dynamic (formerly blue-collar) city, whose image was being reborn by the surge in white-collar population via the dotcom and housing boom. Dr. King, I think this was just as you might have imagined it. There was no dominant group, and no spokesperson for each group, just every man/family for itself. Undoubtedly, some of the families knew each other; we learned a good many of them were already Hercules residents who had moved from smaller and older homes across town. The rest were from other parts of the bay, where prices were much steeper for a house with comparable square footage. So it was a healthy dose of potent ingredients for this cultural stew.

As I had planned, I met almost everyone, and visited some of them frequently with requests for butter, onions, sugar, cinnamon, eggs, recipes — anything I could think of to get them to be "not just be neighbors" but a community. I hated the drive-by waves as they went into their garages and out again the next day without stopping to say hello, talk for a spell, or come by for a cup of coffee. I even signed my husband up on the "write-in" ballot for City Council once, so I could petition door-to-door, trying to get more of them to relate to us, and discover what I could.

My kids owned the street and played with all the kids, and within a short time, our house was the "go-to" place. In the summer of '06, we decided that our short visits to their homes were making us well known, but the neighbors were not engaging each other. I mean Dr. King, what's the point of living in an integrated neighborhood if it's just on the surface? Just like the families that had moved to my Detroit neighborhood with their religions intact, these families came into this neighborhood with that and their families intact, and didn't seem able to outreach for homey love and comfort. I thought this was just the craziest thing. So with that, my kids and I went to City Hall to find out the requirements to block the street from cars and made a flyer to circulate announcing the N. Shelter Bay First Annual Block Party! I was stoked. We hit every house by knocking on the doors to personally make the pitch and left the flyers when no one answered. We had a 30-percent success rate the first round and on the second, an additional 30 percent.

The flyer included contact information, but no one contacted me. It also included instructions for what category of "traditional dishes" to bring so that we would have an authentic international feast. I was salivating. I guess you can tell by now, Dr. King, that I really like to eat, but good food! We were going to have dishes from around the world, homemade by cooks with generational recipes that were handed down—right on our little block. We received the required number of signatures, but a weird thing happened with one of the Mexican neighbors. He barely opened the door, listened to what I was saying, and then started shaking his hand "no." This startled me, so I asked why. He told me he did not "believe in block parties." I was stunned. I told myself, "that's crazy," but luckily I just needed a majority of the neighbors to agree to block the street to traffic. Also, he was toward the end of the block, far enough away from the central location of the action. So I could leave him access, but he would have to go around the block to get to his house.

We began early on the day of the event, bringing our folded tables, chairs and pop-up tents to align on the side of the street. We put up the tables on the shady side across from my house. I arranged everything for easy flow under the tents with separate areas for the drinks, desserts, and main dishes. It was shaping up.

The neighbors began to trickle over one by one. It was as if they were waiting and watching from the windows to see if anyone would come so they would not be the first to arrive (or the only ones to arrive). The first neighbor was the Filipino family right across the street. It made sense too as the gathering spot was literally in front of their house. The husband came by and asked what he should bring, and then stated he needed to do some errands first. I guess he did not read the flyer. So I quickly suggested "your wife's specialty." Then another African-American family came over, started helping set up, and brought some pound cake all sliced up and wrapped individually in plastic sandwich bags. She also brought some sandwiches made from mini-croissants (from Costco) with homemade chicken salad from canned chicken meat. When the first family returned, they came back with king-sized cookies, fruit candies, and franchise fried chicken. I had asked for his wife's specialty, and he returned with this! Oh no, I thought. The Korean family came out and had a foil-covered platter, and a large bowl of something. My smile broadened. Finally some ethnic food I could be happy to try for the first time. Turned out to be Korean ribs. Spicy beef ribs cut through the bone, in thin meaty slices, across the slab versus cut between the ribs like we do. And a giant pan of white rice with Kimchi on the side—apparently staple dishes. Then came the Nigerian family with buckets of guess what—fried chicken! And lastly another Filipino family from two doors down (an elderly couple), with more franchise fried chicken. Dr. King, I was baffled. DID ANYBODY REALLY READ THE FREAKIN' FLYER!!! Did they not understand my vision? Where was my international feast? Had they brought all this damned fried chicken because we were black? I mean, I knew people were busy, as were we, but I had given ample notice. I just wanted one original dish per family. Not a Costco and Colonel buffet. This block party sucked. Nobody tried to engage the other; they only migrated to us. Then the Filipinos segregated themselves "tagalog'ing" (completely made up word) and such, too long to be socially acceptable to the rest of us. I had no real implementation of entertainment, just some stupid brochures about fire safety and upcoming city events from city hall and the fire department. I was so concerned about the food, I did not plan the full event well enough. They made suggestions about next year and how they would help organize to garner more participation. Oh, did I say that out of the twenty-two households invited, only five showed up in addition to us? A sappy turnout.

The conversations were primarily about mortgage loans, how quickly our equities grew in two years, and the landscape bandits that made their rounds to each household soliciting contracts to design and landscape our naked backyards for fees of no less than $25K dollars. I pretended I was engaged, even though I wanted to end it shortly, after seeing the outcome. But the kids had fun. They were just happy to ride their bikes in the street without fear of being hit by a car, and to eat as much cookies and cake as they could sneak without being seen. By 2pm, I was ready to call it quits, and so we did. I was disappointed, but my husband consoled me saying that it was a start. That next year would be better because now they understood more about it.

The funniest thing happened about two weeks after our party. My son came into the house to get me to come up the hill around the block to the next street. The homes above us had a view of the San Pablo Bay, were 500-1,000 square feet larger, and sold for a premium of $50-100k more than our homes. There were also more white homeowners up there. I had only known personally two of the families I met during our successful campaign to prevent Wal-Mart from building a 90,000 sq. ft. store on our waterfront. Well they were having a block party and it put my party to shame. They had three bounce houses for the kids, specifically selected for three age groups of kids. They had two pop-up tents with tables full of all kinds of "homemade" international dishes, desserts, drinks (wine and beer), and a brotha' in the driveway smoking meats on a barrel smoker. I felt sucker-punched. I learned that they had organized, had a committee, formed a Neighborhood Watch group, collected the email addresses of everyone, and $20-40 donation from each household as well, to pay for the bounce houses. And the two founding organizers, two households of white people, doing block parties with *their white American understanding* of how block parties worked. I was happy for them, but jealous and mad too, and now more determined to outdo, or at least try to match them the next year. I had half a mind to go get some of my neighbors and make them walk up the hill so they could see how it is done, but I was wallowing in defeat with a pinch of shame, so that did not happen.

This was the height of the housing boom, and our property values were approaching the one million dollar mark. One of the black families that we did not get to know at all sold their home for the mid $900s and took the $300k profit and ran. It was rumored that they relocated to Houston, paying cash for an even bigger home. We should have been as foresighted as they were, especially being just one generation out of the Civil Rights Era, but we were so caught up in the bubble that any of those thoughts just floated on by without sticking. We had the audacity to think $300k was not enough money to make on a two-year investment. Talk about looking a gift horse in the mouth. As if either of us had ever had the opportunity to save up that much. Hell, neither of us had ever had a bank account with $100k in it. Certainly our parents didn't have the opportunity for an investment at this level of affluence. We, and other neighbors, had the arrogance to think we would hold on until the values went up to $1.5m so we could be millionaires. After all, there had been two homes up the hill that had sold for $1.1m, and $1.2m. We were told that one had been purchased by a former professional baseball player. So we were convinced we were just biding our time.

Shortly after that in the fall my white next-door neighbors put their home on the market and sold it in the spring to black family. They moved to Marin County (one of the whitest and wealthiest areas in the bay area). Now, we were neighborly neighbors, but not quite "friends" yet. I did not know much about them beyond what was visibly present. But can I tell you that their move took me all the way back to Detroit and white flight, Dr. King. I felt they ran because they were outnumbered, which was pure speculation on my part. Like they did not appreciate being the minority (probably the first time in either of their lives), and they did what they had every right to do—move away. That meant they left us to be with ourselves and bask in our multiculturalism without the visible influences of white people. Some would think that this would be ideal. Living the big American dream without the weight of white righteousness. I wondered if any of the other neighbors felt the same way. We felt, along with the other African-American families, we had to uphold what we deemed as *the American way*. However, we represented only nine of the households. Okay Dr. King, this was trippy. So here we were in our big American home with our big American kitchen, feeling aligned with white American standards of what makes a neighborhood valuable, and we were now left to maintain and teach those values to our immigrant neighbors. As if they did not know, and would ask for our help, or even if they cared to aspire to that. But we figured moving *there* meant exactly that.

We pondered a bit about how that came to be, having many conversations about "the shift."

We had assumed there was to be a "coming together" of the AA households. After all, this was our country, and we all understood what it took to get there. Dr. King, we had it. The house, the jobs, the education, three-car garages, two cars, private school, everything! But we soon found out that the unity we sought was formed primarily out of economic interests and protections versus racial unity. There was a guarded alliance that neither of us had ever experienced before in a neighborhood of blacks. This was problematic. Can you imagine that? I never would have believed that we would be prosperous but not be able to celebrate and protect our new stakes in the American Dream. I mean, it was not a requirement, but it was noticeable, awkward, and unexpected.

One of the AA families was blue collar, not college-educated, and had made the investment in their home through hard labor and the sale of their previous home in an over-inflated real estate market. We got along with them okay, but our conversations were limited to food, sports, and church. I mean practically every conversation would get thrown back to a biblical verse or some sports figure, game score, or analogy. This drove my husband crazy, because he liked to chat it up all the time, but more about education, history, politics, movies, relationships and the state of black America. So we would often spend too much time catering to their preferred topics of discussions, and it got tiring after a while. The other AA family was 20 years younger and were never home—working ungodly hours to pay for a house that was too big for a couple in our opinion. Another AA family, that I privately nicknamed George and Louise Jefferson, was just too busy. They both worked in San Francisco and their children went to school there also, so we would see them pulling out of the garage before 6am, and rolling back up after 7 or 8 each night. They did not initiate socializing. The next AA family we befriended was a younger couple, beautiful, at least 10 years our junior, and well educated with a medical degree and a Ph.D. You would have been proud of them too Dr. King. They were living the American dream in full force, and quickly. They also had two boys who played with my son. But that is pretty much as far as the relationship went because we were too old for them, and not hip enough I could tell. So bonding with them was challenging. The last household we interacted with regularly on our block was mixed race; she was AA, and her husband was Mexican. They were both medical professionals, and he was a Chief Internist at a regional hospital. We really enjoyed conversations with them, but he worked off-hours so it was hard to get the four of us together. All this affluence, but no frequent confluence initially. We developed a tighter bond with the last couple over time. However, we had never experienced the nonchalant stances from the bulk of them. We were feeling somewhat like aliens within our own community amongst the other AA families. I do not think you would have understood it at all. Given the work it took for us to get anywhere and break down barriers, you'd think a natural progression would have been to keep bonding and working together. But unlike some of the immigrant families who had their own businesses that were highly supported by their communities, we were all working for "the man" as we used to say, and holding the broader community at bay, still suffering the fear and mistrust from the drug wars, and seeking only the support of our trusted family members. And high-powered and salaried, or not, our employers owned our homes. Be that as it may, we continued our neighborly and bonding efforts. I think I had high expectations of endearment and frequent interactions based on location, like I had in Detroit. All up in everybody's business—every day. Trying to cure my nostalgia for neighborly love. I also needed to know who I could trust my kids with, and with whom I could share my dreams and woes. I wanted it bad and did not want it to take ten years. But that was likely me on my own island, and the reciprocity was not happening fast enough.

However, our family did become the info-depot for local political information, and we were also short-listed as party invitees for them as well. We were happy about that. We happened to be invited to a few social gatherings and were surprised and astounded at how segregated each event was. We attended the parties of the Filipino family, the Nigerian family, and the Korean family to discover that we were the only Americans at each, and the only neighbors from the block. (I should add the Korean family was the same family that protested our moving in.) Sadly, the one who had been so vocal died mysteriously. He was young too, in his late twenties, we believe. My husband noticed one day that there was a limo and many people dressed in black attending their home. He guessed a funeral, but we thought it may have been the elder man we had noticed from time to time. The next day we took flowers to the house and a card, and his sister informed us that it was her brother. We learned later that her daughter also lived there and was the same age as our daughter. Sometime after they became friends and the bridge to our being friendly with them.

We discovered by being invited to these parties that these households were immigrant, with some of the children born here. Some had been in the country for at least a decade, some two, and were corporate professionals (healthcare and IT primarily), business owners, and government workers. However, their closest friends were not outside their demographic. Our family had passed inspection and had earned the right to be welcomed into their homes, their communities, but this would not be true for the other neighbors. We watched, enjoyed traditional dishes, danced, learned some folklore, heard some of their "Coming to America" stories, and witnessed their expressions of assimilation into the American middleclass. We also learned that unlike African-Americans, post-civil rights, they did not appear to need to be validated by their white cohorts. They relied on validation solely from their own communities. The AA parties we attended were also only AAs. So strange to have all that diversity on the outside, but segregation on the inside. I don't think you would have imagined that, Dr. King.

That fall or during the holiday season my husband's boss from Scotland was in town alone. He had to come visit his US team. Many of them were gone on vacation as this Silicon Valley software company shut down during Christmas and New Year to allow the workers to be with their families. Chester was feeling sad for his boss being away from his family and alone. He asked me if we could have him over for dinner to ease his assumed loneliness. I agreed.

We welcomed him as we would have any neighbor on the block and fed him a very fine meal. When he came in you could see awe in his eyes, and this of course made us both feel good. Slightly uncomfortable, but mostly good. Privileged even. Like we were doing the country and African-Americans proud. He actually made the statement that he could fit his whole house into our living and dining room area. We had lengthy conversations about the caste Euro systems and the disparities between the Scottish and American middleclass. He was intrigued by the multi-nationalism we had on our block. We walked after the meal touring the neighborhood and the park along the water, and he took many pictures of the area as well as in our home with his professional camera.

The following week, after the return to work he called his first meeting of the new year with the team. They went over the statuses of various projects in process and outlined further goals. He concluded the meeting (unbeknownst to my husband, and certainly without our permission), with pictures of us, our home, and the neighborhood; there on the projected screen in front of everyone Chester worked with (all white). He remarked how well the company was providing for Chester, offering his personal life (wife and children included) as if it was something that should be tallied alongside his work. Chester was of course thrown off-guard and could only affirm that this was his life. How does one prepare for such a passive act of aggression? He said he left the meeting feeling ambushed, defensive, exposed, and apologetic at the same time. And that he would get sarcastic success marks from various team members on occasions thereafter.

A few weeks after that polarizing event, we happened to be at our Nigerian neighbors' home one afternoon discussing work, the neighborhood, and schools for our children. The husband also worked for the same OEM as Chester, but in a different department and as an individual contributor. We shared with them Chester's gesture of inviting his boss over and how he had "outed" Chester at the meeting. Our neighbor was shocked that we had extended ourselves that way, and in so many words called us stupid. He explained he knew he was smarter than a lot of his colleagues and that he had been there long enough to earn a management or leadership position, but that he refused to voluntarily put himself in the spotlight and there was no way he would ever show or tell anyone at work where he lived — fearing jealous or unfavorable reactions from his American colleagues (white, black, or other). He said it was in his best interest to keep a low profile and be invisible if necessary in order to keep his American employment. We thought that to be so limiting and unnecessarily sacrificial, and against everything our people had fought for, Dr. King. We discounted it as African immigrant-survival psychosis and laughed about his precaution; even though Chester had just experienced a seemingly sense of jealousy that he described.

About a month later the team gathered in the same conference room for an unplanned meeting. Everyone was there with the exception of his boss, who had returned to the physical smallness of his own world. He was on the conference phone. He stoically informed Chester (the lead), and another (pre-determined and discussed, poorly performing team member) that the two of them were part of a necessary lay-off to reduce departmental redundancy and save money. Why was this happening, why to him? And not the others? Could our neighbor's assessment be true? He himself had dodged the bullet. Had Chester's Scottish boss and co-workers conspired to mark Chester in an act of jealous revenge in an attempt to reduce his status, or at least to slow down his acquisitions and possessions of American success? Surely his work had not been diminishing; he was producing more and more each month. What gives? We went into survival mode trying not to waste any time to get another gig for him, feeling hoodwinked for caring and opening our home. Now of course this could have just been the luck of the draw, but as he replayed some of the departmental interactions and subtle messaging in prior conversations, it felt very personal.

To be honest, this was a devastating blow. We had a mortgage, a car note, and preschool tuition to pay. Because of this financial hardship, I began my search for employment in efforts to keep us afloat. And as God would have it, I received a call for a job and was hired, seemingly without any contenders, based on the recommendation of a former colleague and friend. Thank you Debra! Broad community support. Loved it! This lifesaver halted my attempts to make our neighborhood the most "related" multi-cultural gem of the east bay, and thus my block-party efforts were put on the back burner. I began in May '07 and my husband joined the same company that fall. We were again double-income. It was great and right on time, because exactly one month prior to his start, our 3/1 mortgage's interest-only payment (that we rolled into right before the first one expired) reset to P&I fixed, to a whopping $4,875 per month. Okay, stop the madness! Dr. King, we blinked, but then we kept it moving because we didn't have time. With the two of us working 50-60 hours per week in high-pressure jobs that were 20 miles from home, and the kids in two different schools and afterschool, we just could not slow down. We were happy to have more than enough to make the payments, inflated or not. We did that for about four months before we could come up for air and try to see if we could refinance to reduce the monthly payment. In all my life and that of my relatives, same age and older, no black family I knew ever had a mortgage payment of damn near

$5,000 per month, again just one generation out of Civil Rights and not famous, or wealthy. Working middleclass.

But it was happening all over the country. Houses were scandalously being over-valued, while banks and broker houses had concocted mortgage schemes to package and resell mortgage bonds. They were giving secured over-priced mortgage loans and lines of credit without jobs, credit, or any means to actually pay long term, to practically anybody that could spell m-o-r-t-g-a-g-e and had an address. And they let homeowners pull out false equity by the hundreds of thousands if they wanted to. It was not true in our case. We had jobs and a healthy down payment.

In one of our attempts to refinance to reduce our payment to something one salary could cover, in case something happened, we went to an institution and people were literally lined up in the waiting area. We had an appointment, had prepared all of our paperwork ahead of time, and took in our documents for review. The agent looked them over and asked us what the current value was, while checking it against her figures. It was crazy, as if the value was moving like tickertape on the stock market. She then proceeded reviewing our salaries and expenses. She asked us what we each made, although that box was already filled in. She verified if it was gross or net. We told her. Then she took the corrector fluid from her drawer, painted over our salaries, and told us that they did not verify income. She said she could fill in the "stated income" line to match the required amount for approval, because our loan-to-value had dropped since the beginning of the year. Bam! Just like that. She was going to make it work. She repeated her salary question. My husband looked at me, and I looked at him, and we both knew that she was asking us to co-conspire and commit bank fraud. Her sole goal was to make a hefty commission on our jumbo-loan, by any means necessary, with no apparent threat to her of ramifications. I think we asked one or two more questions without answering hers and got the hell out of there. Both of our spider senses were tingling and, thank God we left. Major risk neither of us was willing to remotely entertain taking. It would be a couple more months before we got the energy to do it all over with another lender's application because the paperwork was so cumbersome. And we were juggling balls every day.

Well Dr. King, timing is everything, because within that time frame the property value was sinking just as fast as it had gone up. Our equity was disappearing like water swirling down the bathtub drain. Blink $950k. Blink, blink, $850k. Blink, blink, blink, $700, $600, $550k...what the hell was going on? Forget about refinancing. We then owed $100k more than the value of the house. We just decided to be thankful we could still pay the notes, and would wait and see what happened, hoping for a reversal. There were two other attempts with some other mortgage products from other institutions that solicited us, but none of them worked. In retrospect, each was more dangerous than the first. By the dawn's early light, our property values were bursting in air, and before it was over, it hit bottom at $450k—$200k less than what we had paid!

Like I said, it was not just happening to us. Many of our neighbors were also suffering, and the economy drastically plunged across the country. It was interesting, however, that the AA families became just a bit more accessible after they allowed themselves to come from behind the wall of shame and share their mortgage stories—but they did not do it in mixed company. We all were looking for resources and solutions to this plight we were in. This was worse than the returned check you had talked about that was stamped "Insufficient Funds" on our American Dreams. Because we had put our life savings into it, with no way to retrieve it. It was more like a burning house, because it went up in smoke—no water to stop the flames.

But I have to say also, Dr. King, that kinsman-ship was short-lived, because we were all being fed the same fix-it scams and then it became an issue of trust again. So no one trusted anyone. No one knew what to do. No one had extra tens of thousands of dollars to find a new place, or a rich uncle to bail them out. Not even Uncle Sam. We were first-generation affluence, and then we were not.

And there we were. Together in distress but alone in our misery. Mostly due to greed and the economic policies created in the Bush Administration. Policies that gave millionaires and billionaires more leverage to profit, which in turn gave financial institutions carte blanche to craft all kinds of ratchet-mortgage schemes by way of deregulation. And they preyed upon the masses, especially the poor, in the false acquisition of the American Dream. People robbing and piling up more money than they could spend in five generations. Greed. Greed. Greed. Gluttony on a whole new level. It was the 21st century's version of the colonial land-grab from the Native Americans. But rather than mass murder, and poisoning with alcohol, they proved if you did not know it before, that the pen is mightier than the sword. Nobody died, or felt any physical pain, but the economic tolls were leveling. Our wealth acquisition flat-lined with no crash cart to race down the hallway and save the values of our homes. One ginormous economic crash that rippled across the world. When we had purchased the house, we had savings, another property with a tad bit of equity, stock, and 401k as a safety net.

We sold the second property within the first year of moving, after our college-aged renters did measurable damage to it and persistent complaining from our former San Jose neighbors. Going back and forth to SJ from Hercules was too much of a hassle and we decided to let it go. That actually turned out to be a good thing too, because when the bubble burst, we would have had two houses underwater. So we carried on in the months that followed, hoping for the best. The economy however, began to get bleaker, but we were overwhelmed with the projects at work because we still had jobs...and I need to tell you about that.

HNIC

Dear Dr. King,

I was hired as a recruiter to a healthcare organization's major multi-billion-dollar electronic medical records implementation project. I was told that I would be an individual contributor to manage the recruiting, promotional, and transfer efforts for this business line group to grow from 600+ plus employees. It was explained that there would be 10-20 requisitions per month, a nice manageable flow for an experienced recruiter. I would have the assistance of one fulltime and one halftime person. This was a whole new level of responsibility for me, and I didn't fully grasp just how visible and critical this mission was until my time there was almost over. It could have been daunting if I had known better the actual objections and planned expansion, but that was not made clear in the interview. However, I was a highly experienced corporate and IT recruiter, and due to the pace and fluxes of those jobs, I was fully prepared for this role. I jumped right in feet first, and my head would soon follow.

For the first couple of months the demands were not too great, but began to grow swiftly after the fourth month. The project completion date had been escalated, and we needed to rotate staff and hire new staff members as quickly as possible—for all levels of the operation. After team success in meeting estimates, we were budgeted for increases on my team to meet the increased demands. I first had to hire three, and then three more, then more. When all was said and done, I had a team of eleven as Recruiting Coordinators, Recruiters, and Senior Recruiting Contractors. Two things were blatantly noticeable, which I was not thinking about as they happened: my entire team was women, and there were no whites on my team. I did not plan it. It was the way the roles opened and how the talent showed up. Most of us typically do not think twice about an all-white team, but with an all-brown team, people stop and notice, especially when it is high profile. There were eight African-Americans, including me, one Chinese, one Filipino, and one Egyptian. (My highly visible, all-brown recruiting team may have been my first career-limiting move with this organization.)

However, color be damned, we quickly formed into stealth mode. My ladies worked together, in partnership, and as a unit. We met every challenge thrown at us with a high degree of decorum and professionalism. I used our meeting time for handling issues and training the team in best practices, skills sharing, reporting, event planning, and presentation delivery. We encouraged each other and had monthly celebrations of our successes and birthday acknowledgments. By far, this was the most fun I had with a high-volume, high-stress job. I was not perfect, but I was good at motivating people, loved to take on a new challenge, and eager to learn. There were some personal challenges with one or two managers who did not appreciate my unwillingness to let them tell me how to do my job, or to manage me. We were lateral. I saw no need for them to butt in on the way I did my job, and I let them know that. (That was, I'm sure, my second career-limiting move.) However, for us, it was the best of times. We were pulled in every way possible and had to turn direction at a moment's notice from our Suite Leads and 30 or so hiring managers. But we freakin' rocked!

The exec that hired me transferred to another city and role, after which I had to report directly to the finance director. He and I got along really well. He listened, he supplied everything that we needed to continue to be successful, and he began to train me on report writing, which was one area where I needed some improvement. I loved my work.

I was doing a great job, and then was asked to join a management-training workshop they had purchased for all of their baseline managers. I was really happy about that as well. A short time after that, the finance director reported to me that he would also be transitioning to another business line at corporate headquarters and he would transfer me to yet another manager—his direct report was being promoted to replace him.

This guy and I were lateral at the time, and he was white. I privately nicknamed him Little Goodbar, because he was short and always had a bowl of bite-size candy on his desk that he used to soften his stiff demeanor. He was more than happy to be my "boss." I think he did not like the freedom I displayed and immediately wanted to know everything I did and how I did it. Finance was his world, and Excel spreadsheets were his lifeline and love language. He wanted every recruiting nuance to be reduced to a calculation. Some necessary, some very unnecessary. Mostly about complete control. I also believe that he didn't like that we had fun. We made it look easy because we were laughing and smiling—a lot. You'd think a manager would want his people happy, but his team was pretty stoic, so we stuck out. A bunch of brown people happy for no apparent reason. But I had that effect on my team. Some people are just so rigid and pent-up. He was pleasant about it, but you could tell he did not trust that work was our primary objective. How could we laugh so much with all the crap that was thrown at us on a moment's notice? What was so funny? But I say it was the glue that held us together. The rapid changes, and they were very frequent, had a grinding ripple effect within the entire business unit, and we were the only ones laughing about it.

I also learned later that my predecessor (who just happened to be black) allegedly had risky business dealings. Although my duties were the same, the job title was changed before my entry and my white bosses removed the budget allowance from my level of authority. Which meant I had to ask for every dollar I needed to make our department successful. I had all the responsibilities but no control beyond who I wanted to hire on my team. I was lamenting about the time-suck of asking for money with one of my subordinates whose tenure predated mine. She told me that the company was cynically nicknamed "The Plantation" because the executive and upper management was primarily whitewashed, and the rank and file workers were very diverse—and we are talking thousands of workers. I did have to give them credit for having the most diverse workforce I had ever seen in any white-collar corporation, the most by far. But they clearly had some work to do in the upper ranks.

When I learned about the title change and budget stripping, it really felt like I was paying for the sins of my predecessor. Guilty by black association. I have to tell you though, Dr. King, I was excited to see so many African-Americans doing it. It was surreal, and then I felt bad that I felt that way...if that makes any sense. Stranger still, whenever we had hiring events, and that quickly turned into monthly events with the demands, every time we hired someone black, I felt like I was doing a service, personal, like Harriet Tubman escorting my people to freedom on the Underground Railroad. Or Moses delivering my people to The Promised Land. Those feelings were always lined with some level of guilt, like I had done something wrong. Or "Massa'" was going to find out and send our asses back to blue-collar and agriculture ranks. I even had fears that if I hired too many I would raise eyebrows, and that it would mean my demise. I also felt like I did not want to scare any of the white people. So crazy, but still feeling so real.

They all had merit, and met the qualifications. What the hell is that? Why do those thoughts pollute my/our self-worth, judgment, and creditability? Why did I let them get away with syphoning the seemingly riskier factors of my job to the more "trustworthy" white man? Ugh, Dr. King, that seriously put some chink in my armor, but I rolled with it anyway and just did my job. However, fear had crept in, and I was afraid to ask for money if it had the slightest appearance of a dubious expense. So then I got fearfully stupid.

We were desperately looking for qualified corporate trainers but were short on applicants. We learned of a training conference in San Diego for the Association for Talent Developers, ATD. I requested permission to attend. I got permission and approval to have one hiring manager and one recruiter to accompany me there so I would have adequate help. The way the corporate travel works, Dr. King, is the rank employees pay first for the personal expenses and then have to file for reimbursement of money via expense report. Well one thing I forgot about, that was necessary, was a container to carry our banners in to be shipped. These containers had become pretty standard issue for events and came primarily in elongated plastic bins with wheels, so you could easily move it around like a dolly. We had none within the department because this unit was not accustomed to many events. Although we were one giant company we operated in our own silo and were disconnected from corporate headquarters for our basic operations. So with that, I found a used bin from a vendor in town, for around $50, a substantial savings. Then I decided it did not measure up, because it was grey and had large scratch marks around it and old traces of not peeled-off stickers and marker. Worn like a well-traveled suitcase. So I took it home to spray-paint it black. It took the better part of two hours because I had to use more than one coat for best coverage. Now Dr. King, how degrading is that?

Here I was, in a middle-management position, in corporate America, in a large-ass national corporation with billions of dollars, representing this billion-dollar corporation with issued banners, media, t-shirts and conference toys, and I am in my garage spray-painting the heck out of a plastic bin, so that "I" would not look like poor black trash at a conference! Because I was too afraid to ask for more money out of fear of being scrutinized, over the retail cost of a respectable bin! This was not a startup! Is it just me? Is anyone else suffering this same psychological insanity? I just don't think anybody white would have put up with that, nor hesitated to ask for more money. Anyway, I made it through, suffered no "public" degradation, and made a few hires from the event. Great ROI. Even managed to have some fun while there. But I told myself, actually promised myself, to ask, ask, ask.

That fall Obama was elected president of the US. Oh Dr. King, it was unbelievably awesome! America had a black president, but I will tell you more about that later.

Okay, so I made my ask declaration to stop being scared, and then we were in year-end salary and bonus review. One of my business line executives requested to increase the salaries of every team member who held the same job classification and title as mine. Some of those increases were close to 30 percent. Which required VP approval. The goal was to match the market and have salary equity within the department. Fair enough. Smart move to raise the employee morale and loyalty. Especially since everyone had been grumbling as of late because of the increased work demands with little time for reprieve. Plus, there was beginning to be a retention issue. But we had a mission. With a deadline! Well of course that immediately created an equity issue with me. So I took it upon myself to review the remaining salaries of the remaining managers with my same title (about 6 more) and I found I was on the bottom, by no less than $20k from the next closest salary. Upon further review of their direct reports, I discovered that none of them had a team as big as mine except one other person. After all, I was hired as an individual contributor, but was clearly working a management role with a much broader scope than was told to me at the onset. Okay, ignore it and wait for my review and my increase. Did that, got a 4-percent increase. Standard. In a good year. I do nothing for a while. And then I couldn't take it anymore. Feeling pimped is one thing, but feeling pimped and having proof that you are is another. Now all these incidentals are starting to add up, and it is not making me feel right, and I did not have an advocate. So with a modicum of righteousness, I prepare my request. Hell white people had helped elect Barack Obama as president, so surely I was going to get mine. The freedom gates were truly open.

So, I compile the data, show the equity disparities, outline my many accomplishments to include the money saved on recruitment (not including the stupid bin), and specifically calculate the savings on the time-to-hire reduction. Then scheduled time with my manager and his boss to discuss. I also added in the request for a title change. I did this because the current one was too generic and did not have any name recognition in the HR world. For a professional who wants succession and career path, it is helpful, even if in name only, to have a title that make you look more marketable, relevant, and important with a decent progression in responsibility. I was thanked and asked to give them time to review and approve. Post-mortem, I felt like it was received well and that I had made a "can't say no" case. Of course they would want to keep me happy. I had consistently demonstrated aptitude, fortitude, success, and results! My one weakness was consistent and accurate report writing, but I was trainable and eager to learn, improving, and we were never short on hires, my number one priority! The other mishap, not quite a weakness, is that I sent one email of record to correct a lateral but tenured and vested colleague who tried to correct my team, usurping my authority. Damn! I should have hit the delete button before I sent that email, so there would be no evidence. But Dr. King, how dare she reprimand my team without bringing the issue to me first? I was righteous and frank in my address, but I probably should have verbalized my discontent not knowing how deep her political pockets may have been. So I had one digital fingerprint that could perhaps be used against me.

Be that as it may, I did not let it stop me from making my request; as we know closed mouths don't get fed. And I truly did not think it was too much to ask. So what happened was...my request was postponed because the exec in charge of the whole business unit was leaving the organization and all budgeting was put on freeze until they found a replacement. Which left us with an interim replacement. She was not going to do anything out of the ordinary to call herself into question, so getting a VP's approval on a raise for a baseline manager was not a priority.

A couple of months passed while she matriculated, and I was busy trying to find an advocate to mentor and coach me on the history and politics of the organization. I found one. The same one who had made the request for her team. I was happy she agreed because she seemed to have a lot of political clout within the organization. Score! We had a couple of sessions in her office and a couple of lunch meetings offsite. I felt she understood my ambition and that she also appreciated my work.

At our last lunch, she had asked me if I had a graduate degree, I explained my bachelor's and associate's. She recommended that I consider going back to school for an MBA or MPH in order to be taken seriously and really rise in the ranks. Okay, I would consider, but I knew that was all I could do. We had a fat mortgage payment, a car note, private school tuition, life expenses, two children under 10 years with school and afterschool activities and priorities, and a big-ass house to upkeep and maintain. Not to mention six years of no salary to catch up on retirement and college savings. And she said consider getting a master's degree. Now how in the hell would I squeeze graduate school into my already overtaxed life? What? This does not compute. Well I guess I could do drugs to eliminate my need for sleep. Damn. That was a bit of a wet towel thrown with the force of hurricane winds in my face. That conversation gave me a headache. Taken seriously? Wow, had my fun management style painted a caricature of my professionalism in spite of my results? Were they laughing at me? How many of the women and men in charge had master's degrees? I understand the importance of a well-educated workforce, but this conversation felt odd, in timing and in tone. Most of them had well over 20 years of service at this organization and rose primarily on good work and seniority. Why was the first suggestion for a strategy to go back to school, and I had just been there a little over one year doing excellent work? I had heard this too often when I did not have a bachelor's, and here it was again. How did she know I had my bachelor's anyway—she was not involved in any part of my hiring? Why couldn't we start where I was and coach me to grow and build my organization, create some processes, maybe even some policies, provide some training? Surely there was a knowledge gap that could be fulfilled in this role for better optimization. I didn't like it. It felt the bar was moved intentionally to shadow my potential, legitimate or not.

I continued my efforts, happily, paid some political tithes with folks of influence, and then I was called in one morning for team review. It was a very quick meeting with the Interim and Little Goodbar, and I was asked to reduce my team by three. It made sense because hiring had slowed down and we were winding the entire implementation down. Well another three weeks or so passed and I was asked again to reduce by three more. That was the end of my contractors, and I had five remaining reports, all fulltime employees. Okay, so now we all skittishly begin to look for other opportunities within the giant organization, because now the writing is on the wall. Before any of us could secure anything, we were all let go within a matter of weeks after the last group. It was that cut and dry.

I was furious. Not even a thank you. Sure, Dr. King, we were not the first to be laid-off in such a harsh and unapologetic way, but what really got me was that months prior, we had a full-blown "cut 'n paste" internal hiring event. What that means is that one group of entry-level employees (45) were to be let go from one group and they had 25 slots for the lucky ones to be re-hired into the next group. This was their way of fair-employment-act hiring. What they required us to do was to schedule no less than three interviews with each of them with ten or more hiring managers within two weeks' time. That meant 135 interviews in two weeks, without any notice! I can't even begin to tell you how traumatic that was. Not only did we have to do it at the drop of a dime, we had to also provide career counseling, resume writing, and plain ol' handholding for these 45 people for two whole weeks. They even had the Interim Leader come to a couple of the sessions for Q&A, to ease the pain and stress they were feeling. Pretty much, any and everything else we were working on came to a screeching halt. The paper work alone was enough to drive us crazy, but the scheduling was like playing the game Concentration with two decks of cards, and a fan blowing them around daily. It took some serious orchestration, and all hands were on deck to get them scheduled by the deadline. But we "woman'd" up, and totally aced all the scheduling. Without even one mismatch!

For that one event, management acknowledged and thanked us. This was a grand and humane effort and I was impressed that this organization put out this level of care for baseline, entry-level employees, many with just one year or less of service. Not a very common practice. So all that consideration and handholding was afforded them, the easiest level of employees to recruit and hire, but we were given two hours to get our shit and go. No notice, no warning except what we perceived, and no formal opportunities to be redeployed in another division. I wanted to beat Little Goodbar's ass, and I wanted to blow up the entire building. But I got my things in a box, turned in my key-fob, parking card, got on the elevator (escorted by Little Goodbar turning beet red), and pushed L. I think I drove home comatose, and it would be months before I came out of it. Can I say it was racial? Maybe not, but I can say that it felt like there was no room for me to be me. Like I did not meet the silent requirement of behavioral conformity. Smile, but be serious at all times, until fun and happiness are scheduled, or risk marginalization.

The Whitest Thing I've Ever Done

Dear Dr. King,

Another completely out of the box thing I did was agreeing to host two female high school students from Switzerland. Dr. King, you know what I'm talking about. Black folks were not trusting enough, or accustomed to letting white people bunk in their homes—for any reason, especially foreign strangers. Outside of the racism part, they did not want their home to be judged by white standards, nor did they want to let white people know about how far they had or had not come. Or if there was any dysfunction in the household, they certainly did not want that exposed!

The request was made throughout the school and repeated a couple of times and no one was stepping up, so I agreed. I was willing to take one for the team. Plus, I had lived with white women before. We had the fifth bedroom as our guest bedroom with a private full bath, so I told our administrator if they did not mind sharing a bed (queen-size) then they could stay with us. The deal was to board them, feed them, and bring them to and from school for two straight weeks. My husband had the experience of hosting a foreigner as a college student when his friend came from India. But not as the parental guardian, so this was going to be interesting for both of us.

No sooner than agreeing to host these two young ladies, Imelda and Leone, did a deluge of menacing thoughts enter my head: were they lovers, did they do drugs, would they harm my children, would they steal, would they destroy our property? But mostly, I wondered what would they think of us, and what their report would be back home and to the school? I was able to self-medicate those thoughts into remission by rationalizing the decency of humans to be fairly high if they were paying for their child to be in a private school, and also sending them across the world to expand their experience and knowledge. But I had to carefully monitor my thoughts with a daily dose of affirmations to keep them at bay.

The kids enjoyed their company as did my husband and I. I did a ton of cooking, more than the norm, as I did not have them eat too many leftovers. Had good conversations at the table because their English was pretty good. We took them sightseeing and shopping and to meet a couple of our friends. Actually, the girls were pretty spoiled as I look back. Imelda had a birthday while here so we let her have a few classmates over and made her our traditional birthday brownie tower and sang happy birthday to her. I know she didn't expect anything like that and I think she truly appreciated it. We also retreated upstairs to let them have time together with their invited classmates.

They prepared their last supper here for us as their way to say thank you. And gave us cards, flowers, and trinkets. It was a cheesy pasta dish with mashed potatoes and grilled onions. I do not remember what it was called, but it was pretty tasty, and they were happy to give something back. I cannot say that it was a true cultural exchange for me because between the driving and cooking and cleaning, and my normal life, I was worn out. But I hoped at the very least, Dr. King, we were not an anomaly for them. I hoped that they would go home and report that African-Americans in real life rock! And that would have been my payment and contribution to a worldly conversation.

We received a letter about two months after their return, but I never reciprocated. I started one I think but it was also around the time we began our fight to keep our home, and then I lost the contact information. My four-year-old son however, had fallen in love with Leone. He would run to be near and play with her every day and was visibly upset for about a week after they left. Honestly, I had the thought that a seed was planted in him to prefer white girls over black girls, and it bothered me for a few days. I had to let that go too because love is a whole other ball of wax, and nothing within my control. But I warned my husband that our son falls hard and fast in love and we would have to watch out for his heart.

Dr. King, this school was a Waldorf school. It was private and had a very non-traditional methodology for education called anthroposophy created by an Austrian, Rudolph Steiner, post WWII. His vision, after realizing the effects of war and the war-mongering mindset, was that education needed to be focused not only on the forced mechanics and memorization of academics, but should be taught and aligned with the developmental physiology of the human brain and body. Which was introduced in organic and holistic ways, and at the right time. Kids needed the influences of nature juxtaposed and in some cases, in place of, industrial and digital educational practices. Things like creative play, wonder, arts, storytelling, building, and rhythm were used to foster the natural human intuition and to kindle the innate passion for learning.

I had heard about this school from a white couple, Curt and Kirsten, who I had befriended from the training. I also used to babysit their daughter. They were interesting people, smart, fun, committed, and did a ton of volunteer work that gave them lots of credibility. I pretty much took the lazy route in my search for quality schools, and trusting their assessment of where they put their children, I convinced my husband that our kids should attend too. This was so far away from anything that I had done before.

The campus was in the canyons of the East Bay hills called Wildcat Canyon, and there really were wildcats in those hills. The school owned 11 acres of naturally landscaped land. The children played outside rain or shine. They would make up and play games with the natural surroundings; climb trees, and take long hikes through the canyon. They would garden and build using natural materials. There were chickens, goats and an old white mare named Rocktago, who visited along the kindergarten fence line. It was magical, with thoughtful ceremonies to honor their successes, traditions, holidays, and earth cycles, also honoring their individuality and the human spirit.

After pre-k and kindergarten, the teacher they began their academic journey with would stay with them from grade 1-8, fostering and developing their minds along the way. Unlike the national mad rush to force-feed kids in preschool the basics of reading, writing and arithmetic, anthroposophy defers the introduction of the alphabet, letter construction, and number calculations, until the end of grade one. Then slowly infuses the mechanics beginning in grade two. In theory this made a lot of sense and was great for the high-energy child especially. There was lots of movement throughout the day accompanied by planned and organized activities without too much structure and rigor — two things that were demanded early on in public education, especially in low-income areas. Here, subject matter was introduced, and each child had the license to grasp and understand at their own unique pace. Nothing was forced and shame was not a component if a classmate did not grasp the teachings as quickly as another. In this learning environment, and it truly was a learning environment, each child was honored and his or her progress carefully monitored and documented. No grades.

Once I actually understood what I had registered my daughter and then my son in two years later, I felt I did a great thing for their introduction into school. However, we did not live in a Waldorf bubble, and for us this was beginning to be problematic. And here's why. Part of the agreement was not to teach your child to read on your own. We agreed and signed the contract, and it included other agreements that challenged our everyday habits. Stuff like: no TV, computers or digital devices, or descript toys, no processed foods, and agreeing to complete volunteer hours at the school for classroom time, parent-bonding time, events, and fundraising. And then there was the demographic of the student body. There was diversity and there was another AA family, plus an African family, and three mixed families with bi-racial kids that were amongst the families we observed, so we were happy to not be the "onlys" at this expensive, non-traditional private school, but we were perhaps 5-10 percent of the family population. Sorry, I still cannot help but scan.

I will say that we completely enjoyed that many of the parents were older like us, which felt great. But there seemed to be more people in their individual communities that supported the concepts and methodologies of this type of education than in ours. In addition to our daughter being a smart young toddler, she was also very tall for her age. From when she was four until age seven, she dwarfed her other classmates by at least a full head. Because our families and closest friends knew how bright she was as a toddler and preschooler, it was very, very difficult to feel confident in the fact that she could not read after first grade. Other kids in our families and in our neighborhood were practically reading chapter books by the same age. A bit of an exaggeration, but we were very reluctant to defend the costs we were paying for an elite education. Yet, compared to her closest peers, she was what they considered "behind." Of course we were to blame and blame they did. Now some of this revealed a lot of their ignorance and biases too, but peer pressure is a mutha'...even for a successful, educated, professional couple. We heard remarks like:

"Pay me $900 per month to teach her nothing." Translation, *"If you're stupid enough to pay that kind of money for nothing but babysitting, give it to me."*

"Man, what have those white people brainwashed you into!" Translation, *"You have lost your black ass mind and joined a cult!"*

"She's learning what kind of methodology again?" Translation, *"You will do anything to be like whitey."*

"It's your fault that girl can't read!" Translation, *"Teach that girl how to read, she ain't white! Befo' I call CPS on your wannabe asses."*

And those were only the comments and judgments we heard! Dr. King...why do some black people think that the way it has been is the way it has to be? Or that you are trying to be too white? I mean, I imagine the southern one-room schoolhouses to have had a similar approach. There, education was not just academic, but whole and organic, and very hands-on practical. I mean many of our HBCUs were developed to teach some of those skills specifically. We lost that in industrialization, and some of our humanity with it. I will not go into how much violence is poured into the minds of our youths on a daily, even hourly basis (that would require a whole other book). But you would be thunderstruck at what public-funded education has been reduced to, and how the curriculum has been dumbed-down for the low-income masses. It's like money dictates biological brainpower. Just not right for this country. Just wrong, wrong, wrong.

We stayed the course through all the criticisms and let the process roll. However, as the economy would have it, we were hit with another lay-off and this, plus the increases in tuition that were to be instituted the following school year, resulted in us removing our daughter from the school. It was bittersweet and we were torn, but economics dictated. She was summarily enrolled in one of the elementary public schools in town for the start of second grade. It was a horrible adjustment, and she was the only non-reader of basics for about three months. We totally felt like inadequate parents and uneducated black people with the looks and remarks from her teacher during this period. With shame and guilt to boot.

But boy, oh boy, did she catch up and could not only read with the best of them, but completed her first novel in fourth grade, and has not looked back. To this day she is an avid and voracious reader and honor student. I would guesstimate about 70 novels to-date, for leisure, not school, some of them more than once. How much of that aptitude is a direct impact of Waldorf? Or a result of shame and competition producing a stronger drive? Or due to innate ability and talent? We may never know the full academic impact, but the experience taught us a lot about culture, both white and black; choices, hard choices; and freedom, or lack thereof, to really incorporate self-determination into our lives.

There were some woo-woo moments and occurrences with some of the whites that gave us that uncomfortable, guardedly suspicious and not-interested-in-you-being-my-black-friend vibe, and had us question whether we wanted to be around those people. One time there was a rather rambunctious classmate whose parents kinda just let her rule. She had a devilish side to her, but fortunately only the aptitude and physicality of a five-year-old. She shoved my daughter down once in the kindergarten play area. This was not the first aggressive act. I went to where she was, kneeled down to talk to her when another female parent, white, who had witnessed the entire incident, ran over to where we were. She grabbed the child by the hand and asked her if she was okay before I got two words out of my mouth. Then she ushered her inside the classroom avoiding eye contact with me. That pissed me off so badly. I was not in attack mode, but after she did that, I was. I simply wanted to hear why she did it and was going to ask her to apologize, but that racist witch assumed the worst and jumped to the rescue. I was pissed and hurt at the same time. She revealed her hand and I did not try to fix her. I decided to let her be that way and I was glad. I think if that had happened about ten years prior, I would have made special efforts attempting to unveil to her that I was kind, smart, and important. But I did not. I let her have that party by herself and kept my distance. However, for the most part, the school adventure and the people were very enriching and pleasant. Plus, I made some great friends.

I also met another black woman who was in a mixed marriage with bi-racial kids, and an adopted Asian child. What! Since when did black people adopt Asian kids? Dr. King, she blew my mind. She was tall, model-pretty, confident, and had an advanced degree. I mean, she was the most liberated black woman I had personally known to-date. To be able to tell everyone, and of course this is my guess, but to tell everyone kiss my ass if you do not like my life–it is mine! I was awestruck. She owned it, and did not have to say those words; at least I never heard them. You just got the sense she truly answered only to God. I loved that about her, and she was freedom in my opinion.

My son started at Waldorf during my daughter's last year (of three years total). But we were asked to defer his enrollment because they assessed he was not ready to leave the nest. We enrolled him into a private Catholic preschool, because I had to work, and no school enrollment was not an option then. He started reading the first day. I find it peculiar that he currently does not enjoy leisurely reading that much.

The differences between the Waldorf School and the public school they ended up attending, however, were night and day. The open grass and rolling hillsides were replaced with fenced-in blacktop and concrete play yards. The trees replaced with unkempt potted plants. The animals were replaced with rubber or plastic-coated metal play structures. Natural and ambient-lit classrooms were replaced with fluorescent-tubed high-wattage lighting. Free play and exploration replaced with organized games of competition and dominance. Organic and freshly prepared, nutrient-rich meals were replaced with processed, preserved, and pre-packaged filler food. Thinking and problem solving was replaced with rote and memorization. Progress and development reports replaced with letter grades, ranking and testing, testing, testing. Student body demographic at Waldorf, roughly 80 percent white, student body here 80 percent immigrant, and first-generation American, with 16 different languages. Also, the teaching body was 80 percent white, and mostly female in both institutions. (These are of course, my visual calculations, there is for sure a margin of error, but I don't think I'm off more than 5 per cent).

So the trade off, I felt, was that they would get to know other nationalities and cultures first hand. But stark, stark differences. I partially felt like I was putting them in a prison for little kids. Do X, then Do Y, repeat after me. It broke my heart initially, but we tried to put in as much of the nurturing side of education as we could, after school and on weekends. It's like the adage that says when your neighbor loses his job, it's a recession, but when you lose your job, it's a depression. Those were my sentiments about this transition, but it also illuminated for me key distinctions about economic segregation.

When I was growing up, my mom did not have conversations about whether the schools were "good enough" for her children. The assumption was that it was a school and they would teach. Period. The concerns were primarily about race and prejudice. Would the teachers be racist and treat your child badly? As I mentioned, the white teachers all moved away when we moved in, so we had enriching educational experiences. Those black teachers were going to teach no matter what! But then the school funding shifted to being tied to the sales, property, and even income taxes (in some cases) collected in a particular county. If that county was not rich or solidly comprised of well-to-do neighborhoods, the schools and students suffered. White people did not want their tax dollars going to black schools. Dr. King, that's how they got around desegregation. They drew county lines and tailored the laws to suit their aim for continued segregation, and that was repeated across the nation, in county after county. Understanding this now first-hand with my children was a rude awakening.

Although this public school was recently built, clean, and taken care of, and in a good neighborhood, it was tied to a district that included low-income areas, with high unemployment, and the monies were syphoned by the neediest (poorest) schools first because the population was much bigger and it controlled the votes. The new immigrant student body came from families hungry for the American Dream but unschooled in American classism and educational policies. So for many of them, this school was up a few notches; assembly line or not. They mostly marched along to the beat of the drum of whatever the school district served up and did not do much complaining.

I remember I got so mad at the principal once who talked down (literally and figuratively as she was close to six feet tall) to everybody. They had some school event called diversity or cultural appreciation day or something like that. She was so culturally insensitive that she asked them to wear the clothing styles of their native countries for the parade. It was bad enough that they were going to literally "parade" around the schoolyard. But to add insult to injury, she kept calling their clothes costumes, like it was freakin' Halloween. Truly, I do not think she meant any harm, but it shed light for me where her head was about who they were. I just thought it beyond insensitive, because as an educator she should have known better. Yeah, everybody makes mistakes, but she had time to know better. This school had been diverse for many years, and she had tenure there as well. Like take some time to get to know them, their world, not just whitewash them and do surface level diversity displays and then roll them around like they were on a circus train driving through town. I brought it up to her. Asked her to refrain from calling their clothing costumes and she agreed. Even apologized. She opted for native dress, or regalia, or fashion. So I backed off from my harsh judgment. But I wished I did not have to have that conversation at all. *"Go to the people. Learn from them. Live with them. Start with what they know. Build with what they have. The best of leaders when the job is done, when the task is accomplished, the people will say we have done it ourselves."* Lao Tzu.

There was a national mandate from the George W. Bush Administration called "No Child Left Behind" that created or maybe fortified this level of assembly-line education across low-income and diverse districts because it went one step further and tied testing performance to monies received. His was a fallacious fix for underperforming schools, but observing the two schools for me clearly translated into "No White Child Left Behind."

Oddly, not many of my neighbors on my block had their kids in this neighborhood school. Most of them attended private schools. We had all moved into the area for the size of the properties and the location of Bay Area access. Schools were secondary, it seemed. My friend Michel from MCI was looking for a bigger house at the same time that we were. She tried to coax us to move to Danville like her family instead, primarily because of the great schools and the white-neighbor property value sustainability. The formula that most of our white peers followed; buy the worst house in the best white neighborhood with the best white schools. Either pay it in mortgage or pay it in private tuition. We chose the latter because it was just too white for us both. I probably would have loved being close to Michel, but this was bigger than her. It would be like a concession of "white is right." And here we come chasing y'all so you can't get too far ahead. Plus, the affordable houses in Danville were not new, and new was so very attractive. We also preferred that our children have a diverse start in school initially and not be the "only" for their young self-esteem. So Dr. King, you fought for our rights to be able to sit next to white children in classrooms, but I'm not so sure it was, or is, the best way. And yet ours initially started that way.

Dr. King, here's what happened next. My daughter had completed elementary there and my son was left. His fourth-grade year was just the worst ever. The white principal was replaced by a black principal. She was fresh with a lot of new ideas, and the old guard did not appreciate the new work that was asked of them. One of them boldly stated that she did not want to do more work! That was the first level of resentment. Then the new principal did not back away, or walk gently, or kowtow to their rebuttals, and that created an even stronger level of resentment. Some unfortunate incident happened with some first graders, and the way that incident was documented was not liked by the parents involved. It created a firestorm because those teachers and parents alike lost their minds. They went on the attack like pit bulls and never let up until she was removed. She started in August, and by November they started attacking and went for blood. They spent the rest of the school year organizing, petitioning, and campaigning with the district for her immediate removal. It was the craziest thing I had ever seen. Here they wanted change and improvement, and before they even gave her a chance to do any real and permanent good, they went on the attack. I just do not think if she was white with the same demeanor and actions that it would have went down that way. I truly do not. Call me a racist if you will, but it was something to see the former principal get away with some funky stuff, and she got a pass — for years. No one ever challenged her like that. I ended up pulling my son out of the school for his fifth-grade year and chose to homeschool him instead. And here is where I got confirmation that public education is truly unfairly stacked.

He gets registered with the online program and is nestled under a school district that is one of the higher-performing school districts in the state (mostly white), and about 60 miles from us. They send you all the books, workbooks, teacher's guides, tools, art supplies, supplemental reading materials, and science experiment equipment that you need to complete the curriculum, which you do mostly at home and online. We had monthly visits to the sponsoring school campus to interact with other homeschoolers, and he also had weekly video calls for classroom instruction with the assigned credentialed teacher. We, the parents, were called Learning Coaches. All of the weekly assignments were posted online, and we had to meet the levels of completeness each week. It truly was well organized and structured. The requirement to enroll your child was that a parent had to be a college graduate. I was truly impressed. If I have to critique one thing that they should do better it is make sure the parent is a fit educator. College degrees do not necessarily translate into highly effective teaching, especially with children, and that was true in my case. Life, yes, but pure academics? It was a challenge for me. I wanted my 10-year-old to behave like a college student, so we had many problems. Nonetheless, we did it, and have since moved on, but here is the point of all of this, Dr. King. The curricula and materials sent were so much smarter, broader and more comprehensive than what my daughter had for the same grade. The textbooks and activities were better, and the program included real science experiments as well as art and music classes. By virtue of not having the same level and access of education, this district's schools were behind. It really did not matter how good the children's individual grades were, they were already behind based on geography. Even the sixth grade in the middle school did not match this online school's fifth-grade courses. The standardized testing is based on the level of the broader curricula; it would be hard for them to score higher when less is given. The decks are just not stacked fairly from jump-street. And that should be criminal in America.

Obama is President!!!

Dear Dr. King,

A black man was elected President in 2008...yes, of these United States of America! That is right; I said a Black man is President of the United States and he was reelected for a second term! It is still hard to believe, and I campaigned, contributed, voted and prayed for his election victory. Just like when Nettie swore to Celie after she cried out for Nettie to "Write!" in the movie *The Color Purple*, "nothing but death could keep me from it!" It being voting for Barack Hussein Obama. The first African-American President of this country. The greatest and most powerful position in all of the land. It was record-breaking as well as an historical race on many counts, each time.

Dr. King, where do I begin! My son was in Kindergarten when Senator Obama was running against the other Democratic contender, former first lady, Hillary Rodham Clinton, NY Senator, and wife of the two-term 42nd president, William Jefferson Clinton. Well my son Jacob came home from class and told me he was mad at his teacher because she rolled her eyes at him. I asked him what happened and this is what he told me. "Momma, Ms. _____ told the class that it's a really exciting time for history in the country and she was really happy. She said that for the first time a woman is running for President of the U.S." *(Now you and I both know that was not the first time, but I did not interrupt his story to mention that Margaret Chase Smith (R) and Shirley Chisholm (D) were the first women to run for president, because I wanted him to continue.)* He continued, "I raised my hand and she called on me and I told her that Barack Obama was running for president too, and Momma, she rolled her eyes at me and told me to 'put your hand down'." Now Dr. King, I cannot tell you how wonderful that was for me. It both surprised and tickled me, because as parents we forget how much we feed our children in direct and indirect conversations. This boy was five years old and he knew a little something about politics. Plus, he had the moxie to say something about what he knew. His world was not all ABC and 123, Elmo, Batman, and Ninja Turtles. He knew about Barack. For half of his life now and most of his American memory, he knows a black man (who looks like him) is in the White House and is the POTUS! And that was priceless! I mean were you cheering from the heavens? As it goes Dr. King, Obama not only won the votes of the American public, he won the hearts, hopes, and aspirations of many generations, nationalities, and foreigners worldwide.

I remember the night he won, November 4th, 2008, the networks delayed the historic results to keep hope alive for AZ Senator, John McCain. It seemed as if they were shielding him in some way from a personal defeat, like they were staggering in the results to protect his ego. But the elation and jubilation that I felt, and that those around me felt, was being broadcast on network after network across the progressive and oppressed televised world and radio airwaves. America, and the world, had a new lovechild, and his name was Barack Hussein Obama. The son of a Kenyan, and English-American, the product of three continents (like many of us), all composed into a 6'1" handsome and magnanimous manly frame. I have to believe a spiritual phenomenon occurred the moments after he was declared the victor. It had to be just like the sequential hand-wave we do at sporting events, but on a cosmic level that rolled across the continents and the oceans within minutes. I wondered if there was an actual spiritual glow, or celestial flash, that encircled or colored the earth in those moments like the aurora lights. A harmonic convergence of spiritual joy and hope that had never happened on this planet before! Dr. King, not even you, or Gandhi, nor Jesus himself had that viewership and euphoria from billions of people at one earthly moment in time. Simply astounding and I bore witness! No, I felt witness. This was monumental globally, spiritually, and universally. How could any being live up to that? Anyway, just like the whites who participated in your March on Washington, many, many whites campaigned, supported, contributed, and voted for him. But not all whites were happy about it.

Many were opposed; many from the opposing political party decided to make it their mission to make him fail. There were racist rants, comments, epitaphs, imagery, false accusations, and just plain evil that surfaced on media, social media, radio talk shows, TV talk shows, and news outlets you would not believe. Well actually you would, as you know first-hand. But it was just awful. Imagine that, Dr. King, not conceding defeat and working as a team to help move the country forward for the good of all people. But fight him tooth-and-nail and do everything within their congressional power to make him look really bad, ineffective, and the worst president known. And it was primarily because he was black, cool as a cucumber (even that swagger), and superbly educated by our/their most touted and prestigious school, Harvard Law School. They called him arrogant, an elitist, an alien, a liar, a puppet, and talked negatively about his wife, his girls—and those were just the public slanders. Lord only knows what was said in private. Again, I am pretty sure you have some idea. Nonetheless, he stood tall and true to his calling, fought back on every worthy attack, admitted his mistakes and took actions to correct them. He kept his eye on the prize. In spite of all the nasty and vicious hatemongering thrown at him, he is still holding it down. Like a champ! He has done some amazing and lasting leading, and most certainly will be recorded as one of the greatest presidents this country has had! Regardless of their criminal attempts, he was re-elected for a second term! He is not perfect, but I love him, and I know this country is better for his contributions! You, Dr. King, would be most proud!

FREEDOM? 2010s
(The Global Citizen Years)
We Are the World

The idea of an open world with equal access, peace, justice, and liberty for all, is a dream worth dreaming.

"...We have an historic opportunity for a great global healing and renewal. If we will accept the challenge of nonviolent activism with faith, courage, and determination, we can bring this great vision of a world united in peace and harmony from a distant ideal into glowing reality."

—Coretta Scott King

America the Beautiful...Here We Come!

Dear Dr. King,

I had pockets of employment with a renewable energy company, where I had started as a contractor, then shortly afterwards converted to a fulltime employee. Within months I was laid off and brought back on as a contractor again, and shortly after that I transitioned to on-call. Between those last two transitions and after the, *"We won't be doing any augmentation hiring until the late summer or fall, so there will be no need for training in the summer. We're switching to sales mode,"* speech from my boss, I was again without a job. I was beginning to think my name literally meant wanderer, which translates into one who will never be stable. This teeter-tottering economy was really directly affecting my life. But this time I did not go south, well not figuratively anyway.

My husband and I decided to use the time have a real vacation, and let our children spend time with their one and only grandmother, and to meet scores of their first- second- and third-cousins, aunts and uncles. So we hit the road for a five-week drive across the good ol' USA. "My country 'tis of thee, sweet land of liberty..." here we come!

Our plan was to visit our families in southern CA, Arizona, Texas, Louisiana, Georgia and Michigan. We would start in the Los Angeles area, then go through AZ, from there to TX, LA, GA, MI, and back home, in that order. We would also pass through the various states along that route.

First stop north of Los Angeles, to our closest relatives on his side in Santa Clarita. We had spent many holiday opportunities with these cousins and always had a great time. From there our next stop was Tucson, AZ, to another cousin on my husband's side. This cousin, like my husband, had left Louisiana right after college and became a geologist working for the USGS and was working at the university. He was close in age to my husband, and also had school-age children. He had always been an out-of-the-box guy, and marched to the beat of his own drum. His wife was from Venezuela, and their two children were 18 and 10. The family traveled a lot, loved camping and adventure trips, and was bilingual. At this time our children were 12.5 and 10 so we were looking forward to a lot of fun with them all.

Dr. King, we were stunned to find out that their daughter was gone for 30 days to Alaska for a camping and kayaking adventure—by herself (with a program), without the ability to call home or have any contact. I cannot tell you how that jarred my soul. I was scared and befuddled and could not slightly imagine having that much freedom as a parent, a black parent, even as an adult to go to Alaska by myself. She was aptly prepared, being no stranger to camping or kayaking. Was smart and well-traveled for an 18-year-old. Was even athletic and an excellent swimmer. But no contact—for thirty days! That, I did not understand. I mean, it was recreational, not a military training, so why no contact? They laughed about my befuddlement and treated her trip as a rite-of-passage of sorts and trusted in the program and confidence that their daughter would survive, thrive and grow exponentially while she was away. In their minds, she was an adult and needed to spread her wings. Gain some leadership and self-dependency skills, black bears or no black bears in the wilderness. Grow-up some, take on a new challenge.

Dr. King, could you imagine that? Would you have allowed Yolanda or Bernice to go on such an adventure? All the way to Alaska! And when she was the only black? Perhaps even the only Hispanic. This certainly trumped my concert event of 20,000 people; 20,000 acres of unspoiled land with a kayak and a backpack, and all of its natural inhabitants. It was too much of a giant leap of faith for me.

I could not let go of my fears and teased them that they had just been had. That their daughter had been recruited by a secret governmental agency, and 30 days is what it takes (per all espionage movies) to program humans to be covert secret agents. That she was being trained unknowingly. That she would return more dependent alright, but she would be a badass, undercover killing machine, and would one day get that activation call and go into stealth secret agent mode. I think we had had a couple of glasses of wine when all that came out, so everyone was practically on the floor in laughter. But there was still that small paranoia part of me that believed it was possible.

We left Tucson feeling our trip somewhat small to their daughter's, with ours simply about visiting family and distant relatives in the comfort of our SUV and civilization. I think I worried about her for about a week or two before I could let go. Well...really five because everyone heard about it along the way, and now I am telling you, years later. She is in college now and has not had any unexplainable trips, or calls from the CIA (we guess).

So on we went, east on I-10. Next stop, Houston, TX, to see my brother and my husband's nephews and niece, and the Johnson Space Center. After that we made our way on to Dallas to see more of my family. We stayed there for two days to participate in the wedding of my eldest sister. She got hitched to a man who appeared to really love her and she was very happy. My son got to give her away. He was so charming.

We also got to see my super-cool former neighbor who I have been patterning my "neighborhood mom" life after, and oh what a sight she was for my eyes. I completely loved every moment. I acknowledged Bettie Joe, and shared with her who she was for me growing up, and the impact she had on my life. She of course had no idea, but I could tell she got it. I certainly felt loved all over again by her and I think she felt the same love coming back to her from me.

From Dallas to Baton Rouge, we did a route that took us through Karnack, TX, birthplace of Lady Bird Johnson. She welcomed us, via a series of banners on the street lamps that lined both sides, showing her headshot. We did not know if it was a permanent installation or some holiday or ceremony. But we were not curious enough to stop and find out.

It was both ironic and a drive back in time in this small rural town. No sooner than we entered Karnack, did Sheriff Scary decide he needed to tailgate us. We were not speeding, but as soon as my husband saw him in the rearview, he got very tense. He immediately checked our speed and set the odometer on cruise control exactly two miles under the speed limit just to be sure. Well we were not sure if he was riding so close to intimidate us because we had CA plates (people have a lot of crazy perceptions about Californians, some of it justifiable), or because we were black. We also were not planning to stop and ask. Thank goodness we did not need any gas. I'm certain my husband's blood pressure was through the roof, but he just rattled off a string of superlatives to keep himself from losing total control. I was scared, but just prayed that Sheriff Scary would leave it at that, seeing the kids in the car. The irony was, Lady Bird had no influence on him regarding our rights—granted by her husband, President LBJ—to drive through his town. He stayed on our tail until about half a mile across the city line and then turned off without incident. I tried not to dwell in it too much. I did not want him to take my mental power away for the remainder of the ride. If I were by myself however, I don't know that I wouldn't have lost it all together. I was just thankful we made it through.

We had so much fun and love in Louisiana with the Stevens' branch, and even toured a swampy Bouef Bayou and ate some alligator. Ewww! But it tastes like chicken. I was really drifting in thoughts of slaves and how they endured the not-too-forgiving landscape of the South, with the heat and the humidity. I was not dwelling on slavery, but when we did the swamp tour, it crossed my mind more than once to wonder how they could have possibly made it through, especially in the dark. I imagined how many were eaten by the alligators, bitten by the boll weevils and the snakes, and just did not survive.

It also struck me a few times on the drive from Louisiana to Georgia, how many had crossed the now-cleared and paved paths that we easily drove through; which you yourself had driven through many times. There is something about the heat, the pasty humidity, the swaying Spanish moss, and the invasive ivy covering all those trees lining the highways that kept those thoughts creeping in and out of my head. We were going to stop in AL to see my relatives and visit Birmingham, and Selma, but we spent a couple of extra days in Baton Rouge, and had to withdraw from that plan.

Dr. King, we visited The King Center in Atlanta. A museum founded by your beloved Coretta to honor your memory and vision. It was beautiful. We learned more about you that we did not know, and there were many, many visitors. I was encouraged to know that people had genuine interest in understanding more about you and the movements. But I kinda wished they were not all there at the same time we were. I tend to get a vertigo sensation in museums when they are too crowded and have difficulty experiencing the exhibits. Nonetheless, it was very moving and inspirational. Oddly, the most striking to me were the sculptural display of the "Marchers," and the "farm wagon" that pulled your coffin. Seeing those two exhibits moved me to tears.

Detroit was something to mourn. In fact, my daughter actually apologized to me that my childhood home was no longer there, as it was in Baton Rouge for my husband. I was touched that she felt the need to comfort me in such a way, but she did not understand I did not really feel anything in particular about that. Most of my happiness there occurred outside with my friends and in the schools. So I had no nostalgia for the house, I did however have strong feelings for my friends. I wanted to see them all, get caught up on the neighborhood gossip, you know, like old times. But that was just a fancy, because there were only two or three families that I remembered still in residency there. One of my dearest friends, who still lived there, I nicknamed the "Pope of Pinehurst." Her self-appointed nickname is "Qatz" (Cats). She created that as a teen, and I get it now, because she definitely has nine lives. And like me, had suffered some tragic losses; half of her siblings, through fire, disease, and a terrible car accident. But she is still doing her thing. She is an American treasure, and I say this in all earnestness. She has a heart as big as Kansas. She grew up on Pinehurst and has moved away and back, but is a neighborhood gem for the generational knowledge she has in her head about her community. She knew all of us kids, the mothers, and many of the grandmothers. Having her own children, she knows all of her children's generation, and her children's children, now a grandmother herself at the age of 50. She is what our ancestors called the village shaman, not for performing medical fixes and healing, but for the intimate details she holds about many a households and families. A walking encyclopedia of lives, loves, losses, triumphs, and defeats: of a neighborhood that has been transmuted. She has loved on everyone there, probably for at least a ten-block radius. And that for me is an American rarity and classic. Not many people can claim that because we are such a transient society; but oh, what living history she is. Someone needs to document and curate her world. It would be better than Google mapping. Human relationship mapping.

Detroit was just a skeleton of itself, Dr. King. If anyone wants to do an archeological dig about the plight of the African-American family in metropolis USA, during the industrial age, this city is the place. It was in ruins; the thousands, literally thousands, of abandoned homes, businesses, churches, strip malls, and factories were just eerie and ghostly. I can only liken it to how Tulsa, OK, must have looked after the whites attacked and burned down the entire area known as Black Wall Street in '21. Parts of the city were just devastated. I did not realize how destroyed it was, hearing the reports from afar. However, as bad as it was, what I really saw was the potential. For example, in CA, especially in the Bay Area, there was a higher than normal vacancy rate for a brief period after the recession. But people rebounded quickly and were moving in with pop-up businesses to begin again and rebuild.

In Detroit however, there was a lingering sadness in the air, like an abatement of the human spirit, not just abandoned buildings and factories, and that is perhaps what my daughter felt. But the potential, oh the possibility of a bright future for Detroit, Dr. King! It could return to its greatness with the right critical mass of people with business, education, and development goals. Something that perhaps an outsider could see more clearly. The mere fact that it is a beautiful location, with the Great Lakes, and just across the river from Ontario, Canada, means there is all sorts of potential there, especially with the extraordinarily cheap property values. There was a time in my 20s and 30s when I used to be embarrassed to say I was from Detroit. Michigan would always be my first answer, and I would hold my breath hoping the questioner would not ask further. But I understand now, it truly does not matter where you are from. People can be from anywhere and grow up to be anything if their heart is in the right place and the drive is within them. Location is truly temporary, and I mean physical and mental. And now I know Detroit is a great place to come from.

We left Detroit after four days and saving my cousin's life by performing the Heimlich. I would tell you about it, Dr. King, but this cousin would probably kill me. Notice I said cousin and not he or she. Outside of that event, we had a few scary episodes of crazy weather that had us praying to Jesus to spare our lives. The first was a hundred-foot wall of dust, better known as a dust storm in the Phoenix area. There was also the highly dramatic thunder and lightning storm on our arrival to Atlanta. Then we had the scariest near-tornado driving experience through Nebraska — corn country. We were about 30 miles east of our destination, spotted funnel clouds in the distance headed in our direction. Birds were being blown into our windshield. We started praying to Jesus, when we saw the truck driver brake to lag behind us, and stop under the last overpass visible. I also started videotaping the funnels and recording our names on my mobile phone. I also texted my friend in CA, to tell her where we were and how to contact my family just in case something happened. We raced through the rainstorm passing miles of cornrows off I-80, and miraculously got to our motel in North Platte. We were very grateful to be alive.

The storm was instantly forgotten when the kids saw the pool and all of their fears dissipated. My husband chose to stay in the room to watch TV. We hit the pool. We were anxious too, not having had a swim since we left Louisiana, almost two weeks prior. It was a pretty clean inn, one of those franchise ones that are family friendly and have "free" continental breakfast for guests. The poolroom was spacious and included a hot tub. The door from the lobby entered near the shallow end. We walked along the edge with about ten people in the pool and another four in the hot tub. We had to walk to the deep end where the hot tub was before we saw a couple of vacant lounge chairs on which to rest our towels. No sooner than we dropped everything, when everyone, and I am not joking, everyone, got out of the pool and hot tub and headed toward the door.

I could not believe what I was seeing. I looked at my kids and wondered if they thought what I knew. My son asked where everyone was going. I shrugged, said I did not know, pretending I didn't. And could not believe it was happening again. I was worried how the event would affect them. It had been a long time since it had happened to me, and it was the last thing on my mind, so I did not know what to say. I think I said something like more room for us, and ran and jumped into the water screaming to usher in fun. I was glad if all the others were going to leave that they got out quickly 'cause they might not have had time to pee in it. Hopefully.

I certainly was not expecting this event in the Bible belt, in 2012 no less. But I surely kept my eye open for the chlorine guy. No sooner than having that thought, the door opened and in walked my husband. He was feeling left out and came down to join us. I told him what happened, which I probably should not have, because his "I'm coming to join you" smile instantly evaporated. And then he spent the next thirty minutes gurgling about that and the racist guy, just the night before, in the hot tub at an inn in Iowa City, who said to him that black people could not swim because of our butts. It was such a time-suck, but eventually he let it go with a round of Marco Polo, a couple of freestyle races, and silly synchronized swimming gestures.

The next day we hit the road shortly after breakfast and continued our trek back on I-80 to our next planned sleepover in Salt Lake City, UT. I have to confess we drove into Salt Lake carrying every religious and racial stereotype about Utah and Mormons, who were reputed to be racists, and also because we had somewhat been re-immersed in racism. I was hoping it might not be that way, especially after seeing the giant granite bust of the Great Emancipator, Abraham Lincoln passing through Laramie and Cheyenne, WY. But after observing many ranch-style homes with lots and lots of land, those thoughts crept right back in. I expected to see households with "Big Love" (meaning tens of children and many wives). It was so bad in my head. I actually thought they'd be waiting and walking around just to confirm my biased thinking; parading in full-length shirts or dresses with long-sleeve cotton tops and bonnets. I mean…I went 19th century in my thinking; almost back to 18th century prairieland thinking. Silly me.

So you can imagine how dismantled we were when we drove into downtown Salt Lake, not far from the university, and heard blaring Hip-hop music coming from a park across the street from the motel. We could not figure that one out. A live Hip-hop concert in Utah; it rattled our cages for sure. Then we observed scores of students and young adults, very diverse, all around and walking downhill from the campus to attend. I felt like I was in hipster uptown Oakland for a brief period. It was very diverting, but we had no complaints about it. We were actually quite relieved. We were also hungry and tired. We hurried ourselves to check in, wanting to feel the vibe of the streets, and walked to a nearby restaurant. The energy was great and we had a fairly decent meal at a franchise restaurant. It would have been even better to find an authentic family-owned one, but we were too tired to do the research or ask around. Of course the kids wanted to swim again because our room opened to the pool area. So who was I to say no? It was after all the last stop before we would drive the entire way back home to CA. The pool was empty this time, so instant relief. Maybe everyone was at the concert, but the kids did not care, they just wanted to play in the water.

About forty-five minutes later a white woman came in. She parked her belongings near the hot tub, which was at about 3 o'clock from where I was sitting. She walked over to the pool. Got in. Did a quick lap or two. Got right out and went into the hot tub. Hmmm, I thought, thank you for not being a jerk. I was in and out of watching the kids, relaxing, and reading a local magazine I found on the table. Out the corner of my eye, I thought the woman was trying to get out of the tub, but she was actually slightly bobbing a bit, up and down. Maneuvering herself somewhat. It caught my eye and I turned to see. Oh my, I could not turn away, like a deer in headlights. Dr. King, she had turned herself to face the wall of the hot tub, with her elbows on the outer edge, just enough to hold herself in a frontal position to the water jets. I was fixated. How in the world, what in the world, what the heck? I mean...I could not stop watching! I knew she could feel my stare, gawk, but she pretended not to, or couldn't care less apparently. Her objective was clear. Her skin started blushing red, and within a couple of minutes she was the color of a lobster. Then, with a slight roll back of her head, she let go of the edge. Turned around and water-walked to the other side. Grabbed the rail. Hoisted herself up. Got out. Blotted herself with her towel. Passed through the glass door that opened to the outside patio. Sat down. Lit a cigarette. Took a very long drag and exhaled. And that was that. I'll be damned if that didn't just beat all. I did not know if my mouth was touching the floor, but I was paralyzed in disbelief. Not of the act, in and of itself, but that it was done in public seemingly without a care as to who was watching.

Now Dr. King, I have no intention of copying that act, but I have to say I was completely envious that someone could have so much freedom. How does a person get to that level? Some would call it disgusting and nasty or completely inappropriate, and maybe it was all of those things too. But all I could see was freedom; a level of freedom that I have yet to embrace. And that made me sad.

I snapped out of my fixation, because my attention was redirected back at my daughter. She was coming out of the pool and was heading in the direction of the hot tub to warm up. I yelled something to halt her, having now in my head more thoughts of so many others, who had been in there, and what was left behind, bubbling in the suds. I told her it was for adults only, and too hot for twelve-year-olds. She forced the issue, but I jumped up and started gathering our things, called out to her brother, and told them we had to go. We left the pool in a puff of smoke. Man. That was a trip. Chester laughed about it when I told him, and he wasn't mad at her. He was just bummed he didn't get to see it. I knocked him upside his head with my towel. Men.

Dr. King, this country is absolutely beautiful! We were all in awe for nearly the entire trip. We felt extremely fortunate to have had the opportunity, although we did not think that way initially because of my lost employment. We felt extremely blessed to have so many relatives with whom to spend quality time. The love they poured on us made up for the money I was not making. It felt like hot, sweet, salty, and buttery cornbread with a big bowl of southern gumbo at an all-you-can-eat homemade buffet table. There is just no substitute for black family love. None. And it was just what I/we needed to send us back to the Wild West, to rebuild our American dream for the next stretch of our lives. For the most part, with the exception of three of my husband's nephews, our families live pretty segregated lives in their communities and churches. They did not appear to have a need to desegregate necessarily. That is not a judgment or conclusion about anything. It simply may be purely circumstantial, but it was noticeable to me coming from California.

Many of our family members still seemed to be in recovery mode from the depression. Funny, Dr. King, "they" keep calling it everything but a depression (economic bust, economic downturn, slow economy, sputtering economy, financial crash, financial crisis, Wall Street crash, great recession). That is all about keeping people from really organizing, hitting the streets, and calling our leaders to account. But in my eyes, it was really a depression! For millions of homeowners across the entire country to lose millions of jobs, millions of their homes, most of their equity, and also their life and retirement savings—and to say it was a recession. My God, I would hate to see what a depression looks like! But that's how the political machine spins it, so that Americans cannot really call a duck a duck.

We're all so plugged into the news spin-cycles nowadays; they could easily have us all believing anything on the surface. Because most people will not go any deeper than that. The messengers have figured out with enough messaging and promises to "get better," "bounce back," and "upturn," people won't organize and spend time with each other to see what's really going on, and to see how widespread it is. Sometimes I feel like we are all on a remote-controlled socio-economic dial in this country, Dr. King. Like enough history has been lived, human behaviors recorded, data collected and analyzed, by the one percent who control the economy, that they know how and where to shift the tides, what to shift our attentions to, and for how long. Just like they do with gas prices. They can do it with the right amount of media blitz to keep enough of us engaged, thinking we can change anything we want; keeping enough of us just above water and busy enough holding on to what we have, so that we only have time to look at the immediate and not focus on the bigger picture, or the long-term effects. It is highly conspiratorial, but so completely doable with today's technology. And I am not convinced it is not happening that way already.

The landscape of this country is majestic as the song says. Each state seems to have its own personality that almost hits you like a new radio station as soon as you cross state lines. All in all, we touched 18 states: AZ, NM, TX, LA, MS, AL, GA, TN, KY, OH, MI, IL, IN, IA, NE, WY, UT, and NV, close to 8,000 miles in total: a great geography lesson for the kids and a trip of a lifetime. To boot, we had a family member to board and feed us practically every eight hours. We were so blessed in fact, that we only had to spend money for a hotel six nights out of 35 — it was just awesome!

Quite surprisingly UT and WY spoke to me as potential places to live, or at least visit again long term. There was something about the natural landscapes, the outcrops, mountains, and the air that welcomed me and at the same time beckoned adventure and a sense of serenity. I have now visited just about two-thirds of the US. It seems we finally have achieved a kind of free access, but freedom should mean something more in the world of today. I do wish you could have seen all the landscape of the country through the eyes of free access. I know you spent a lot of time on the road, and a lot of time on airplanes, but I do not know how much you actually were able to see and experience stress-free, and have time to appreciate. Or maybe you did, and it was the "mountaintops" that further inspired you to keep going forward. But "America the Beautiful" is still beautiful. "...From every mountainside, let freedom ring."

Energy, Technology & Me

Dear Dr. King,

My last most recent stints at corporate America involved two very different and emerging technologies for the world. One was in a renewable energy company. The other was at a cloud data storage company. If these two companies are a snapshot at what today's generation of the middle class will look like, then you should know that black people are in trouble because we are not in. They are very diverse with the population of the world, so they are truly global organizations. But our representation is nothing like the middle class of the industrial age.

I was hired at the energy company to co-develop their new hire orientation. It was also the first job I had in a while where I was found on the Internet by a recruiter, and got the interview without knowing anyone personally connected to the opportunity. So that felt really great!

It was one of those warm and fuzzy, very liberal, very Democratic organizations started by really smart people who love this planet and were passionate about keeping it healthy. Not quite environmental extremists, but definitely devout activists. They put their money where their mouths were, and it had a tree-hugging, rogue, save-the-world type of vibe, and I honestly felt right at home. Prior to that job, my only concern about the earth was the land my house was on, as the grounds were formerly owned by an oil company and it was a brownfield (land that was highly contaminated and polluted by petroleum byproducts) that had to be decontaminated, cleaned, and EPA approved livable before the homes were built. So I was happy to learn more about the environment and to learn about renewable energy.

It was a very diverse organization, with a lot of young energy, old experience, passion and expertise. Again, I loved it. I had started this job in July, and all was well with the hiring ramp-ups. I also helped with recruitment as needed. I held weekly new hire orientations that I truly felt made a strong impression on the new employees, and wish that all corporations started their employees in similar fashion. It was a bit wonky with energy tours, brownbag lunches outside, quizzes, a video of me giving a mock commencement speech, dressed as Michelle Obama, and beer toasts at the end of the training. But I think this orientation really gave this company the edge on getting employees instantly related, somewhat loyal, and on task sooner rather than later.

I was really happy with the role and I think I let my happiness show too much. Dr. King, sometimes I feel like you have to just be a stoic, hardcore serious, or superbly expertise as a black employee to be less vulnerable and less visible, just like my Nigerian neighbor said. He is still working today, and has survived several bouts of lay-offs, and even an acquisition and merger. But it is difficult for me to hide my emotions. I do not have that poker face. My high school coach told me I always wore my next move on my face. I guess I never mastered shaking that.

Here again was someone, *white,* who seemed to be weird about my happiness at work. This was tricky because we worked close together and reported to the same boss. She reminded me of one of those white women that had little or no "voluntary" association with black people. I could be wrong but that was the feeling I got. It is true I was having the best professional experience ever there. I also made it look fun and interesting and there perhaps began the chess game I think, to move into my position. She always wanted to know what I discussed with our boss, what project she had me working on, and everything else she could find. She really pissed me off once when we were on the way to a job fair in downtown Oakland. It was mid-afternoon and we were on a major avenue in downtown, and had come to a red light. A tall African-American teenage or young adult crossed the street in front of us in the crosswalk. He was clean, wore his hair in locks and his clothes were loose. As he walked in front of her side, she looked to her left and pushed her lock down on her SUV. He was not even looking at us, and danger just flashed in her mind to lock the door. I was in the passenger seat and I said nothing. We were three blocks away from our destination and I did not want my much-needed energy to be off when I was attempting to attract recruits. So I just logged it in my list of things to watch out for with her, and then understood why out of roughly 40 sales people on the team thus far, there was just one African-American. Dr. King that was quite outside of the norm because in my experience, the way the majority of blacks got into corporate America was through sales or customer service roles. That would be our general entry, almost guaranteed, but not if the gatekeeper was uninterested, or fearful.

Our relationship was cordial, even friendly at times, but perhaps there was some sort of perceived threat, like she wanted to be sure I would not surpass her professionally, or in likeability, or social ability with our boss as well as the other executives. It seemed she was fine to have me on her team, but only if my rise was less than hers. My radar should have gone off when she mentioned once that she was getting bored with her role. But I was too busy to make it mean anything about me. It really should have gone way off when she asked me where else I was looking. But I guess I was steeped in denial, hoping my work and loyalty would mean something.

We were cruising along, the summer flew by, and hiring began to slow down at the onset of the fall. I think they just needed to have time to let all the new talent settle in and get to the point of performance. It was either that or the stockholders put on the brakes, or they over-projected sales. At any rate this slowdown gave me time to catch my breath, to hone my tracking and reporting, and to refine and assess what elements of the training could be improved, omitted, or tweaked for optimization. I still had no full contract or stock by November and then was informed that they did, in fact, over-project hiring and that I, and a score or so of others, would be let go. I swear Dr. King; I cannot even begin to tell you where this news sent me. I was thinking I needed an exorcism, or something for some bad karma somewhere. I, for the life of me, could not believe I was hearing this — again! What was it? My career choice? Or just me? I know I did great work. Was it purely the luck of the draw? I know that they appreciated it. They told me on numerous occasions. I know that I was even liked by many, so I just did not get it as a simple calculation.

The corporate environment has changed so drastically, Dr. King. There is no job security anymore. A person can lose their job for any variety of reasons without cause, notice, or apology. Especially in CA, there is what's called "at will" employment. Which translates into, any employer can fire you just because. *Just because I don't like you. Just because you are too happy. Just because I feel like it.* My colleague, however, was spared. I was mad I didn't have my full comprehensive contract inked, as I never got the stock that other new hires received. They were working on the proper classifications and I was too accommodating to demand it for myself. There was a part of me that was afraid to demand anything, because when I spoke up at the other job, I was subsequently let go. Here I did not open my mouth, but I still got the same result! I had only inquired gently, via email once before on the progress of my complete offer because I knew everyone was super busy.

My boss poured hope into my return by telling me to hold on to my equipment because she would find a way to bring me back as a contractor if she could. As it turns out, she did. She called me back in February, but it was only part-time, and it was to package the program, deliver a few orientations, and provide ad-hoc recruiting support. I basically had revolving door employment (two months on, one month off, etc.), from that point on until the onset of the summer of 2013, doing basically whatever was asked of me. I even agreed to represent the company as a Junior Achievement Coach to a class of 11th graders at an East Oakland high school. And that was completely outside of the scope of the role of a contractor. But I was willing to do whatever it took to demonstrate my commitment.

My new hire program had been taken over by my colleague while I was on my road trip (the one that I had only taken because I was told there would be no need for training until after my return). Hindsight. I did not really look for anything else because I really wanted longevity there. I thought I would get a chance when my boss told me that they were budgeted for a fulltime recruiter, but she had transferred the role to my colleague, and I would have to ask her for the position. As much as I hated to do it, I did ask, and she was already poised with her rehearsed rejection. Dr. King, I so regretted that, but I did not want to leave with the "what if" question in my head. So it was checkmate for me, and for the life of me, I could not understand why. Can I say this was racial? Absolutely not. Maybe it was one of those arbitrary situations that I'll never know. But it certainly feels like black people really have to watch their backs in corporate America. We have no room for misperceptions, or slip-ups, or misunderstandings, or miscommunications. You can work as eagerly and as hard as the next guy, but you are walking on thin ice most of the time, and that is very unfortunate. I do not know how we will get over these hurdles. Be more litigious? Develop our own? I don't know. Am I a sample population, no, but I also know that in these circumstances, I am not an anomaly. I have had peers that are afraid to take a vacation from work. Afraid of becoming a 1099 worker, or simply unemployed. So when they are on vacation, they are still checking in on their mobile devices the entire time away.

My most recent full-time job was as an Engineering Sourcer/Recruiter with another small Silicon Valley company that was in growth mode, in process of securing Series E round of funding. This company was very progressive, had lots of money and a great niche market in an emerging technology that was beginning to explode. I came in with a loosely defined role, yet again (why can't I learn?), with other carrots (variety of roles) dangling before me. I agreed because I was out of work, we needed the income, and they allowed me to work from home. My initial reaction was hesitant, but life demands money and I was short.

This was the first time recruiting was my primary responsibility for more than four months since 2001. I was truly rusty. I had forgotten many timesaving and organizational tricks that would have made life initially easier. Additionally, technology had changed as well, tenfold since that time, so there was a bit of a relearning curve. However, the methodology remained the same, so I was not in doubt that I could come up to speed and do a good job.

First impressions are very important, and I certainly blew that by showing up almost an hour late to my first training with everyone. I had the location wrong and found myself at the office 65 miles away from my home, after driving close to three hours, and then had to rush back to the car to drive another 10 minutes to the actual location. I missed the warm and fuzzy part of the training provided by the host company, as well as the introductions. The senior recruiter that hired me was likely somewhat embarrassed as I was her catch, and she was a powerhouse expecting me to be a mini version of her. Well not mini, as I am hardly smaller than most women, but someone that mimicked her style of work and work ethic.

My work started innocently enough, learning the HR team and workflows, the hiring managers, VPs and the newest recruiting strategies and reporting processes. I jumped in with all intentions of doing splendid work. I was also initially excited to know that perhaps, after demonstrating quality results, I would have the opportunity to move into a new role with more variety called HR Business Partner. This would have been an ideal role for me and I expressed real interest. We were still growing and the company was preparing to do a great business, and I felt lucky be a part of the team.

We were ramping up to 300 employees, from the mid-200s, when I came onboard. There were three blacks, including me, that I could count. We had remote workers, so I could be off a bit, but after our conference, I did not think so. Two of us were in HR and the other one was in marketing. He was a newly hired Harvard grad. If I'm to be honest my first thought was, "Damn, does a brotha' have to have a Harvard degree to get up in here?" But I let it go. The company was diverse however. No one could argue that. Some of everybody worked there, from all over the world, but the University Recruiter had no immediate plans to go to Morehouse, or Howard, or Tuskegee to do any recruiting anytime soon as far as I could tell. You could say it was not missed by anyone, except for me of course.

The first thing I had to figure out was what I was looking for with all of my managers. Then, get through the deluge of applicants that had already submitted resumes before I could move beyond that, or so I thought. Having been on the submittal side myself more than a few times, I was compelled to at least look and respond to them first before opting for alternative sourcing techniques. I just had a strong sense of compassion there, and perhaps that was to my disadvantage because there seemed to be a preference for passive candidates rather than active ones. One thing that was very awkward for me was that I had a difficult time adjusting to the sourcing role. I had been used to jumping in doing my thing and figuring it all out. But here I was hand-held a bit too long and created a persona of incompetency because my lead led the meetings and was very good and quick at what she did. For me to jump in most of the time felt exactly like mush to me, so I am pretty sure I came across as incompetent on more than one occasion. I wished she had taken me off her tit the second week there and let me figure it out on my own. But she was very guarded with the clients and the stellar reputation she felt she had secured with most of them. I was not going to have room to lessen that if she could help it. It may be a weak muscle for me there because I retract and observe more in situations like that rather than speak up or out too quickly. And this train was moving too quickly for me to trot along. So in retrospect, I participated in my demise by holding back too long. However, things were moving along and I was doing my best to keep up.

Dr. King, in the high-tech world of engineering, the technology is swift and the competition is dog-eat-dog. Everyone wants to be first to market, and get there as quickly as possible without taking any prisoners, and technology seems to replace or upgrade itself well at the speed of a dotcom minute (my version of a NY minute). One company invents a new technology; shortly thereafter another is on its heels with a newer improved version, and then the next. There is no time to rest on your laurels from the successes of the first product. You have to keep it moving. It is a fierce environment that is only softened by large salaries, extreme budgets of food, dining, entertainment amenities, flex scheduling and lax dress codes to keep the employees in the office longer and engaged in their work practically 24/7 with email and mobile access. Dr. King, these are knowledge workers with engineering degrees primarily. The problem with the lack of blacks in this industry is that Gen X and the Millennials were caught up in the massive downward spiral of public education. So the normal percentages of people with strong interests in the math, science and engineering fields were reduced more dramatically by the lack of a quality education afforded at low-income and non-white public schools. Really, no feeder system for a large quantity of African-American tech workers to begin with. Many other nations were investing in the science and math training of their students and produced large quantities of engineers and knowledge workers, and many of them, made their way to the LOO (Land Of Opportunity, b.k.a. US) to get those jobs and get those jobs they did with extended work visas. So Dr. King, it was like policy makers were more interested in opening opportunities and investing in imported knowledge workers, tens of thousands, than investing and developing the minds of its citizens, black citizens. Adding yet another layer of angst to the racial disparity conversation by calling it a digital divide.

In my role, however, I was screening and sourcing candidates from around the globe. A good percentage of this company's workers could work remotely, so it was interesting to me to interview and potentially hire people from the

UK, France, Italy, Russia, and Germany. I have to admit I had racial fears about the candidates like they would see me on the web camera and treat me as if I did not matter, or did not know what I was doing. So I primarily entered the calls with the pretense of showing them how smart I was. I would always take a deep breath before I engaged with one of them and stared intensely looking for a reaction, surprise, dismay, or an air of superiority to my blackness. But one hundred percent of the time, there was none. I did not perceive any indifference at all and was comforted by the seemingly international acceptance. It could have been simply that I was holding the key to the particular job, or it could have been simply their humanity. In either case I was pleased.

We had a conference in the early fall to promote our organization, attract industry leaders, and to build upon the technology. It was attended by tech workers from across the globe. The attendance reported at approximately 2,500 people. And Dr. King here is what was sad about that for me. I was one of the five, yes five blacks in attendance. I scanned and scanned and looked and looked, but could not find more than that. I mentioned this to one of my coworkers and told him I would give him $20 if he could find more. I kept my $20. And, no I was not blaming the organization per se; but it was a strong statement about the lack of black workers in the tech industry as a whole.

It was not long after the conference that I was let go Dr. King. I had two more administrative mishaps, and one verbal mistake, before I was told my services were no longer needed. This was one of those times where I got off to a bad start and then it seemed that every little mishap was amplified thereafter diminishing my reputation. I could never tell if any of my clients appreciated my work, until I told them I would no longer be working with them. A few of them seemed genuinely surprised and expressed slight confusion and warm acknowledgments for my work. That shocked me because they gave me the impression on our weekly video meetings that they had no real appreciation for anything I did. I was somewhat saddened for my personal loss, but I was more concerned if they would discount black workers more because of me. With me gone, they were down to two blacks out of 300 we had grown to. One of the VPs said to me after receiving the news trying to have me leave on a high note, "not all flowers thrive in the same environment." That put it into perspective for me somewhat, but I still worried if they would hire any more African violets without someone like me to urge them along. C'est la vie.

WHAT'S THE FUTURE?

(Will It Get Better?)
Women, children, men,
Take it into the palms of your hands.
Mold it into the shape of your most
Private need. Sculpt it into
The image of your most public self.
Lift up your hearts
Each new hour holds new chances
For new beginnings.
Do not be wedded forever
To fear, yoked eternally
To brutishness.
The horizon leans forward,
Offering you space to place new steps of change.
Here, on the pulse of this fine day
You may have the courage
To look up and out upon me, the
Rock, the River, the Tree, your country.
No less to Midas than the mendicant.
No less to you now than the mastodon then.
Here on the pulse of this new day
You may have the grace to look up and out
And into your sister's eyes, into
Your brother's face, your country
And say simply
Very simply
With hope
Good morning.

—From Inaugural Poem, "On the Pulse of Morning" by Maya Angelou, 1993

Dr. King, A New Dream Is Needed

Dear Dr. King,

We are coming upon the 50th anniversary of your tragic murder, and it is really the best of times and the worst of times. It appears there will always be extremes in this country and in the world. I think for us black people, we were not ushered into a burning house so much as we have been walking on continuous lava flows with some areas cooled or hardened enough to enter and stand. Yet others are still very hot and burn everything on contact. Some of it a fast and deadly burn, while other parts are slow moving and permeating. Laws were passed, but justice is still not just, and changed laws do not change morality.

We have a new president who claims he's not a racist, but he is certainly playing one on TV. He usurped the electoral vote, allegedly, with the help of the Russians, yes, the Russians, conservative gerrymandering and voter suppression. He lost the popular vote, to what would have been our first female president, by over 3,000,000, but since he's been in office he appears to be on a mission to lock down the borders and remove 3,000,000 "brown and black"people from our country through stricter immigration laws and enforcement. He appears to want to create the permanent "white" billionaire class in power and have everyone who doesn't look like him, think like him, and behave like him in second and or third class citizenry. And unfortunately, after just one year, he is off to a good start. His campaign mantra was Make America Great Again, in which everyone I know, black and white, is code for Make America White Again.

Black people got stuck with unity, and I mean this in a contradictory way. As a people, we feel we are accountable for all the ills of everyone we look like. Like we are permanently living with "my brother's keeper" syndrome. Except many feel the contract was signed without their permission. My cousin said to me in a phone conversation recently that she felt they dropped the ball on teaching my generation (whom I dubbed "The Benefactors of the Dream"), how to stay unified and prosper as a people, because they were too busy running to the "free" access and money to make their claims. These runs were mostly north and west, to leave behind the suffocating forces of Jim Crow, but also to grab at "the dream" via the industrial revolution. That grab required assimilating, and she said much was lost in the translation. The reaches they made propelled them into unchartered territory with no map, no tour guide, no rule book, and no emergency plan; much like the slave-ship voyages, but by their will, unchained, and with far less physical constraints. However, reach they did, and by the time they reached the destination and began to build their dreams, other planned forces were in design to decimate and strip those dreams away. Drugs, red-lining, economic segregation, gerrymandering, imaging, white appropriation, birth control, abortion, sterilization, disease, mass incarceration. "The Wheel of Racial Misfortune." Some call it attempted genocide. All malicious with varying degrees of death, destruction, and dismemberment, born out of evil and fear of retaliation. Some of its effects were instant. Some slow and painful. Some invisible but invasive. Some highly toxic and deadly. But even with all that aimed directly at us, WE ARE STILL HERE! We are survivors, and even "thrivers," but not without our battle scars.

As a people, we have achieved "integration" and "assimilation" into almost all systems and excel in many of them. Even reaching to the highest of the high in many. Have even created some of our OWN systems. But we are not a people in the sense of a unit of one with the same hopes and aspirations foundationally supported by a unified, in-sync, and close-proximity monolithic culture. Those days are gone. I feel close geography is required at least to gain any type of renaissance. And therein lies the unity problem, because that is not going to happen any time soon.

Unlike sea turtles, there is no natal homing device; we don't have a working internal compass leading us by magnetic pull to an "earthly" place where we hatched. It has been distorted and off its axis for centuries. You can say it is Africa, but no one I know wants to go there to live right now.

You can say it is the South, but I have few relatives there who consider it the best place on earth. No one is planning a pilgrimage to reclaim the South. It almost feels like it would be a step backward.

Free will, yes. Free access, yes. Most of the time. But freedom, as we know it, is an illusion. Can't have it without consequences; can't have it without imposing on another's. Wrong dream for this time, but right for its time. Wrong word for these times. We need another. And I do not know what that word would be.

The dream is bigger now. Or at least different. My kids have attended schools with people from all over the world. They have friends of many nationalities, hold hands, pray, play, and dream together. We can check that one as mission accomplished. Sure there are pockets in our country, which are still very segregated and hold on to prejudices very strongly. But I do not think it is a majority, and I do not think the Millennials and Generation Z? (those born after 1990) are so plagued with the trappings of race the way prior generations have been. They have just been caught in the recent crossfires of its stronghold on the older generations. But they are coming into their own, finding their human voices. So there is real hope there.

Many of my peers have done extremely well and have professional careers and lives they love. They own properties, are leaders in their fields, highly degreed, and are world travelers. And they had to work a bit harder for it, in many cases, harder than their white counterparts, but they made it. Some have taken blows for the team.

They have persevered. But they do not exactly feel free. However, you would be extremely proud of them.

I think I have voted in every presidential election since I was 18, thank you! But I only started understanding politics, and what it means to speak up, get out and participate, after I met my husband. So we are doing things at the community level and have a core group of friends who are also very politically active. No one as bold and bodacious as you, but we are in there and enrolling others. And now we all need to turn it up a notch or two.

You might be glad to know that you have a holiday, streets, schools, museums, movies, sculptures, and volumes of books to commemorate your life, vision, contributions, sacrifices, courage and perseverance to fight for what is right. Not all of them represent your true legacy. Some of the schools and streets signs are in areas that need radical improvement. And worse still, many schools have whittled down your contributions to a March and a Speech, but I know better.

The most recent installations to honor and re-voice your legacy, I personally call The Rock, The River, and The Tree. (I have a habit of secretly renaming things and people, and this is in homage to Maya Angelou.)

In Washington, D.C. there is a commemorative stone sculpture called the *MLK, Jr. Memorial* at the Washington Mall. It has two main features: *A Mountain of Despair,* and on the backside, *A Stone of Hope,* which is a 28-foot replica of you emerging out of the stone. So I think of it as The Rock. It looks pretty impressive from the photos I have seen. It is nestled between the Abraham Lincoln and Thomas Jefferson memorials. I plan to see it this summer.

There was a movie released in 2015, called *Selma*, all about the struggle and your organized campaigns for our voting rights. Since it is a motion picture and thus moves from frame to frame, I call it The River.

And The Tree...well Tavis Smiley, a TV journalist, author and civil rights advocate, one of your most dedicated supporters, wrote a new book (in 2014) about the last year of your life entitled, *Death of A King*. He said it was his love letter to you to pay homage to your legacy and sacrifices. The book stands on its own merit, however, Tavis is now being accused of sexual misconduct, and since O.J.'s not guilty verdict, as soon as a famous black male gets accused of anything, the populous trend has been to also incriminate (or devalue) their body of work, almost immediately, and certainly before any trials. It should be called the "O.J. Effect" perhaps. However, I read and appreciated the book, and I call it The Tree for the obvious reason that it is paper. I think you would be pleased with them all, and I know you pray that they are not in name only, but somehow in their limited communications get people to move and act accordingly.

I met Martin III, in 2014, in Oakland, at Allen Temple Church in east Oakland, CA. He seemed like a gracious man, a gentleman's gentleman. I only spoke with him briefly, but that was my first impression. He came to speak about the state of race relations, President Obama, and The King Center. He also spoke about the books of your intellectual works and research that is continuously being edited and published by Clayborne Carson at Stanford University, via the Martin Luther King Papers Project. I cannot wait to read and learn more about your brilliance.

I went to meet Martin because of my personal mission. I was not even supposed to be in the same room with him. But I followed him pretending to be one of his entourage, and then the door was shut in my face when I got to it. I waited and snuck in when the guard wasn't looking and someone came out. Martin was kind enough to talk to me and to take pictures with me also. He seemed genuinely interested in my book idea. That made me really happy. My mission was to ask him to write the Foreword or Afterword to this collection of letters to you. I sent emails to the woman he told me to a couple of times, but I didn't get any replies. So I just let it be. It's not too late. He could still do it. Maybe he will contact me post-release. Either way, I'm okay.

Dr. King, what I realize more about you as I grow older, is that you were definitely a Godsend, because most people do not normally get away from their own self-seeking ambitions and think globally until they are much older than 39. Much less stand up and speak about it. You matured so quickly. Became a man's man! Truly became a man of God. Representing his unconditional love of humanity. You were certainly connected to the

Love Supreme. No one can dispute that! Your resolve, my oh my! If that could be bottled and distributed broadly—WOW! What a different place this world would be!

I do not know where we are headed in this country. Relations are now polarized again and rightly so. There is still much injustice, and unfortunately many of our people are still bearing the brunt of it. Life is not valued anymore. And black lives, it seems, lesser still. It is way too easy for people to kill these days. Like it is everybody's right, no matter how minor the infraction. And practically everybody has a gun. Not just pistols, either. The average person can have collections of militia-type weapons and will use them, it seems, at the drop of a dime. We are a violent society, no doubt. And that violence is amplified over and over by the continuous stream of senseless mass shootings of various people, and even the children, Dr. King—while in school. They are killing the children! The country was certainly born through extreme uses of violence, so perhaps it is just the natural progression. I don't know, but I do believe love, and only love, will overcome it. We certainly need love to pour out and pour down like a mighty stream all over and around this country and the world. So there is still much, much work for us to do.

The world has developed technologies that would blow your mind. Technologies that can communicate to thousands of people in an instant. One is called social media. You peer into a screen (like a TV screen) that has a keyboard, a camera, and a microphone and speaker so you can talk or send messages to practically anybody in the world, any time of day, with the same access, and without leaving your house. You'd think it would be easier for us all to get on the same page—the love page—and all get along, but wherever we go, there we are. So people are just not ready to give up the ghost. We are all up in arms about the lost levels of personal privacy because of it. There is a part of me that thinks the loss of some privacy may be the very thing that causes people to begin to have more compassion, empathy, and understanding—and therefore more love for each other. A bit like that seminar I did that opened my eyes. I think it can give people a broader understanding of each other—if they cannot travel. And perhaps, just perhaps, they can begin to see that nobody is perfect and everybody has faults. Then maybe the shame and guilt people carry that makes them do stupid and strange things under the guise of keeping it in the dark, will help them see that their faults may not be such a big deal, and all that ego craziness will just melt away. I know some things are better left unsaid and unheard, but I was just running with that for a bit as a possibility.

Anyway, Dr. King, I think your dream has been fulfilled to some degree and that the new dream has to be expanded or redirected to mental freedom, as soon as we can tamper down this newly unleashed and boldly stated rise in racial hatred and white nationalism. The laws have been changed, and there is still plenty of injustice. But if people can truly get to that sacred place in their hearts and live "To thine own self be true," and achieve mental freedom, then we may have a solid chance at breaking down these racial walls. And that is what I wanted to tell you. I love you. I wish you had countless clones here. But we will get there. God willing.

Thank you for your vision and contributions to humanity! We are better for it! You made a real and lasting difference. I know because we cannot stop talking about you!

Godspeed,
Wanda

Dear President Obama, Before You Leave Office...

Dear President Obama,

(Dated: April 2015) Congratulations! I really mean congratulations! You actually stepped into that space and made "freakin'" history! It was brilliant. Oh and your family, how lovely! You guys are just so swank! I loved that you were willing to get out there and bust the lid off the flea jar we had all been bouncing under. Thank you, thank you, thank you! I never thought I would see a black president in my lifetime, and a black family in The White House. And that gives me hope for this country. I so loved that you put in a basketball court! It is, after all, American-made. I just got so tickled by that.

I had fun when I found out Michelle and I have the same birthday, but I am one year older. I started taking pictures of myself to replicate some of her photos. I even considered auditioning to play her comedic double on TV, or in the movies, but I chickened out. I got as far as posting it on social media. I saw her in person in San Francisco once, at the Fairmount Hotel, in 2010. She came with Jill Biden, Nancy Pelosi, and Kamala Harris to promote women in politics, and campaigning for midterms, of course. She is just as awesome in person!

When you were elected, I was a bona fide middle-class American, maybe even on the lower side of upper-middle-class-dom. Today, I am holding on to middle-class-dom by the skin of my teeth. But primarily in idea, not in ownership and assets. We bottomed out in 2011 with the foreclosure of our "close-enough" dream house, after a double-barrel round of lay-offs for both my husband and I. I do not blame you for our circumstances; it truly was a combination of being in the wrong place at the wrong time and without thorough, long-term planning. I/we own our part in our misfortune. But I do wish with the whole mortgage and financial crisis and subsequent bailout, that you would have tied some enforceable accountability requirements to the banks before you gave them our money. Like make sure responsible homeowners got a fair shot at refinancing. It really felt like you set the banks up to turn the knife, after they had already stabbed us, multiple times.

I personally love that you moved forward and secured the Affordable Care Act; it has already made a difference for us. But being in the world of IT for my career, I have no idea how the website fumbled at the onset the way it did. I only wished you had a cleaner start with that website and avoided all the drama that followed. I know it was a massive unprecedented effort, but someone jacked you on the technological side, because that crap should have never happened. *But I ain't mad at you for that either.*

I really hated that the attacks came out the way they did at the beginning of your presidency from Mr. Joe "You lie" Wilson, to Mitch "One-term president" McConnell and his allies. But I am pretty sure you had some idea of what you were getting into. I just wish you did not have to bear all of that. **No one on earth knows what it's like to be you! No one! No one, not one! Not even your 43 predecessors — because they were not black! You, Mr. President, are in a class all by yourself, and I hope at the very least that you are not lonely!** No other president has taken the bashing and threats and hatemongering and political attacks that you have. It is shameful. I believe in freedom of speech, but that crap was just wrong. I often wonder if your "congressional adversaries" (and that phrase sounds like treason in the current climate) had spent just one-tenth the time and energy to support you instead of tear you down, where we would be now as a country. But we will never know that. Sure, I can point the finger at you for all kinds of political, social, moral, financial, and institutional ills, but really where would that get me right now? Nowhere. I do not have the time anyway. And I truly am of a mind to stop complaining and get back to work.

So for my personal losses, I am over them now. It was extremely hard when they happened. I am sure it was harder for my husband, being a man. A black man. An older black man with school-age children. In California no less. A former homeowner for 33 years. The first male in his family to graduate college. A decades-long, solid career as a computer developer. With a heart of gold for the success of our children in these schools. But I think he is coming out of it too. He surprises me with his tenacity for trying new things and going with the flow. I guess that is part of the reason I fell in love with him.

You say you are fighting for the middle class, and I believe that you did. But I cannot say I even know what middle class is anymore, given my paths. I think it was originally deemed to define having the earnings of the average American, like in the middle. But we have billionaires now, so how can a majority of a people reach multi-millionaire status to get to the middle of income earners in America? I am being somewhat hyperbolic, but really what does middle class mean? Is it having a job, and a mortgage no matter how much debt that mortgage represents, with some savings, and maybe a 401k? Or is it having a college degree and living in a decent neighborhood, with no mortgage debt (renting) and a specific income level? Or is it owning a house outright and earning just enough to maintain it and pay your taxes? Or is it having access to travel and the freedom to make enough to keep you and your family housed, clothed and fed, with adequate health care? Or is it having the mindset that you are not poor, no matter what your circumstances? I still feel middle class, maybe I am in extreme denial, but I do. Today I have no job, no savings, debt, and am 52. And oddly enough, not suicidal, homicidal, or even angry with you, nor with the world, like some of my brethren. Not even left without hope. Yeah, there's that word again—hope! In my case, it still springs eternal. I do not know why, and have to say it is God in me that keeps me from completely losing it. Also my kids. Close in age to yours. I have to show up for them. Get kicked down, get back up. Get kicked down, get back up. Get kicked down, get the hell up! So I am here, getting up, and now embarking on a new career because that HR world just has not been stable for me. I am taking a word from T.D. Jakes and trying to "monetize" my passion, and not just continue to do what I was trained to do. So we will see what happens. (I do not think employers will be calling me anyway with this book out there!) So I may have to make my own income stream(s). It might be easier for Taylor Swift to get another boyfriend than for me to get another job (just over broke), with all my kissing-and-telling. Actually, I am sure Taylor will have no problem getting boyfriends. Maybe I should write a song about it instead. But "Que sera, sera, ..." this book is gonna do what it's gonna do. And me, well I'm gonna do what I'm gonna do. I think I am an emotional worker first, then functional, and then committed, with a healthy dose of hyper-creativity underlining all of that. My cup certainly runneth over in that department. I have to believe in the work before I get my head around it, and then I can produce quality and sometimes-extraordinary results. So perhaps my career mojo will come in the arts or communications industries.

I never thought I would be 52 trying to figure this out still, but here I am. I could easily fall back on being a wife and mother and dedicate my life to solely making my husband and kids happy. But I think that breed of woman expired with the 20th century. There is just too much stimulation in the world today for me to be content with fulltime family matters only. All this, and I am a relatively happy and joyous person. My friends seem to thoroughly enjoy my company, so I must be okay and not crazy. But none of this is your problem. It is my American story, and I was just rambling a bit. But here is what I would really like for you to read and think about, maybe even respond to—if you would be that generous with your time.

You have just under two years left, and you have made your declarations in the State of the Union 2015; nothing earth-shattering, but it felt like you meant every word and that you really want to leave us in a much better place before you exit. I truly believe you do! But like every other American, I have my own thoughts about priorities and sometimes wish I could wave a magic wand to make them happen. **In my serial bouts of mental wrangling, there are five things that I truly wish you would do before you leave office. So here are my Top Five:**

1) Level-set education in this country! Equalize the playing field. End the economic segregation of quality primary and secondary education! I know that this request is an oversimplification, and I will present no research or fact-based suggestions as to how this gets accomplished. But I also know the solutions are not rocket science. As one example, the monies from the military budget that was recently cut can be earmarked to increase teachers' salaries across the board, and reform and standardize a global, comprehensive curriculum that is currently only afforded privately (you know, the same level of education that Malia and Sasha are experiencing, that Chelsea Clinton received, and all the presidents' school-age children before them). For every American: black, white, rich, poor, first-generation, or tenth-generation, quality public education should be our inalienable, foundational birthright in the pursuit of our happiness. Because you and I know that the current state of public education is arguably the new Jim Crow — as well as the prison systems, with the low-income schools set-up being the pipeline to prison. We've all witnessed the maniacal and expedient deterioration of the public-education system, and the growth and expansion of the private tutoring corporations. It has been going on for decades, but George W. put it on speed-dial. *No Child Left Behind* is an assault on the minds of our most vulnerable citizens. They are being strip-mined of their innate genius. Please fix it. Our children deserve better.

2) Apologize for slavery. What? Negroes, Black Americans, Afro-Americans, African-Americans, and I, have been wanting and waiting for an American "President" to apologize to us all for the heinous, centuries-long, terroristic destructive reign of slavery; not just congress. None of your predecessors have dared to do it despite the fact that every other abused foreign nationalist has been given an apology with reparations to boot. Even the Jews (a religion and not a race) have had America and American Presidents apologize for the Holocaust in some manner, and that happened in Germany. And Israel is still in the pockets of America for it. So I ask, especially in this "hyper-racial," misnamed "post-racial" period in our country's history, and on behalf of the white side of your ancestry, and by the powers bestowed upon you in the full authority of your office, will you apologize to your native sons and daughters, as well as to the peoples on the continent of Africa? The world really needs for this to happen.

I do not fully understand why this was such a difficult thing to do/admit by your predecessors, while in office or post-office positions (I mean I do understand the racist part of it), but the time has come for this statement, proclamation—and you, Chief Executive Officer, are at the helm.

2.a.) As a product of that apology, every black American should be able to receive a tax-credit for a DNA analysis to identify our ancestral place of origin. I know we will never have reparations (a civil war would likely ensue first, if that were decreed!), but in lieu of that, how about the tax-credit? America owes us at least that!

3) Finish the ACA and make it a single-payer system. We are almost there, and it can be done. Let's finish it.

4) Rethink and change how we categorize Americans. Take race off the table. What if we reclassified how we classify people? Sort of like a job reclassification, but a people reclassifying that is NOT ROOTED IN RACE. What if all birth certificates are stamped "American." Not Black, not White, not Asian, not Hispanic, just American. I cannot think of one benefit I am allotted today because I check the black box. Isn't the genesis of the race classification tied to geography anyway? If I am born in America, I should be American. Period. Then we would factor in where the parents were from, only to determine if the newborn is first generation American, or second-generation American, or third, fourth, fifth, etc., as best as we can determine. Kind of a radical approach, but humor me here.

Now let's take it one step further. What if then also, your tenure, or seniority, for lack of a better term, was tied to some tax benefit based on your American-ness. Like some type of a sliding scale having the oldest generational Americans pay less in taxes, or gain more tax reductions via credits. May sound a little off the chain, and I have not even expressed this idea to anyone to hear if it is, but it makes sense to me. I know personally, I think it is unfair for others to come here and reap the same governmental benefits that those who have been here for generations, who have put generations of blood, sweat, and tears into creating, fighting for, and implementing. It appears that immigrants can, in some cases, extract the same if not more benefits, or safety nets than those of us who have been in our great country for generations. And many do it without having to vote, or pay taxes, or be documented, and that is just wrong to me. It is like they reap the rewards without fully contributing, and I do have a problem with that. That is all of this thought bubble. I just wanted to put it out there to see what you thought.

However, I do think if we just start with "American" documentation, we can at least begin to minimize or maybe begin to eradicate the race conversation. I have been thinking of many, many things, and continue to get all kind of out-of-the-box ideas. But I will not share them all.

5) Fix the water crisis that is beginning to cascade. I am not all the way tapped into how the infrastructure, distribution, and rights to adequately articulate how water works, but I just have a strong feeling that with all the hydraulic fracking and commercialization of drinking water happening today, we are headed for a serious water war if this issue isn't dived into and plugged up before it becomes disastrous. Survival of the richest, or whoever, has the most arms calamity. **Drinking water is our basic human right.** Please do what you can do now, and do not let the greed and corruption that is trickling in create an unprecedented crisis and have us all turn on each other for basic survival. That is not the country I want my kids to inherit.

I could go on, but I wanted to limit it to five. I could especially go on about the wars, killings, drone attacks, infrastructure, race relations, tax reform, solar, etc., but for me, these five things are on my shortlist. It does not mean that I am uncaring about the rest, because I do care, but for the things that would affect my life right now, right today, this is where my head is. It may change tomorrow, but this book will have already been published, so I will stand by it and defer my other thoughts for another time and platform.

Oh, and as a sidebar, and completely within your control, please do not go on another sketch comedy show with people like "what's his name." The one who asked you "how does it feels to be the last black president?" I hated that show. It was completely beneath you. He was disrespectful whether it was scripted or not, and that was not funny! You are bigger than that. Do not lower yourself to do another, pleez! Find other ways to reach your younger constituents. The community college thing is a GREAT start. More stuff like that.

May God bless, restore, and protect you and your family! I will forever be grateful for your service and sacrifice! All of it! Whether I agree or not! In my eyes, the Obamas (and Grandma Robinson) rock!

With God's blessing,
Citizen Wanda

Dear Black People

Dear Black People,

I love you. You are beautiful...classically beautiful! I am here, I am also one, and I am one with you. Like you, I yearn for peace, justice, equality, prosperity, and freedom. But I also yearn for the solitude of individuality and authentic expression. Two extremely difficult freedoms to acquire in a race-based society. Yes, our ancestry and our skin binds us, but our spirituality and humanity goes deeper than that, deeper than the assertion and recognition of race. I want to get back to that. We were not blind when we didn't see race. We were blind-sided and became blind because of it. And constant and persistent focus on that keeps us lost. And that is the truth!

There are times when I want to set this mutha' off, and times it feels truly like I can't breathe. But until God takes my breath away, I will continue to exhale and inhale each and every breath exemplifying His glory in this beautiful, bountiful, temple I was given. And really that is what we all must do. Live our highest self! Thanks Oprah!

I have been blessed and fortunate enough to have experienced the love of a black father, grandfather, six brothers, eight nephews, hosts of male cousins and uncles, my husband, and my son. Full circle. I hope that I will also experience the love of a grandson. What I can tell you about black male love you already know, but to reiterate, it is all consuming, insanely loyal, warm, protective, funny, complicated, piercing, demanding, gentle, spontaneous, hard, righteous, and profound. It is truly all of that. And I am better for it.

To be doubly blessed, I have also experienced the love of a black mother, grandmothers, two sisters, nine nieces, hosts of female cousins and aunts, and my daughter. Full circle. I also hope to experience the love of a granddaughter. What I can tell you about black female love you already know, but to reiterate, it is essential, profound, nurturing, emotional, liberal, protective, generous, complicated, tender, sacrificial, trusting, moody, insanely loyal, uncompromising, and strong. And I am better for it.

God has truly blessed me.

I have also personally experienced the deaths of those types of love, from sudden death, diseased death, aging death, accidental, suicidal, homicidal, and natural spontaneous abortion. What I can tell you about losing black love you already know, but to reiterate, it is painful, heart wrenching, gut wrenching, mournful, conflicting, tragic, indigestible, and sorrowful. It hurts!

So I understand intricately what it's like to be you/me.

I am feeling this race conversation is a perpetual trap, and I for one am ready for mental freedom. It is the next frontier, and this freedom white people cannot give us. That is something we have to attain on our own, within our own individuality and spirit.

So as a people are we Black? Yes. But aren't we also American with African ancestry? Just like Negro, Black is an oversimplification, and in reality, especially in this country, our country, it denotes negativity. I am tired of being in defense of my natural self. So why are we holding on to this black-ness and why are we giving white Americans a free pass to be American first? How come we are African-American, and they are American? What benefit has that provided us? How come when we hear reports describing each other, they say "man" in reference to themselves, and say "black man" in reference to us? Is a black man black first, or a man first?

Now before you go crazy, and start sending me nasty-grams and posting retaliatory "keeping it real" hash tags all over cyber-space via social media, let me explain what I mean. I'll start by saying, I'm not asking you to be white, lose your culture, admonish your race, or pretend like your skin color is not dark/brown/black, or that it does not say something to the rest of the world about you and your ancestry. That is not what I mean. I am asking you to consider that in Africa, before the European invasion, Africans were "Africans," identified by their indigenous lands, families, tribes, nations. Black was not in the language of their identity. Negro (Spanish for black) was what the Spaniards decided to name them out of their fear, ignorance, and as an oversimplification. They identified them by the easiest common denominator. All of the other derivatives and translations of Negro ensued, each one more derogatory than the last. We reincorporated the term "Black" post-civil rights as a term of endearment, as our self-pride and identity in an attempt to restore pride in our God-given beauty and to dissuade ourselves from adapting the European standards of what is beautiful as a culture. Our aesthetic self-determination. Shortly after that we changed again, and today we're African-American. But aren't we really American first? Why aren't we claiming that? I think the hyphen helps circumvent our true ownership. We need to rethink this.

We should reclaim our birthright and lose the hyphenation. Just as in the Bible, in The Book of John, it begins with the Word. Our words have power, and how we use them, more power still.

I do not want to spend the next 50 years with a large percentage of my mental energy in a racial context. As I said in my introduction, it's stealing my grace and joy. For me, having race at the frontal cortex of my every interaction perpetuates and makes more pervasive, more real, and therefore everlasting, the conversation of race. Which is, really, first a social (because that's what the society said we were), cultural (because we said okay and became it), and then psychological (now what the hell does that mean?) prison. And having it remain that way means they win. We lose. Perpetually. Yes, you belong to a family, a community, a geography, a race (man-made), a world.

This does not mean ignore and pretend that racial realisms in the world do not exist: like ignoring a speeding car and walking out into the street and thinking it will not hit you, because ignoring dangerous things can do grave harm. But regard it as something we do not have to allow to occupy our pre-thoughts, and after-thoughts, about how things are. Can you even imagine that?

What if we individually tried on viewing the world, instead of immediately assessing and judging people by their demographic — and this would be for white people too. What if we lived by **"There are two types of people in the world — me and everybody else?"** You know, like our fingerprints. You are uniquely you. You came into the world alone, and you are going to die alone. You are the only you there is on this earth, out of seven billion people and counting. **NO ONE ELSE IS EXACTLY LIKE YOU.** So try this on: you truly only know yourself, and everyone else you do not know, and you have to learn about those you interact with. Does shifting the paradigm provide any mental freedom for you? If you looked through this lens instead of the familial, tribal, cultural, and racial viewpoint(s) or perspective(s), would it shift the focus for you?

We have all heard the adage: Expecting something different by doing the same thing over and over is the definition of insanity. So how can we expect anything different if we do not start with the first thing each of us can do, individually and collectively, by recreating the views and language for how we speak about race? The thoughts come first, and then the languaging. We cannot solve racial indifference using the current vocabulary and vernacular. Many of the terms were designed to be divisive as their very definitions; giving us the short end of the stick. **So like AA (Alcoholics Anonymous), here is my 12-Step Plan:**

1) Lose black, hyphenations, and the "N" word as descriptions of who we are. Just stop. Stop saying them. Stop answering to them. Stop singing and dancing to them. Stop endearing them. Stop. **Lose also: "underprivileged," "under-served," "minority," "at-risk-youth," "inner-city," "person of color," "born a slave" and "came from nothing"** to describe ourselves and especially, our youth. Quit tagging them/us with inferiority! Stop participating in the self-marginalization. It is self-mutilation and AIN'T HELPING NOBODY!

2) Self-Determinate. We share ancestry, historical, and social injustices perpetrated upon us, but we are tribal, all people are tribal. Black is not a religion to believe in. Treat your immediate family as your nation. That is powerful to even say. A nation, my family. We often use village, but nation has a higher calling. More purpose! You will be the leader. Manage your nation for education, health, prosperity, and sustainability. If we do that, the collective nation of our people will be powerful.

3) Run, don't walk to the nearest voters' registrar and get yourself registered. And then vote. Period! Stop thinking that someone else is going to speak your truth. Speak your own! We have to participate in this system, like it or not. If we do not participate, we have no voice, and our needs are not going to be addressed. It is our birthright and our complete responsibility! **Get involved at the local level. Start with your community and your elected officials.** Go meet them, make them talk to you. Tell them your stories and needs. Help them understand broadly. You cannot hold them accountable if they do not know you and your concerns.

4) Create and control our image(s)! You better believe a picture is worth a thousand words. It is, it is, it is! We have got to fight fire with fire on this one. For every negative image you see, add ten more positive ones to deprogram the negative views. We can do that every day, all day long, on every social media outlet we interact with. Even if it is nothing but a selfie of you looking good and smiling. Just do it!

5) Begin to recognize everything as a system. Most "systems" were designed and created without your input or best life in mind. Understand that systems were made up by someone, and that it is not, or does not have to be "the way it is" — forever! What can be made can be remade. Step back, review that system. Choose to be a part of it or not. Do not just fall in line to what is served up. As the Scarecrow in the movie *The Wiz*, played by Michael Jackson, said, "Never accept any situation...question, argue, and explore." Do that, but do so with the best outcome in mind.

6) Begin to develop and create your own systems. System think. System think. System think. If you can't beat them (whoever you deem "them" to be), or can't join "them," create your own! This includes businesses. Make the current system irrelevant to your survival and success. We are all endowed with unlimited creative powers.

7) Buy some land. And grow something. If you cannot buy land, plant something in the land you are on. If you cannot plant in the land you are on, get a pot or bucket. It sounds esoteric, but something very profound and grounding occurs when you dig into the earth to produce something from it. Make it a practice. Maybe even grow some of your own food.

8) Get your DNA analyzed so you know. Just get it done. Take the guesswork out of your ancestral regional origins. It makes a difference.

9) Learn our history. Read an African or African-American book regularly. Know your history, not just for the sake of information, but so that you understand how not to repeat and guard against tragic mistakes we have already lived through. *"Education is a companion that no misfortune can depress, no crime can destroy, no enemy can alienate, no despotism can enslave. In solitude a solace and in society an ornament. It chastens vice, it guides virtue, it gives at once grace and government to genius. Without it, what is man? A splendid slave, a reasoning savage."* **Joseph Addison**

10) Travel. Get out of Dodge. Wherever your Dodge is. If you live in your own bubble your whole life, you have a very limiting perspective. Reading books can help, but truly, life is the best teacher! Get your passports. Make it a priority. Go see the world. Period. Globalize you. Just like that Oleta Adams song, "Get Here" says, "...by railway, airplane, caravan, cross the desert like an

Arab man, just get here/there." There is even a Megabus now. Travel.

11) As always, and this one should be a given, but to reiterate, speak out against injustices, all injustices, ALL THE TIME! We have to remain hyper-vigilant about this. If 2014 did not convince us that speaking up is imperative to our survival, I do not know what will. It has already been said by the glorious man I wrote this book to, *"Injustice anywhere is a threat to injustice everywhere!"* Dr. Martin Luther King, Jr.

12) Meditate. Pray. Forgive. We have many, many churches. We go to them all the time. But do we really go in? Into that sacred place that only you can reach? That sacred place of the Most High that gets you infinitely connected to what is truly sourcing you? You have to get there. It is your Divine assignment, and it takes practice. Be still. Let go. Peace, Grace, and Purpose are there waiting for you.

So this is my armchair philosophy, or street prescription, to help eliminate or cure the internal psychosis of post-traumatic racial stress syndrome. I am here with you in the daily battlefield and taking it one day at a time. I am sure I will have my critics, and that is okay. We have a world to heal, and it all starts with the willingness to communicate. But please do not hate on me for the sake of hating on me. That would be wasting more time. I hope you like my book. I know that I am not speaking for everyone. Remember individuality and mental freedom is the new frontier. The rest I think will follow. Almost like a natural byproduct. So I encourage you to begin your own book, or blog, or journal. It is very cathartic and healing. Just start. You will be transformed.

I love you! I honor you!

Your sister,
Wanda

Dear African Immigrants

Dear African Immigrants,

Welcome to America! I love you! I'm so glad you are here, especially by your own free will. Way to end a cycle! I love that I am able to see the faces, hear the voices, and feel the warmth of the peoples of my ancestry in-person rather than on a "please help" television commercial, an exotic worldly magazine cover, or "give now" postcard. I am glad I've gotten to know the wonders of the many of you I have encountered and embraced. Through you, I have gained more information and understanding about the beauties and the ills of our motherland; from fascinating countries like Ethiopia, Somalia, Egypt, Eritrea, Kenya, Cameroon, Nigeria, Sierra Leone, and other places. But please, please, do not adopt a posture that holds the same prejudges and behaviors mirroring the 20th-century oppressors...because that is just very wrong. You need not fear us; we are you. You need not distance yourselves, nor step on our shoulders without even a "hello" or "thank you"; please do not go there. It plays right into the hand of racism and does not serve our humanity.

You may not completely understand the mindset of the media blacks you have come to know through the screens that have cleverly, narrowly, and bitterly defined who the-lot-of-us are in this country. You may be confused why we are in the richest land in the world and still have so far to go on the trajectory of true and sustaining systemic success. But be empathetic, not critical, as you also wear the gilded mask. Yes, take the high road, but do so with grace and humility. Although the rat-a-tat melodic accents of your voices conjure up a romantic charm and innocence about who you are, to Americans white and black, seeming to give you more instant access than the distant sentencing those of us born here are accustomed to, we are all swimming in the same cesspool. Be mindful and in remembrance that your land has also been contaminated, and many of your minds poisoned by the evil white men did and still do. Some of that poison has virally and in perpetuity infected vast areas of your entire continent, leaving physical and emotional ghettos for you to flee from. And solemnly pray for a return to its indigenous, homogenous, "Eden-istic" (I think I made this word up), continental wealth, while you pursue your wealthy aspirations here.

We are more alike than not, and I honor you.

Your sister in ancestry,
Wanda

Dear Rational White People

Dear Rational White People,

I love you. Damn, it must be hard to be you too. But, on an incalculably different level of hard to be us. Everybody blames you for everything. Hell, if you just got here, or were born in the latter half of the 20th century, you inherited most of this paralyzing bullshit too. The good, the bad, and the ugly of it all. So I know: Right! What do we expect? All this crap ain't exactly your fault. Some of it, but not all of it. However, many of you can do something about it. I know that most of your ancestors could not have had the foresight and had no idea that this would last for centuries, generation after generation after generation after generation. What's done is done, and you did not exactly do it.

So what do you do now? For starters breathe; it is heavy but not impossible. We went to the moon, broke the sound barrier, split an atom, cloned a sheep, talked to each other across continents without wires, even found the Titanic. So I know we can do this too! We do not want to take over. We just want to stop being feared and marginalized. We want a "just" country with "real" democracy, and "equal" opportunity. In the truest sense of those words.

What this means is, take down the systemic laws, walls, policies, institutions, and practices that block equality! Take them down! Just like the Berlin Wall. Bring them down! You know what they are. If you think that it's not real, and people are just looking for a patsy, please know that it *is* real, and take another deep breath. Admit to someone close to you that there is still a race problem, like the first step of AA. You had a four-hundred-year head start before you "legally opened" our country. Step out of your mental isolation and privileged comfort zone(s), but not in a philanthropic way; opt for a more humanistic, peer-to-peer approach, and simply reach out and get to know someone who is not robot-white to include in your inner circles. Like really GET TO KNOW THEM. This post-traumatic racial stress syndrome is not just on us. It is on you too. Cause. Affect. Cause. Affect. I mean affect as in the verb, not the noun effect. It is my call for you to do something. So come out of the closet, or let the curtain down and get to know us. That will be the first and most meaningful step. It is recommended to repeat something 21 times until it becomes a habit, or causes your brain to rewire and shift. When you have accomplished that, rinse, repeat; rinse, repeat; rinse, repeat. **Do this until you shift the initial mindset of FEAR. You know the second most powerful force on the planet—love's evil cousin.**

We are more alike than not, and I honor you.

Your sister in country,
Wanda

Dear Everybody Else

Dear Everybody Else,

I'm sorry. And I love you too. Being born the eighth child in a family of nine means I was born into a tribe. That means I had to meet, greet and gingerly fall in love with ten immediate family members, four extended relatives, and hosts of other cousins, aunts, and uncles within a very, very short time period once I landed on earth. So I have a huge capacity for loving almost anybody, and an unselfish nature to render it. In other words, I think — it is real easy for me — to get you! If you take all of that, plus my attending three high schools and playing sports, having decades of extremely high-volume, face-to-face contact, via customer service, sales, recruiting, and training jobs, it means that I am, connected to the people of this world. Which means, we are all connected.

I am sorry that I was *mis*-educated (until I wasn't) with Eurocentric values as the premier way, and that everything else, every other race, and culture, including my own, was below that/them. You know the deceptive and dehumanizing "Hierarchy of Hate" (did I just coin this phrase?) we learned to use to systematically devalue peoples from foreign lands, including your homelands of Mexico, South America, Eastern Europe, Africa, Australia, the Middle East, Asia, India, and Israel. (Here, I've got to remind everybody that **WE ARE ALL GOD'S CHOSEN PEOPLE…and some of us just don't know it yet)!**

Needing to feel better about my race in my uninformed days, I nestled you under me, to stroke my ego, and considered you less than what God made. And for that, I sincerely apologize. Please forgive me. Thank God I learned better by taking the time and interest to engage and learn from you first-hand, instead of accepting what was being fed to me through the visual images on the screens and in the abbreviated, one-sided, and highly agendized chapters of those books. I hope you will do the same too. I am so moved and inspired by your personal stories, your lands, your courage, your sacrifices, and your choices to make America your home. However, I often feel that you too have been duped and taken in by what has been fed to you, and have played the same game of caste and annexation with us here because your skin is not as dark or your hair not as curly. Your worldwide accents appease and soothe with rhythms that evoke exoticism and mystery, rather than fear, creating open doors in many cases. But lest you forget, we black people built those doors! With forced bloody planks of hickory, oak, maple, ash and pine, from the very first trees that were chopped down by slave labor, which made a clearing—an entry, for your prosperity. Please be thankful instead of resentful that they found us first; it could have been you! Yet, many of the same things that have happened to us, have in various degrees happened to you, by the same oppressing stance, here in America, and in your homelands—in most cases through shorter stints, and/or with high-impact, devastatingly destructive events rather than extended centuries. However, your ancestral skeletons wept too.

We are more alike than not, and I honor you.

Your sister in claiming American ownership, Wanda

Dear God...Not Another 50 Years of Race

Dear God,

Wow, I do not know if this was my assignment, but this is what came forth, so this is what I did. I hope You like it. I have no idea where all these words came from—well some of them, just not all of them. But I guess that's not totally true...because I am talking to You. I am truly amazed by the experience. You certainly know how impatient I can be and how I start a lot of things without finishing. But I could not stop this, so I have to think it is You. You must be trying, yet again, for the umpteenth-thousandth time to get us to see for ourselves, that we are only perpetuating Hell on earth instead of Heaven—all over eight pounds of casing—(give or take a few). We could have it all, but for the hate.

Repeat:
WE COULD HAVE IT ALL, BUT FOR THE HATE!

God you are patient with us here on earth, although many say we are nearing an apocalyptic end, of Biblical proportions. But I keep the hope of this walk, because You send evidence every day in birthing rooms across the globe that You are not giving up on us yet. Giving us more and more opportunities to get it right.

Will it be baby Jacob or Jamal, or Isabelle, Matteo, Samuel, Natalie, Don, Immanuel, Nate, Elizabeth, Tai, Kamalpreet, Taylor, Niles, Ashanti, Prakesh, Mickhya, Ilhami; or August, Santana, Marte, Arik, Connor, Dominique, Talet, Sven, Amalia, Sydney, Jaden, Isaiah, Diamond, C.J., Mia, Frances, Whitney, Ceadin, Noah, Courtney, Bryce, Ryan, Mikhail, Satchel, Nick, Olivia, Lekzy, Michael, Neviah, Akili, Trevor, Matthew, Destiny, Maya; or Chloe, Kyle, Braelyn, Dexter, Shiloh, Jordan, Delanye, Kendall, Hudson, Carter, B.J., Nathan, Susie, Micah, Shamar, Ajani, Isabel, Gareth, Eron, Logan, Jasmyne, Summer, Royce, William, Kayla, Sebastian, James, Vanessa, Kade, Nijal, David, Layla, Rucker, Brayden, Simone, Kao, Sterling, Austin, Rio, Nyla, Karmine, Malik, Anastasia, Nathan, Corbin, De'Jah, or Alden?

Or maybe, just maybe, it is the little Messiah in us all. You are certainly the most High in patience and in love, and I exalt Thee.

In terms of human evolution, would it be possible to upgrade Your perfect works? Or should I say debug Your perfect works, to give the next human release 2.0 an increase in ability to easily access that corner of the brain where the understanding of unconditional love resides? Maybe even put it on autopilot. I think our hearts get it, but that free-will stuff has screwed it all up big time. Please forgive my unholy language. I do not mean it in an irreverent way. Or God, if not that, could You send someone who is willing to share freely with the masses, for the love of You and not money or power, the chemical formula for the pill, or the language code for the app, to access that area within our current human prototype, perhaps, at least until the upgrade arrives. As I am sure some "thing," like an evil virus, did a hack job and reengineered Your original programming.

I know that *The Ten Commandments* was the original app served up on Your fierce stone tablets. And it was the bomb too! Ten easy links about how to *apply* our lives on earth, this glorious life giving, life-sustaining paradisiac planet. But we are about to mess this up for good too, without Your Divine intercession. Please help take race/skin color out of our human calculations of character. Although the variety is beautiful and a wonderful bouquet of hues and hair textures (like all of your earthly creations), it has caused centuries of hellish havoc, and we are just not getting it!

I love You! I praise You! I thank You!

Your child,
Wanda

P.S. Thanks again for this book. I will forever be grateful. Amen

THANK YOU, THANK YOU, THANK YOU...

I want to thank people I have not met who have each contributed to me a sense of freedom. Most of you are celebrities or are public figures. And since you are confined from the general public, I may never have the personal chance to say it, face-to-face. I'm writing it in the book on the off chance that you will read it. So here we go, and in no particular order...

Ryan Coogler!!! — Wakanda FOREVER!!! **Dude, you slayed it is all I can say. I do have an essay I wrote about it that should be floating on the internet soon, so more about it there. The box office and history will say the rest. Simply though, thank you for your imagination and helping us see. We can't unsee Wakanda!**

Whoopi Goldberg — For your locks. You gave me permission to let my hair 'do what it do' and still feel beautiful.

Chris Rock — For *Everybody Hates Chris*. Some of the show inspired the idea for this book. And my kids have learned a lot about my Detroit days because of it, with my edits of course. And for just being the bold truth-telling badass you are. You rock!

Don King — For your crown. I laughed a lot about it over the years. But I so understand it completely now.

Oprah Winfrey—For not letting your physicality keep you from pursuing your dreams. And for being your highest self, and raising your bar, over and over! I still think you need to be canonized! And I know you are not Catholic. But black people need a saint for this century, and you are the closest in my view. And I do not care what "err-body" else says about that! But please do not play another middle-aged woman getting beat by the police. Get your sexy on the screen!

James Carville—For being a Democrat and so, so smart! I just love you and Mary! Love that you demonstrate freedom from stark, opposing views. Still have to get your book too. Oh, and I love your initials. Destined for greatness JC!

Spike Lee—For putting it out there and doing your craft, by any means necessary. Many are not pleased by your brash style and comments. But you get to be you, and I love you for it! You represent! Say hi to Joie, I feel like I know her.

Rachel Maddow—For being you. There is something about your bravery I admire. It may be easier, I think, to be a lesbian and comedic, like Ellen, who is awesome too. But it is something else to be strong and confident and serious. And I know you are not the first, but I love your candor, rigor and due diligence.

Denzel Washington—For excellence and doing Hollywood, your way! You are the man!

Melissa Harris-Perry—For the braids in corporate America! And on TV too!

Morgan Freeman—For being the soothing voice and face of God.

Shaun Robinson—For being the sexiest and most youthful 50-something on TV! You are truly representing and I love it! I also love that you went to CT too!

Michael Jordan—For flying and being masterful at your game! You just lifted all of sportsmanship higher!

FLOTUS, Michelle Obama—For choosing not to conform to that (prissy white) what others think the FLOTUS lady should act like, dress like, and say to the people! Classy because you say so! With your self-described grace and dignity! Oh, so beautiful!

Henry Louis Gates, Jr.—For documenting and telling our stories in only the way you could. You are a national and global treasure, and your works are priceless. I love you for your commitment to history, our history!

Cornel West—For mixing it up and making everybody think and rethink, and think again. You are a genius, and I adore your depth and love. I love your unyielding passion for the truth and your courage to seek, speak, and put it out there. Can we talk?

Stevie Wonder—For your gracious heart and brilliance. If only the sighted could see what you see. You are masterful, supremely musical, rhythmical, and so, so loved!

Will & Jada—For being you, but for being a couple/family too, the way you define it. I do not know exactly what it is, but I have been a fan of you both before you got together. When you show up together, I am all smiles. And I can't help it. So whatever that is, I love it! And I just adore Jaden and Willow!

Venus & Serena—For adding powerful, bold, bright, and brilliant color to tennis whites! And serving it up on a whole new level!

Lady Ga-Ga—For just being fearless. And full of love! My, my, what an original you are! Girl you got some chops, and some guts, and some chutzpah, and some jazz. You are a gem, and I cannot wait to see what is next.

Tavis Smiley—For your everlasting black love! I love your personal story and how you championed life! Just love it! I hope you resolve the current allegations in a way that provides the healing that is needed for all parties involved.

Muhammad Ali—What can I say? You are simply the bomb! And still the greatest! You demonstrated not only conviction, but also heart, power, self-determination, and self-proclamation! You sir, are a man's man and a demonstrative force of nature sourced through your Higher Power! I also like that we have the same birthday. Thank you! I love you! R.I.P.

Chris Matthews—Thank you! We met in, 2014, at USF, and I told you that you were the first white man of your generation who I love. You appear to be (on TV)—smart, sensitive, fair, fiery, and a staunch, loud, and consistent advocate of humanity—and I believe that's who you truly are, and I admire you for that!

Diana Ross—For your feminine prowess. You are still the boss! Your beauty, class, grace, and talent just gives me the chills. Thank you for

Mahogany, *Lady Sings the Blues*, and *The Wiz*. So indelible, so powerful, so inspiring!

Tina Turner—For your strength and beauty! Madam, you are in a class all by yourself! I really do not even have the words, except, exceptional! I don't even know how you did it, but I am forever grateful that you graced us with all that passion and power and talent you have. A truly unstoppable force of nature.

Alice Walker/Steven Spielberg—For *The Color Purple*, the book and the movie. Simply a masterpiece and the biggest Academy Award snub. It should have dominated and won all 11 nominations. There has never been a movie so ingeniously filmed, in my opinion. Every scene is practically iconic! Every character so real, revealing, relatable, relevant, and memorable. And oh my, oh my, the cinematography! The music (Quincy Jones!!!)! Just simply brilliant! I have seen it at least 4 times a year since its release, and I can recite many lines and scenes. Not one inch of wasted film, not one wasted word! Pure genius.

Janet Jackson—For taking "Control." I think we had the same number of siblings, with the same gender profile, 6 boys, 3 girls, and I am also the baby girl (but not the youngest), but I was so with you in that song and understood it completely. It gave me some courage to step out and take some chances with my own life, and it was great to do it with a beat. I love you! Thank you!

And there are so many more! I could write another book...

AFTERWORD

At the end of the day, now that you are at the end of this book, at the very least, I hope you enjoyed it. At the very best, I hope you read something that inspired you to do life better, whatever that better is for you. Because the one freedom you do have right now, and always will have, is the freedom to choose. I simply hope you choose peace and love, over war and hatred. Our world seriously needs a reprieve on the latter. Because **ALL LIVES MATTER!**

May God continue to bless you!

Your sister in God's favor,
Wanda Lee-Stevens

Share your comments or contact me:
www.facebook.com/AuthorWandaLeeStevens
www.twitter.com/50YearsWLS
50Years@wandaleestevens.com

Name:	Wanda Lee-Stevens
Birthplace:	Detroit, MI, USA
Nationality:	American
Gender:	Female
Race:	Human
Ethos:	Midwestern, Afrocentric-Urban, 1960/'70s
Culture:	21st Century, American-Blended

ACKNOWLEDGMENTS

You think that writing a book is a solitary assignment. At the onset I truly thought I was going to perform a solo act, but it really takes a village to produce a book. Fortunately, I have been blessed yet again with the willingness, encouragement, emotional support, financial support, patience, care, generosity, talents, the overall camaraderie and love through this process, from my village. You truly do not know how much you impacted me and kept me going. It may have been something as simple as a phone call to cheer me up, that walk to clear my head, that talk to fill in the blanks, a dinner together that fed my belly and my soul, that bottle of wine to calm my nerves, that genuine enthusiasm you showed when I told you what I was up to, or that prayer that truly lifted me higher. All those big and little things alike, kept giving me the juice I needed to persist and not give up.

It has truly been transformative, and I am better for it. My patient writing coach, Rebecca Salome (www.rebeccasalomemidwriter.com), is wonderful at getting to the nitty-gritty and heart of what you want to write. She works her magic to birth it out of you (like a "midwriter" of sorts) — all while keeping you on track and rigorously in that "through line!"

And my wonderful life coach, Margaret Pazant

(www.facebook.com/MargaretPazantCoaching), a big shout out! She is expert at getting *you* out of *your* own way, and getting *you* to own *you*. No joke!

So, without further ado and in randomized order (desperately hoping to not forget anyone), I want to say thank you, thank you, thank you! It truly could not have been done without all of you! I am grateful to God for all of you and grateful to God for the inspiration, vision, and talent.

So a Big "Thank You" to my village:

My husband, Chester, and my children, August & Jacob Stevens—my wonderful family who has been the most patient and supportive; Aline Stevens & the Stevens Family; Pastor Bennett & Angela Bradley; Carita Bowers; Tracy Hester; John & Gayle Cummings; Josie B. Cummings; Robert D. & Cynthia Taylor; Ronald & Brenda Arthur; Queen Anne Cannon; Darnell Jones & Patricia Lee-Jones; Rebecca Salome; Margaret Pazant; Candy Bright; Darlene Kong; Debra Salan; Donald & Kimberly Richardson; Douglass & Clevette Lee; Anthony & Elaine Rice; Dewine Lee; Warren & Pam Lee; Natasha Lee; Anthony Lee; Ron & Brendyl Lee; Deborah Lee; Lorenzo Lee; Lamont Lee; Marcus Lee; Monique Phillips; Dr. James Mendez & Barbara Gallman; Manny & Myrna de Vera; Charlie Davidson & Selina Williams; Eloy Bustamante; Deacon Wilbert & Sister Connie Sims; Ron & Bettie Joe Singleton; Nikki Lancaster; Leah Hoskins; Alex & Laura Lee; Margaret Pazant; Larobb & Janice Lee; Nancy Lee; Barbara Andrews

& the Andrews Nation; Evan Felter & Ileana Barragan; Floyd & Yajaira Gray; Debra Curtis-Petties; Edward, Dezzie, & Deidre Moseley; Rafael & Rosalind Porter & the Porter Nation; Thomas Gradie, Margaret Hanlon-Gradie & Amalia Gradie; Lisa Holcombe; Brad & Genie Foon; Paul & Adele Laput; Jojo Soriano; Horace Cardoza & Kim Ennis; Paris Hill; Kathlyn Hughes; Liana Lei; Ilhami, Eve & Isabel Topaloglu; Madeline McNab; Steve Young, Kelley Flynn & Maya Young; Sylvia Villa-Serrano; Don & Michelle Mancha; Viktor Manrique & Richard White; Brenda McCuistion; Charlie Acquino & Barbara Luck; Michael Hopper & Payge Means-Hopper; Helena-Joyce Wright; Alison McKee; Hercules Library & the Hercules Library Commission; John Sherman Mills; Dovie Jones; Kim Archie; Adia & Shiloh Bradley; Cynthia Castain; Andree Driskell; The Bart-Williams Family; Bridget Laurent; Curt & Kirsten Hill; Dr. Joyce Graham; Sondra McNary; Dr. Marianela Carter; Prescott Cole & Barbara Lipson; Barbara McDonald; Clark Edwards; Shawn & Eldreai Ellis; David, Colisa & Isaac Fowler; Nigel & Felicia Gopaul; Dr. Rucker & Candace Johnson; Jenifer Chan; Mark Boggs; Jonathan Dickson; Matthew Barker-Benfield; Michael Guzman; Maya Willner; Dwayne & Elaine Hylick; Liane Ingram; Gina E. Johnson; William & Janice Leighton, Gayle & Ceara Threets; Nick & Ruma Tenbrink; Tony Scholis & Mechele-Neeley Scholis; Mitch Saunders; Chris & Michel Shadowens; John Connery & Pam Levinson-Connery; Craig & Lillian Samuel; Doris Rutland; Lou Kern & Kathleen Burke; Hunter Roberts; Todd & Lori

Risby; Carol Jackson-Pringle; Tonya Patton; Atemu & Nora Aton; Rosie Obetz; Gisele Mills; Loretta Love-Huff; Steve & Terri Fanning; Melayne Curry; Rob Limon & Maria Laxo; Colleen George; Damon & Kameelah Whitaker and all of you that have been wishing me well from afar, thank you!

God bless!

Last but not least...

My oldest and best friend Kimberly Richardson, Detroit native, is my homegirl if there ever was one. She is one of my staunch supporters and fans—in her words. If I am her Oprah, she is my Gayle! *(Sorry Kim, you haven't written your book yet, so I had to take the Oprah position.)* We live over 3,000 miles apart and do not see each other regularly. However, Kim is one of the strongest, most generous, loving, intelligent, loyal, and brave, girls—women—I have ever known.

We had parallel lives for the most part from ages 6 to 16. Same neighborhood, same friends, same ambitions bred in elementary school, and then same high school. And when I moved and left our high school at 16, and later moved to CA, our lives became very different.

However, she and I spent countless hours on the phone talking about the good old days for the following 30 years. We still do this at least six or seven times a year. It is hard to believe that we have kept in touch for so long; but I am grateful we never stopped being friends and sisters—45 years and counting!

Our many hours of recollection, praise of, and gratitude for our youth, are the primary reasons I started to write this book several years ago. I felt our upbringing was a great American story (especially our elementary school and our teachers who were just simply wonderful). But in the beginning, I did not have the courage to tell my story as myself, and so I started it as a fiction novel and wrote just three chapters. I later attempted it again with a fiction series, under the title character, "Brandy." I wrote three short stories for that series under the pseudonym, Sadie Augustine (a hybrid of my grandmother, mother, and daughter's names). Brandy gave me the courage to write as myself after its very modest success.

So I thank you Kimberly for being you! You are not just my best friend, but my sister, kindred spirit, and my Gayle! I love you! Here's to our continued dreams!

PRAISE FOR WANDA LEE-STEVENS'

50 YEARS of ASSIMILATION
From the Midwest to the Wild West and All the Blackness & Whiteness In Between

*****

5.0 out of 5 stars
More of this, please!

"One of the things the world needs right now is ordinary people telling their stories, especially people whose experiences have often been marginalized. Wanda Lee-Stevens' 50 Years of Assimilation delivers, offering the reader a deeply personal story of what it was like coming of age and surviving as a Black woman in post-Civil Rights USA. Her book is honest, insightful, courageous, and full of humor...the particularity of her experiences makes them interesting, but the authenticity of her voice, and her willingness to include the less flattering details about herself, renders her stories both funny and relatable.

Throughout the book, Lee-Stevens pulls no punches in reporting the personal impacts of racism, yet she always resists the temptation to infer explicit racist intent...Refreshingly, it is neither a breathless exaltation of progress nor a grumble about how much injustice remains. It is simply a frank, first person, account of how life has actually unfolded for one particular black woman from the heart of the rust belt...But one of the book's surprises is the way it offers white men like myself a window onto another side of our supposedly colorblind society. Without demonizing anyone or ducking responsibility for her own missteps, Lee-Stevens helps readers appreciate the very real challenges, mundane and outrageous, subtle and blatant, that she and others must overcome to achieve the American middleclass existence that some of us treat as a birthright."

Gregory A. Mengel, Ph.D, Co-Director
Beyond Separation, Oakland, CA

*****

5.0 out of 5 stars
Well-written and thought-provoking...a MUST read!

"They say that everyone has a story...well, some are better than others and Lee-Stevens' telling of her life story is absolutely wonderful! Humorous at times and thoughtfully written, '50 Years of Assimilation' was more than a good read and really challenged my thinking. Though it discusses American racial dynamics over the past five decades, Lee-Stevens' experiences are as relevant today as they've ever been. I thoroughly enjoyed the book and would highly recommend it to anyone living in the great U.S. of A. or anyone abroad seeking a real-life example of the 'black experience' in America."

Tara Murray, VA

*****

5.0 out of 5 stars
Courageous Storytelling!

"I could not put this book down. I flew through Wanda's story and savored her sage wisdom. She has captured our collective American story by fearlessly revealing hers with authority, grace and humor! Her courage to 'tell it like it is' without pretense was refreshing and heartwarming. Despite many challenges and losses Wanda lands on her feet and marches on, just as Dr. King would have wanted. Her authentic voice guides us through the trials and tribulations of assimilation into the dominant culture and back out again. This book is a much needed, account of race relations through the lens of an extraordinary, ordinary American. I was inspired and informed at a time when we need clear perspectives, compassion and healing more than ever.

Thank You Wanda- for sharing your intriguing story and insightful recommendations on how Americans can come together and take care of our collective destiny."

Kay O'Neill, Co-Founder, Open Access
Menlo Park, CA

*****

5.0 out of 5 stars
A moving experience...

"As an older mixed race man, reading Wanda Lee-Stevens' brilliant telling of her life story was a moving experience for me. Wanda is a talented and insightful storyteller. 50 Years of Assimilation is a delightful must read for anyone willing to update their thinking about race in America. I thoroughly

enjoyed the book and would highly recommend it to anyone interested in a real-life example of the 'black experience' in America."

Boyd Watkins, San Francisco, CA

*****

5.0 out of 5 stars
Entertaining and thought provoking!

"This is a thoroughly entertaining and thought-provoking coming of age story about an African American woman's journey from the Midwest to California. I enjoyed the writing style, which was a series of letters to Dr. Martin Luther King. For me, these letters served as questions and commentary about how Dr. King might feel about all of the major social accomplishments as a result of his efforts-- including the election of President Obama. It was also a melancholy reminder of how little has changed. This is a good read to remind us that in spite of the challenges that many African Americans face, resilience keeps us going."

Gayle Cummings, Assist. Dean, Public Health Touro University, Vallejo, CA

*****

5.0 out of 5 stars
A must read!

"I found this book to be a thoughtful and well written story of growth, disappointment, tragedy, courage, love and joy. Lee-Stevens does a beautiful job telling her story as a unique individual while also weaving in the racial and cultural experience of a Midwestern woman born in the year of

MLK's "I Have a Dream" speech. I am still thinking of many of the injustices, adventures, and everyday experiences so vulnerably shared in this book. A must read."

Barbara Lipson, Sr. Program Manager
SEEDS Community Resources Cntr, Berkeley, CA

*****

5.0 out of 5 stars
Sweet, funny, smart!

"I met Ms. Lee-Stevens at a conference and decided to buy her book as it takes courage to write about yourself, especially if it includes talking about race in the US. I wanted to know more about this woman who is only a few years younger than me and from a very different world (I am white and from San Francisco) - despite us both being American.

Her style of writing is humble and funny right off the bat and that is great for drawing a reader in. The more I read the more I admired and felt closer to her. The format is her writing to Dr. Martin Luther King Jr., telling him how life is here in the US, and for her as a Black woman, since he was killed. This way of presenting her stories adds a deeper dynamic than a straight narrative of her life. It allowed me to understand more the impact of the post-civil rights times on a real person as well as on her family and community. Our lives had many more similarities than I would have thought and learning that was worth the price of purchase.

I felt like I grew in awareness and compassion right beside Ms. Lee-Stevens as she shares her personal growth - and am so grateful for her willingness and ability to take me along. Her honesty and love will help anyone ease into facing the legacy of white privilege and oppression in our country and want to do something about it. She doesn't come from a blame or shame place at all, just from her truth and that's powerful."

Alison Worcester, Social Justice Advocate
San Francisco, CA

****

4.0 out of 5 stars
An Important Read: Educational, Entertaining, and Compelling

"With care and adeptness, this author guides the reader through a time, a culture and a lifetime of profoundly complex, harrowing and at times funny adventures and misadventures across race and gender. The intricate weaving of historical knowledge, anecdotal accounts, personal narratives and shared community contexts are all, illustrative of Lee-Stevens' craft, artistry, and luminescence. This book has lessons for us all; you will find a part of yourself and some aspect of your own story on its pages."

D.L. Proby, Oakland, CA

ABOUT THE AUTHOR

Wanda is a small business owner and former Human Resource professional. Her resume writing, talent sourcing, talent management skills, and her natural ability to relate to people from all walks of life evolved into an organic passion for entertaining, storytelling and writing.

She is a Detroit native and has lived the last 30 years in Northern CA. Wanda is a graduate of the University of San Francisco, with a B.S. degree in Organizational Behavior. She enjoyed being a "'self-study" of how the organization called America has shaped her life. She is a wife and mother and resides with her family.

77655093R00208

Made in the USA
Middletown, DE
24 June 2018